Rebirth of the Silk Road and a New Era for Eurasia

Edited by

Tadahiro Tsuji, Yiliang Wu and Yugun Riku

Yachiyo Shuppan

Copyright © 2015 by Tadahiro Tsuji, Yiliang Wu and Yugun Riku

All rights reserved. No part of this publication may be reproduced or transmitted in any form or by any means, electronic or mechanical, including photocopying, recording, scanning, or any information storage or retrieval system, without written permission from the publisher.

Published by
Yachiyo Shuppan Co., Ltd.
2-2-13 Misakicho Chiyoda-ku Tokyo
Phone 03-3262-0420
Fax 03-3237-0723
www.yachiyo-net.co.jp

ISBN: 978-4-8429-1648-4
First published in JAPAN on March 20, 2015

Contents

Introduction   1

Chapter 1
New Silk Road and Central Asia from a "Geo-Economic" Perspective   9
   I. Introduction   9
   II. New Silk Road: Background   10
   III. Economic Relations between the Three Central Asian Countries/Regions   14
   IV. Central Asia's Renewed International Relations   20
   V. Conclusion   25

Chapter 2
Forming a Beads-type Industrial City along the New Silk Road   27
   I. Introduction   27
   II. Why a Beads-type Development Strategy?   28
   III. Possibility of Forming Beads-type Industrial Cities in the New Silk Road Region   33
   IV. Policy Measures for the Beads-type Development Strategy   37
   V. Prospect of Economic Development in the New Silk Road Region   40

Chapter 3
Dynamic Catch-Up and the Possibility for New Regional Economic Development   45
   I. Introduction   45
   II. Globalization of Corporate Production Activities and Emergence of a New Internalization Division of Labor   46
   III. Dynamic Catch-Up Model   51
   IV. Conclusion   56

Chapter 4
EU Trade Policy towards Central Asia States:
      Implications for China and Japan   59
   I. Aims of EU Trade Policy towards Central Asia   59
   II. Features of Economic Relation   65
   III. Conclusion: Implications for China and Japan, Prospect for New Silk Road   71

Chapter 5
Measuring the Transportation Competitiveness of the New Silk Road — 75
- I. Introduction — 75
- II. Transportation Competitiveness — 76
- III. Transport Competitiveness of the New Silk Road — 80
- IV. Current State of Transportation on the New Silk Road and Potential Improvements — 88

Chapter 6
Economic Development in Central Asia and Infrastructure — 95
- I. Introduction — 95
- II. The Current State of Integration with the Global Economy — 95
- III. The Necessity for Trade and Transport Facilitation (TTF) in the Economic Development of Inland Areas — 99
- IV. The Current Status and Problems of TTF in Central Asian Countries — 100
- V. Conclusion — 107

Chapter 7
Chinese Regional Development and the New Silk Road:
An Examination of Existing Major Cities and Emerging Small-to-medium Sized Cities in the Central Region of China — 109
- I. Introduction — 109
- II. Economic Growth in Existing Major Urban Cities of the Central Region of China — 111
- III. Growth and Development of Small-to-medium Sized Cities of the Central Region of China — 114
- IV. Conclusion — 119

Chapter 8
Pattern of the Newly-Internationally Traded Products in Central Asian Countries — 123
- I. Introduction — 123
- II. The Trade Growth and Newly International Traded Products — 124
- III. Evidence of International Trade in CA5 — 130
- IV. Conclusion — 139

Chapter 9
New Silk Road and Economic Development in Kazakhstan — 143
- I. Introduction — 143
- II. Economic Development — 144
- III. The New Silk Road — 148

IV. The Influence of the New Silk Road on Trade and Economic
   Development of Kazakhstan 151
V. Conclusion 155

Chapter 10
Economic Overview of Uzbekistan:
   Cooperation, Free Industrial Zone Establishment, and Financial Stability 157
I. Introduction 157
II. The Republic of Uzbekistan's Cooperation with the Asia-Pacific Region 158
III. Free Industrial Zone Establishment 162
IV. Financial Stability 165
V. Conclusion 174
VI. Economic Development and Forecast for Uzbekistan:
   Economic Development in Uzbekistan up to 2011 and its Forecast for 2012-2013 176

Chapter 11
Importance of Innovative Endogenous Industrial Policies for Shrinking Cities
   along the Silk Road 183
I. Introduction 183
II. Shrinking Cities in the World 184
III. Shrinking Cities and Depopulation in Japan 185
IV. Model on Economic Resilience in Shrinking Cities 186
V. Policies to Enhance Economic Resilience 188
VI. Economic Gardening 189
VII. Implementing Economic Gardening in Silk Road Cities in China 191
VIII. Conclusion 193

Chapter 12
Economic Development of the New Silk Road Area and Its Links with Japan 195
I. Introduction 195
II. The Economic Importance of the New Silk Road Area for Japan 195
III. The Importance of the New Silk Road Area for Japan in Terms of
   Diplomatic Relations 199
IV. Japan's Role in the Economic Development of the New Silk Road Area 200
V. Conclusion 204

Closing Remarks 205

Index 209

Acknowledgements

First and foremost, we have to express our thanks to Mr. Shigeru Asaumi, President of Sea Enterprise Co., Ltd., for his sincere support and dedicated involvement. Without it, our research would have never been carried out, especially during the fieldwork in Kazakhstan and Uzbekistan.

We would also like to show our gratitude to professors and researchers at Shandong University, Shaanxi Normal University, Lanzhou University, Beijing Normal University, and Shanghai Academy of Social Sciences in China, al-Farabi Kazakh National University in Kazakhstan and University of World Economy and Diplomacy in Uzbekistan. Discussion with them was highly insightful and invaluable.

We also wish to thank all the people who helped us arrange the fieldwork in China, Kazakhstan and Uzbekistan. We were offered rare access to the Khorgos International Center of Boundary Cooperation from both the Chinese and the Kazakh sides, which was a great opportunity for understanding the differences in the progress of economic cooperation among the countries concerned.

We are honored to be awarded the Nihon University College of Economics Center for China and Asian Studies Research Fund and we would like to express our sincere gratitude to the esteemed judging panel for awarding us the fund.

Contributors

Tadahiro Tsuji (Introduction, Chapters 2, 6 & 12, Closing Remarks) is Professor of Economic Development, College of Economics, Nihon University, Tokyo, Japan.

Yiliang Wu (Introduction, Chapters 2, 5 & 12, Closing Remarks), Ph.D. (Economics), is Professor of Economics, College of Economics, Nihon University, Tokyo, Japan.

Yugun Riku (Chapters 2 & 3), Ph.D. (Economics), is Professor of International Economics, Distance Learning Division and Graduate School of Social and Cultural Studies, Nihon University, Tokyo, Japan.

Kenji Akiyama (Chapter 1), Ph.D. (Economics), is Director, Kanagawa University Center for Asian Studies and Professor at the Graduate School of Economics, Kanagawa University, Yokohama, Japan.

Mitsuo Honda (Chapter 2), Ph.D. (Economics), is Emeritus Professor, Nihon University, Tokyo, Japan.

Naohiko Ijiri (Chapters 2 & 8) is Professor of International Economics, College of Economics, Nihon University, Tokyo, Japan.

Kiyomi Suzui (Chapter 4) is Professor and Dean, Faculty of Foreign Studies, Kyoto Sangyo University, Kyoto, Japan.

Naili Zhang (Chapter 7), Ph.D. (Economics), is Director of Japanese Economic Research Center and Professor at the School of Economics, Shandong University, Jinan, China.

Takaaki Maeno (Chapter 8), Ph.D. (Economics), is Research Assistant at the College of Economics, Nihon University, Tokyo, Japan.

Shuichi Ikemoto (Chapter 8) is Professor at the College of Economics, Nihon University, Tokyo, Japan.

Bulat Mukhamediyev (Chapter 9) is Professor of Economics, Department of Economics, al-Farabi Kazakh National University, Almaty, Kazakhstan.

Abdujabar Rasulov (Chapter 10) is Professor of Economics, Department of International Economic Relations, University of World Economy and Diplomacy, Tashkent, Uzbekistan.

Bakoeva Gulbahor (Chapter 10) is Teacher at the Department of International Economic Relations, University of World Economy and Diplomacy, Tashkent, Uzbekistan.

Mirodil Mirzakhmedov (Chapter 10) is Director at Akkurat Avto LLC, Tashkent, Uzbekistan.

Takashi Yamamoto (Chapter 11), Ph.D. (Economics), is Professor and Head, Department of Economics, Takushoku University, Tokyo, Japan.

Introduction

This book summarizes the results of a joint research project by the Nihon University College of Economics Center for China and Asian Studies entitled "Research on the Economic Development of the New Silk Road Regions". Participants to this research project include members of the New Silk Road Research Team at the Nihon University College of Economics and specialists from Japan and elsewhere, who worked jointly for three years from 2011. The genesis of this research dates back to 2003, when a team consisting of faculty members from the Nihon University College of Economics engaged in a joint endeavor to address regional development issues from a multidisciplinary perspective by combining international trade theory, economic development theory, and spatial economics. The research team made several trips to China, which was growing at a rapid pace. The team began to recognize the importance and potentiality of economic development of the inland regions through our field surveys of Lianyungang and Xuzhou. We researched how the geographical and spatial alignment of China's core cities impacted the economic development of each city. The results of our joint research were published in 2007[1]. Our research pointed to the widening economic disparity between western and central China with cities in the coastal regions in the east, which began the process of industrialization at a relatively early stage. As one solution, we proposed the construction of a trade transportation route connecting Europe in the west through the improvement of highways and railways and the establishment of efficient custom inspection systems. By doing so, we argued that the development of the western regions was indeed possibleas access to transportation connecting western China to its neighboring countries would improve and geographic conditions for economic development would be enhanced.

Subsequently, the subject of our research expanded from China to the interior regions of Eurasia. We continued our joint research project with a particular focus on the economic development of the New Silk Road. A succession of studies led us to realize that there were limits to building a New Silk Road through the efforts of any single country. We also proposed the formation of "Beads-type" industrial cities by connecting cities along the New Silk Road with a modern transportation system. Our proposal was based on theoretical research related to industrial agglomeration and urbanization, which occur as the economy develops[2]. This approach, referred to as the Beads-type Development Strategy, constitutes the theoretical backbone of this book. The term "Beads-type" has the following spatial connotation: With the development of the New Silk Road regions, a transportation web spanning the Eurasian Continent will increasingly play an important role as a transportation route for international

---

[1] Refer to Honda *et al.* (2007).

[2] Refer to these individual pieces of work: Wu, 2000, 2006; Tsuji, 2006; Riku, 2006.

trade, with economies along this route becoming increasingly entwined and promoting further globalization. As such dynamic changes ensue industrial agglomeration will progress further and create centers of economic transactions in the major cities of each country along this route. Moreover, as a convenient gateway for external trade, new cities may emerge as production hubs along the border. Beads-type expresses the spatial characteristic of such economic activities along the New Silk Road. Mindful of this spatial characteristic, the Beads-type Development Strategy along the New Silk Road which we propose will provide impetus to the development of not only western China, but relevant countries along the route, and in particular the inland countries of. Additionally, the industrialized countries located on the far eastern and western ends of the Eurasian Continent should benefit from this strategy as well. Consequently, we emphasize the importance of mutual trust and cooperation among countries if they are to benefit from this strategy. In this book we have delved further into the possibility for economic development of the inland regions of Eurasia and illustrate the present problems and solutions obtained through our observations.

The inland regions of the Eurasian Continent are rich in natural resources, and as such, the regional economic cooperation of this region has moved forward with the involvement of neighboring countries and industrialized nations in other areas. Central Asia, which is located in the interior regions of the Eurasian Continent, is growing in importance. However, this does not necessarily mean that this area will regain the economic prosperity it once enjoyed. According to conventional views of economic development, landlocked interior regions of a continent are at a geographical disadvantage in a modern society with advanced marine transportation. Therefore, economic development is extremely difficult for such areas.

In order to eliminate the transportation disadvantages of these landlocked regions, international institutions such as the United Nations, the Asian Development Bank, and the European Bank for Reconstruction and Development have taken the initiative to construct railroads and road networks in rapid succession. Russia and China have actively involved themselves in this region as well. In this way, an east-west land distribution route spanning the Eurasian Continent has become a focus of increasing interest.

We next turn to the theoretical possibilities of constructing a New Silk Road and promoting economic development in the inland regions along this route. Since the 1990s, "industrial agglomeration" and "industrial clusters" have been widely acknowledged and actively debated as a phenomenon whereby enterprise clusters form within a relatively small area. Pioneering research by Krugman and Porter have been a focus of attention with regard to debates concerning the spatial aspects of economic activity. Porter posits that the source of production superiority of a particular industry in a particular region is derived from competition and cooperation among enterprises situated in that particular region. In contrast, relying on Marshall's concept of economic externality, Krugman explains the spatial heterogeneous distribution of economic activity from interactions between scale economies and transport costs. The arguments of the two economists do not differ greatly in that they both consider the source of production superiority as endogenous.

This is a method of analysis called the new economic geography or spatial economics, which combines traditional trade theory with economic geography. Krugman, who proposed this method, employed a two-region model that allowed for spatial element mobility to explain how differences in spatial factor endowment ratios and the spatial division and specialization of production are endogenously formed. Krugman demonstrated that agglomeration of economic activity occurs as a result of site selection by companies and workers (= consumers) in a scale economy with low transport costs, and that differences in spatial factor endowment ratios are determined endogenously. It is our contention that if transport costs can be reduced by building a transportation network spanning the New Silk Road regions, this would trigger industry agglomeration in base cities along this route.

The above is the fundamental theoretical premise on which this book was written. We believe that this basic analytical perspective can be applied to a project with a subject matter that spans multiple countries, in addition to studies that limit the research target to the spatial division and specialization of production of one domestic economy, as was the case with our previous project. Within the interior regions of Eurasia are the five Central Asian countries of Kazakhstan, the Kyrgyz Republic, Tajikistan, Uzbekistan, and Turkmenistan, surrounded by Russia, Iran, and the Caucasus nations (such as Georgia). The possibility of economic development for these countries, situated in the interior regions of the continent, can be revisited from the perspective of the spatial division and specialization of production, which we propose in our book. Can our development strategy initiate the economic development of the Central Asian regions? What are the conditions for this to happen? What are the conditions lacking in these Central Asian countries? How should neighboring countries involve themselves in the economic development of this region? We offer our most recent research findings from multiple viewpoints to address these issues and comment on recent economic trends. The book is structured along the following chapters.

Chapter 1 discusses the geopolitical significance of the Central Asian nations, which connect the east-west corridor of the Eurasian Continent, from the perspective of political science and economics with a particular focus on China's economic relations with Central Asia.Central Asia has an abundance of natural resources including fossil fuels such as oil and natural gas and is rich in iron ore, copper, uranium, and rare metals. Infrastructure development is rapidly underway so that trade can be facilitated. However, due to political considerations on the part of the investment recipient, transportation routes are being planned in such a way that they circumvent concerned countries. As a result, economic development in this region is raising political concerns. We also argued that there are many challenges to economic development of the New Silk Road, such as the U.S. military deployment in Central Asia in its battle against terrorism, inherent political instability within the region, and China's economic expansion and the threat it may impose on neighboring nations.

In Chapter 2, we present the concepts of a Beads-type Development Strategy and the formation of Beads-type industrial cities to illustrate the theoretical basis of our research in examining the possibilities of economic development in the interior regions and its mechanism. We posit that economic development of the interior regions could be triggered autonomously in the context of advancements in trade liberalization worldwide, progress in transportation technology, and remarkable improvements in infrastructure development. This could lead to industrial agglomeration and the creation of new sites as drivers for growth under conditions different from the past. In this way, we conclude that the New Silk Road regions could constitute an important land transportation route connecting the east-west corridor of the Eurasian Continent providing economic benefits to the entire continent.

Chapter 3 describes the presence of a dynamic catch-up process inherent in emerging countries that is different from the past "flying geese pattern," which was supported by the notion that the effects of industrial relocation will spread internationally. The dynamic catch-up process is a hypothesis based on the collective experience of the emerging countries of East Asia. We posit that the catch-up process proposed by this hypothesis is applicable not only to East Asia, but also to regions along the New Silk Road and in particular the interior regions of western China and the Central Asian nations. We argue for the necessity of a Beads-type Development Strategy that integrates the regional economy and initiates a strategic endeavor to strengthen inter-regional coordination and benefit-sharing through the utilization of the labor, capital, and technology in which each country enjoys a comparative advantage.

Chapter 4 describes the EU's trade policy with Central Asia and identifies the characteristics of the trade relations between the two. We first conclude that the chief objective of the EU's trade policy toward Central Asia is the diversification of energy imports, a strategic initiative consistent with geopolitical considerations. We next illustrate the imbalance and asymmetry of trade between the EU and the Central Asian nations. We also show the vertical nature of their trade relations as well. Finally, the completion of an east-west Eurasian corridor would connect China and Europe through a Silk Road railway and a road system, increasing the importance of Central Asia as a transportation hub, even though we do not expect that the Central Asian nations will emerge as "the next market" in the near future.

Chapter 5 is a discussion concerning the competitiveness of the New Silk Road as a means of transportation. In this chapter we first use a theoretical model to explain the concept of the competitiveness of the New Silk Road as a means of transportation and introduce an original index to describe transportation competitiveness. In addition, we use the gravity equation to develop a mechanism to measure the transportation competitiveness index and apply it to the 2009 trade data. We determined that the maximum allowable distance for land transport on the New Silk Road is around 7,500 km. There has been a trend toward expansion of the maximum allowable distances in recent years, indicating that the New Silk Road's transportation competitiveness is improving.

Lastly, we examine the present state and problems surrounding railway transportation, which impacts the transportation competitiveness of the New Silk Road, and comment on possibilities for the future.

Chapter 6 focuses on infrastructure to consider whether necessary conditions are in place for the successful application of the Beads-type Development Strategy to the New Silk Road regions. Beads-type industrial city clusters as sites to drive growth in the region need to be formed if economic development is to be achieved using this strategy. This can only happen if each base city is closely linked with one another. Infrastructure is a prerequisite for this. We conclude that building infrastructure goes beyond creating the "hardware." It is vital that infrastructure development include the "soft" aspect, as well as regional economic cooperation.

Chapter 7 attempts to apply the theoretical framework of economic development of the New Silk Road to the central China region and analyze the present situation. In this chapter, we classify the main base cities in the central region into "existing main cities" and "emerging medium to small cities." We describe the development of these cities within the context of economic development of China as a whole and examine the potential for the formation of a Beads-type industrial area. We have observed that the existing main cities which have traditionally developed as manufacturing sites, despite their inland location, are recently establishing export processing zones to promote exports and increasingly gaining importance in their function as hubs for land transportation. The active economic development that we witnessed at these main cities is creating synergies via distribution networks linking the cities, resulting in economic development that is spilling over into the emerging medium to small cities. We conclude that although regional economic disparities in the inland regions of China still exist, we find evidence of change as well.

In Chapter 8, we conduct a positive analysis on the relationship between the state of transportation infrastructure and the growth of total factor productivity, or TFP, using panel data derived from observations of main cities along the New Silk Road. We selected 17 major cities as our analysis targets along the route from Rizhao in the Shandong Province of China to Urumqi in the Xinjiang Uyghur Autonomous Region. We observed that the growth of TFP increased as railway and highway standards were upgraded to higher levels. Moreover, we confirmed the presence of a spatial spillover effect as well. We conclude that incentives for investments in transportation are important if there is to be a rebirth of the ancient Silk Road and the completion of a new Eurasian Land Bridge.

In Chapter 9, we conduct a positive analysis using the gravity model to determine the impact of numerous infrastructure projects currently underway along the New Silk Road and the impact of regional economic integration measures on international trade and the economic development in Kazakhstan. In our analysis we used transportation time as a measurement of distances (obstacles) between capital cities and further assumed that transportation time is affected not only by distances, but that it changes depending on road conditions, i.e., speed. For our analysis, we used panel data collected from 10 Central Asian nations and relevant neighboring countries from 2002 to 2011. We confirmed that the reduction of transportation time led to increased exports among the relevant countries, and this was pronounced in the Central Asian nations including Kazakhstan. It was also evident that this led to GDP expansion as well.

In Chapter 10, where we discuss Uzbekistan, we look into the present state of the Uzbekistan economy from the perspective of mutual exchange with neighboring countries and as a site for industrialization, and examine the country's financial markets to ascertain its future economic outlook. We find that Uzbekistan has actively promoted mutual exchange with Japan, Korea, and China both at the government level and at the private level after establishing diplomatic relations with these countries. This has benefited the country's international trade. Furthermore, it is evident that the country's economic policy is conducted strategically as witnessed by the establishment of a free trade zone in Navoi, which serves as an international distribution center connecting Asia with Europe. However, it is necessary for the country to use every measure available to form large-scale financial markets where financial products such as derivatives can be traded in order to address the domestic problem of capital shortages. Since Uzbekistan was spared from the effects of the European financial crisis and declines in primary commodity prices, the country's short-term economic outlook is favorable. However, we conclude that the country must contain inflation and develop human resources in the long run.

In Chapter 11, we discuss the relatively recent topic of the "shrinking cities" problem using examples of cities in China to determine the cities' sustainability and economic development strategies from an economics perspective. Since the growth of cities depend on their production capability to generate value, if a city's productivity and production capability declines and its relative advantages start to lose their appeal, companies will migrate away from such cities and their population will decline. In light of demographic changes occurring in China, it is very meaningful that we seek solutions for China with reference to various cases around the world. We argue that raising the performance of small and medium-sized enterprises holds the key to a city's economic resilience and suggest that Economic Gardening, a method conceived in the U.S., can be a powerful means to assist small and medium-sized enterprises.

Finally, Chapter 12 discusses the importance of Japan's role in bringing out the economic potential of the New Silk Road. Although economic ties between Japan and the New Silk Road regions are gradually developing in step with Japan's interest in the regions' natural resources, the volume of international trade and direct investments remains insignificant. However, improvements in transportation competitiveness of the New Silk Road regions have the potential to radically change the economic power map of the Eurasian Continent. If that is the case, the development of Central Asia will benefit Japan. Therefore, we advocate the importance of Japan's increasing involvement in the New Silk Road regions.

As shown above, we have theoretically investigated the possibility of economic development along the New Silk Road regions applying disciplines such as political economy, economic development theory, and spatial economics. At the same time, we have reviewed some of the real problems that these regions face and offered specific solutions. Chinese President Xi Jinping made the headlines when he visited Central Asia in 2013 and he put forward his plan for a "Silk Road Economic Belt." This plan was by no means an accident. In light of our research regarding the economic development of the New Silk Road regions initiated ten years ago, the "Silk Road Economic Belt" plan is an inevitable present-day product of technological advancements in land transportation, which has opened up new possibilities for the Eurasian Continent. In addition, the plan is consistent with the shared expectations among each of the countries that a New Silk Road can promote economic development. However, the important question is what can be offered in terms of a concrete roadmap in carrying forward this plan that can satisfy the interests and expectations of each nation. We are confident that we offer in our book hints to resolve this question.

References

Honda, Mitsuo, Yiliang Wu, Yugun Riku, Naohiko Ijiri and Tadahiro Tsuji (2007), *Industrial Agglomeration and a New International Division of Labor: a New Analytical Viewpoint of the Globalizing Chinese Economy* (in Japanese), Bunshindo.

Riku, Yugun (2006), "Economic Development and Industrial Agglomeration in Developing Countries (in Japanese)," *Kiyo* (Nihon University Economic Science Research Institute), 36, 251-263.

Tsuji, Tadahiro (2006), "Industrialization and Industrial Agglomeration in China's Coastal Region (in Japanese)," *Kiyo* (Nihon University Economic Science Research Institute), 36, 265-279.

Wu, Yiliang (2000), "Limited Labor Mobility and Industry Accumulation: Relevancy of Industry Location Facing Borderline (in Japanese)," *Keizaishushi*, 70 (1), 55-69.

Wu, Yilinag (2006), "An Analysis on Trade and Foreign Direct Investment from a Viewpoint of New Economic Gepography (in Japanese)," *Kiyo* (Nihon University Economic Science Research Institute), 36, 227-249.

Chapter 1

NEW SILK ROAD AND CENTRAL ASIA FROM A "GEO-ECONOMIC" PERSPECTIVE

I. Introduction

The Silk Road once flourished as an overland transportation route between East and West, linking China with the Middle East and Europe. Its social and cultural impact in many different areas was profound, through the trading of goods such as silk and spices, the interaction of diverse peoples and ethnic groups, and the diffusion of religion and technology. However, with the discovery of the new continents and other lands in the Age of Discovery the Silk Road's role as an economically important trade route was taken over by sea transportation, leading to a decline in the activity and fortunes of the Silk Road.

Today, however, the economic growth resulting from global sea trade has led to renewed interest in the role of overland transportation. The European Union (EU), a giant economic market achieved by regional integration, and also China, which now serves as the "workshop of the world" and boasts the second largest GDP of any country after years of high economic growth, now attract enormous attention as huge consumer markets. In East Asia, major drivers of the global economy Japan and South Korea together with the rapidly developing ASEAN nations are important international markets. Thus, overland trade routes linking the EU and East Asia are once again the focus of great interest, as a "New Silk Road".

The east-west interaction of the New Silk Road extends from the Far East to Europe or the Middle East. Significantly, the New Silk Road also passes through and around the geopolitically important regions of Central Asia and Russia. In fact, the development of the New Silk Road is closely tied to the economic growth of the countries of Central Asia, located around the middle of the Eurasian continent. At the same time, the political and economic development and stability in these Central Asian nations are vital to the development of the New Silk Road, and a crucial factor in its success in the coming years.

This paper focuses on the geopolitical significance of the Central Asian region in linking East and West across the Eurasian continent, and examines the economic relations between China and Central Asia from a political and economic perspective. "Geopolitics" is a technical term that literally means the study of how geographic conditions influence political circumstances, but since we are chiefly looking at the geographic conditions and economic development of Central Asia in this paper, our approach could better be described as one of "geo-economics".

"Central Asia" commonly refers to the five nations of Kazakhstan, Uzbekistan, Kyrgyzstan, Tajikistan, and Turkmenistan, but since the economic and political conditions in the countries differ widely, we limit our focus here to three regions/countries: the Xinjiang Uyghur Autonomous Region of China (hereinafter simply "Xinjiang"), Kazakhstan, and Uzbekistan. As a major supplier of energy, Kazakhstan is an important trading partner to China -the biggest in trade value among the Central Asian republics- and it is also important for being the first country encountered along the Silk Road trade routes from China. Uzbekistan is the most populous of the Central Asian nations and consequently offers a consumer market of great promise. It is also politically influential in Central Asia for its strong regional leadership. Xinjiang is located in the far west of China and borders a number of Central Asian countries. It is strategically vital to China, both politically and economically.

II. New Silk Road: Background

1. Independence and Economic Liberalization of the Central Asian Republics

The collapse of the Soviet Union in December 1991 and the end of the Cold War brought about massive changes in international politics. There was a distinct shift from political to economic concerns, as economic development became a key priority. After the Cold War ended, computer and Internet technology became widely available for civilian use, whereas it was previously used principally for military applications. This led to the information-communication technology revolution and became key in the advance of globalization. Market economics came to be the accepted principle of economic management and friendly relations between countries became vital to economic growth.

After independence, the countries of Central Asia at the fringes of the Soviet sphere, which featured centrally planned economies controlled by the Communist Party, were forced to make the transition to market-based economic systems. As independent nations, they had to establish new political systems and move from a socialist planned economy to a market-based economic system, and to strive to achieve economic growth under a market-based economy. In the transition to a market-based economy, they had to liberalize their economies, which necessitated the review and reform of their government management and administration systems, for example by making new laws to provide assurance to private-sector companies and by setting out to privatize state-owned enterprises. In addition, in order to achieve economic growth, the countries were required to deregulate their economies, liberalize trade, and welcome foreign investment, all while maintaining political stability as an independent nation.

These Central Asian countries varied significantly in their implementation of the abovementioned reforms in terms of the difficulties they faced and their commitment to the challenges. While Kazakhstan, Kyrgyzstan, and Tajikistan made the transition quite abruptly, Uzbekistan and Turkmenistan took a more gradual approach to the crossover. In the 1990s, throughout the years after independence, the countries generally remained mired in an economic slump with high inflation, but after the turn of the millennium, their market-based economies seemed to reach a critical mass, putting them on a solid track to economic growth. Although some of the weaknesses resulting from economic liberalization are reflected in their economic performance, on the whole they now look able to sustain a high level of growth.

The collapse of the Soviet Union gave rise to a great deal of chaos; however, it also led to the opening of borders and trade routes, paved the way for the export of energy resources onto the global market, enabled dynamic exchanges with other worlds and made possible many advances. In the pursuit of economic growth through a market-based economy, there is naturally an emphasis on international trade. Since the Central Asian republics were suppliers of primary commodities in the old Soviet economy, natural gas and agricultural products became major exports. Their production of strategic resources such as oil, natural gas, and rare-earth metals -in which they are relatively predominant- has played a significant role in the development of their national economies. However, to develop their economies further, the countries need greater liberalization of their international trade and an industrial structure that features more high value added products. They also need to attract more foreign investment and to establish more stable and open political and economic systems.

2. China's Economic Growth and Development of its Western Frontier

In 1978, China too implemented reforms and opened up its economy, and in 1992, it adopted a socialist market-based economic system, which led to rapid economic growth, predominantly in coastal regions of the country. Then, around 2000, China forged its "great western region development strategy", which marked a shift in the focus of the government's development polices from coastal to inland regions. This led to rapid construction of infrastructure such as roads and electric power facilities in inland regions. Thus, China is well on its way to comprehensive development over its entire territory.

The question of how to develop the economy of its inland regions to ensure stable growth of its national economy became a major challenge for China; trying to reduce the economic disparities within the country has been one key concern. There was a need to open up the inland to the outside world, particularly Xinjiang, to establish a doorway into Central Asia and facilitate free trade. Xinjiang is not only strategically positioned in a geopolitical sense, it is also vital as a pathway into the country for oil, natural gas, and other energy resources on which China depends for its economic development. At the same time, it also serves as a departure point for trade with Central Asia, and by extension as a trade route to the Caspian

Sea, the Middle East, and Europe. In other words, Xinjiang is both a point of entry for energy supplies and a point of departure for export commodities. Furthermore, it provides an alternative source of energy supplies to those coming in by sea to the coastal regions, thereby greatly enhancing energy security. Xinjiang is also used for nuclear testing, as well as being the location of various military facilities. For this reason, the government puts great importance on the region and, through its "great western development" policy, is implementing special measures to promote investment and attract companies to the region. It is fair to say that the stability and development of Xinjiang is closely linked to the stability and development of the country as a whole. (Mackerras and Clarke, 2009, p.100)

Geographically and in terms of natural environment, Xinjiang is blessed. As already mentioned, it is located in the far west of China, a frontier outpost on the Chinese side of the "Eurasian Land Bridge" that leads to Europe. It is also an important base for the distribution of goods, as a trade gateway that borders the countries of Central Asia, through which the Eurasian Land Bridge runs. In addition, Xinjiang boasts natural conditions well suited to agriculture, livestock farming, and forestry, blessed as it is with water, good soil, and long hours of solar insolation. It also has an abundance of energy resources in the form of oil and natural gas, as well as rich deposits of mineral resources, including gold, copper, and rare-earth metals. In fact, it produces most kinds of mineral resources. On top of all this, Xinjiang is also blessed with tourist appeal, due to its natural scenic beauty and historical interest in Silk Road ruins and relics.

There is, however, one element of instability: the problem of minority ethnic groups, such as the Uyghur independence movement, and the terrorist activities of religious extremists. In view of these threats, the Chinese government is striving to stabilize the region as it pursues a development strategy that prioritizes development and growth. It is building overland routes for commercial transportation and creating links to coastal regions. At the same time, it is extending links into Central Asia by building highways and railways, thereby opening up overland transportation by road and rail. China has also set up the Kashgar Special Economic Zone and the Khorgos (Qorghas) Special Development Zone with the aim of expanding and accelerating its trade and investment with Central Asia.

3. Geopolitical Importance of Central Asia

Geopolitical significance is above all a question of geographical conditions.

Central Asia is surrounded by the great powers China and Russia, and it also borders politically sensitive parts of South Asia and the Middle East, such as Pakistan and Afghanistan, as well as the Caucasus region, considered an international crossroads and home to the Caspian Sea basin, which is immensely rich in oil, natural gas, and other energy resources. As an intermediate link and transit point between East and West on the Eurasian continent, Central

Asia is itself abundant in oil and gas, and other strategic energy and mineral resources.

In the 19th century, Central Asia came under the direct rule of Imperial Russia. After the Russian revolution of 1917, under the centrally planned Soviet economy, the region was employed for the cultivation of agricultural crops and cotton, and it became a center for the cotton industry, metallurgy, and other heavy industries, as well as for the development of energy and other natural resources. However, this narrow concentration of particular industries did not allow the region to develop in a balanced way. Later, following the collapse of the Soviet Union in 1991 and the end of the Cold War, the countries of the region gained independence only to find themselves enmeshed in the hardships of transitioning to a globalized, marked-based economy.

The five independent nations that emerged in Central Asia are divided chiefly along ethnic lines, but each of the countries is multiethnic, with the presence of various minority ethnicities and some ethnic-based conflict. There are still remnants of the systems and political culture of the Soviet era, and although the ideology of communism has largely disappeared, the idea of centralized rule by a national government that plans all economic activities has been prevalent. The strong presidential-style system of government derives from the First Secretary of the Communist Party system that preceded it, and although elections are held, political competition is severely restricted and the authority of the president has been further enhanced through national referendums and constitutional amendments. As a result, the national assembly and judiciary exist in little more than name only. Despite the fact that the countries can potentially have mutually advantageous relations with their neighbors, their presidents tend to distrust each other, and political liberalization and economic reforms seem to be continually delayed. Also, at the domestic level, there is a clear divide between winners and losers: generally the groups that hold political power are doing very well, whereas their opponents tend to be excluded from sharing in the prosperity of the country.

Xinjiang is located on the fringes of central China. In the mid-18th century, the area was conquered and ruled by the Qing Dynasty and later it was absorbed into China. The Uyghurs are the region's main ethnic identity, but the regional government is dominated by Han Chinese. In response to the autocratic rule of the Han, a nationalist movement has sprung up, based on an Islamic revival and a renewed ethnic consciousness among the Uyghurs. In 1933 and again in 1944, attempts were made to establish independence from China, under the name "East Turkestan", but within months the uprisings were subdued. The nationalist independence movement continued, but since the communist party came to power in 1949, Xinjiang has been held firmly to the bosom of the People's Republic of China. Even to this day, however, the Uyghurs continue to pursue their separatist aspirations and assert their Islamic identity, and revolts still occasionally occur. Thus, the Uyghur issue remains a source of potential instability in Xinjiang.

The collapse of the Soviet Union and the end of the Cold War opened the door for Islam to become a prominent influence on the societies of Central Asia. Although the form of Islam practiced in the region is generally moderate, this religious revival gave rise to an element of fundamentalist opposition and has also led to social confusion and even acts of terrorism. The region is rich in energy resources, but the presence of diverse ethnic groups and Islamic religious fundamentalism and the imposition of authoritarian political rule have brought about an element of political instability. Although some of the countries have a wealth of natural resources, others are poorer and not so blessed with resources. The region is geopolitically important, but it is characterized by complex historical, ethnic, religious, and cultural factors. Undoubtedly, these countries have a vital bearing on the economic development of the Central Asia region. The big challenge is how to achieve political stability and economic development in the region over the coming years.

III. Economic Relations between the Three Central Asian Countries/Regions

The three countries/regions of Central Asia focused on here are located in the middle of the Eurasian continent. They are landlocked regions with no direct access to the sea. Because the trade needed to drive development relies on overland transport, development up to now has been limited. Here, we examine the general economic conditions of these three areas of Central Asia, as well as their economic relations.

1. Outline of the Three Central Asian Countries/Regions

(1) Xinjiang

Xinjiang is located in the northwestern-most part of China, occupying one-sixth of China's total landmass. It is the second-largest province/autonomous region of China after Tibet. It is also very important geopolitically because it borders eight countries, including India, Pakistan, Afghanistan, and Kazakhstan.

Xinjiang's relatively small population of 22 million is made up of one-third Han Chinese, with most of the remaining two-thirds Uyghurs. However, there are 47 other ethnic groups present. Since they made up the great majority of inhabitants, the Uyghurs were granted self-rule and allowed to use their language officially. Since the 1950s, however, the population of Han Chinese has risen sharply, due to government policies designed to increase their presence, and ethnic tensions have heightened. Uprisings and acts of terrorism have occurred, prompting crackdowns by the Chinese government. Large numbers of Uyghurs and minority ethnic groups live in poverty, and the economic disparity within Xinjiang is higher than anywhere else in China. This disparity, associated with the ethnic problem, influences the stability and development of the region in complex ways.

At the same time, the Xinjiang Uyghur Autonomous Region is blessed with an abundance of energy resources -oil, natural gas (approx. 30% of China's total deposits), and coal (approx. 40%)- as well as mineral resources, including iron ore, copper, and rare-earth metals. The region also boasts a wealth of renewable energy resources such as solar and wind power, and is a rich agricultural resource as a producer of cotton, vegetables, and fruit. It is major center of cotton production, accounting for approximately 40% of China's total output. Livestock farming is another big industry, particularly for wool and mutton. It is also a very appealing tourist destination. In view of all these factors, the Xinjiang region clearly possesses a huge potential for economic development. In order to maintain security and promote economic development, the Chinese government has stationed large numbers of military troops (Xinjiang Production and Construction Corps) in the region and it pursues policies aimed at increasing the presence and influence of Han Chinese by encouraging their resettlement and promoting Chinese-language education. The challenge of integrating Xinjiang into the country's economic development strategy is a serious issue for the national government. Currently, political power is held by the Communist Party, comprising mainly Han Chinese. The Chinese government clearly regards the Xinjiang region as a key focal point of national development.

In the years ahead, Xinjiang will play a major role in China's domestic energy production. In particular, a natural gas pipeline extending from the Tarim Basin to Shanghai is expected to become a vital element of China's long-term energy security. In the 21st century, Xinjiang is likely to become one of China's key energy centers.

(2) Kazakhstan

In 1989, current Kazakh President Nursultan Nazarbayev was the First Secretary of the Kazakhstan Communist Party. In 1990, he was elected the first president of the republic and ever since December 1991, when the country became officially independent, political power has been narrowly concentrated under an authoritarian regime. Furthermore, Nazarbayev has been increasing the powers of the president, to dominate the country and run the nation largely for his personal benefit.

Kazakhstan was part of the former Soviet Union, making up the largest territory of the empire after Russia. It is blessed with massive deposits of fossil fuels and precious mineral resources such as uranium, copper, and zinc. The country also has a large agricultural sector, focused largely on livestock and cereal production. The export of oil, grains, and other commodities to neighboring countries has been a wellspring of growth for Kazakhstan's economy. Due to the country's rapid transition to a market-based economy and its abundance of oil, it has attracted substantial foreign direct investment and achieved a high level of economic growth through resource development and energy exports. These factors have made Kazakhstan the richest country in Central Asia in terms of per capita GDP.

However, as a result of the country's heavy dependence on energy resources and the financial resources earned from them, the global financial crisis of 2008 had a severe impact on the economy, causing Kazakhstan to fall into recession. A country that achieves economic growth relying on natural gas exports puts itself at risk of so-called Dutch disease, whereby appreciation of the nation's currency makes the export of manufactured goods difficult, leading to the decline of its manufacturing industry. To offset this risk, Kazakhstan now needs to cultivate a greater diversity of industries, such as transportation, pharmaceuticals, communications, and petrochemicals.

(3) Uzbekistan

Like his Kazakh counterpart, Uzbekistan President Islam Karimov was the First Secretary of his country's Communist Party back in 1989, becoming the president of the republic in 1990 before being elected president in December 1991 after independence. Similarly, as in Kazakhstan, his rule has been characterized by heavy-handedness and increasing authority, resulting in what is now effectively a dictatorial, authoritarian system of government.

Uzbekistan is a doubly landlocked country, in that it is necessary to cross through two or more other countries to reach the nearest sea port. The country is largely arid, with only 11% of its area consisting of irrigated, arable land, along rivers. A full 60% of the people reside in cities with a high population density. It has the highest population of the Central Asian republics (approx. 26 million), which makes it a promising consumer market.

The country's main export is natural gas, which accounts for approximately 40% of the country's foreign exchange earnings (2009). Other important exports include gold, rare-earth metals, and cotton. Uzbekistan is the second-largest exporter of cotton in the world, and the fifth-largest producer. Gradually, though, its export mix is diversifying away from cotton, due to increasing volumes of high value added fruit and vegetables.

Due to the high international prices of its main exports, growth has topped 8% for the past several years; however, Uzbekistan has made little progress so far in transitioning from the centralized command economy of the Soviet era to a market-based economic system. Although the investment environment is not very attractive, the impact of the global financial crisis on the economy has been small, due to the country's relative isolation from world capital markets.

2. Trade Relations between the Three Central Asian Countries/Regions

Trade between Central Asia and China has risen sharply over recent years. Over the 10-year period from 2001 to 2010, the total value of trade between the two grew by an average of 36.7% per year. Trade with Central Asia makes up only 1.8% of China's total trade in value terms, but from Central Asia's point of view, China is a vital trading partner. Overall, the main products exported to China by the Central Asian nations (according to 2011 trade statistics) are energy resources and raw materials, typically oil and other mineral fuels, copper and copper products, mineral ores, inorganic chemicals, and cotton and cotton textiles. Kazakhstan's exports are concentrated more in oil and other mineral fuels, and Uzbekistan's main exports are cotton and cotton textiles. Energy resources account for an overwhelmingly large part of export value. In contrast, China's main exports to Central Asia are manufactured goods such as machinery, electrical equipment, steel products, automobiles and auto parts, and clothing and footwear. Chinese exports previously consisted largely of products made by labor-intensive light-industrial enterprises, but in the past 10 years, there has been a steady shift to products made by more high-tech, advanced manufacturing.

Their basic industrial structures make the economies of China and Central Asia complementary: Central Asia supplies energy and raw materials to China, and the latter supplies manufactured goods to the former. For Central Asia, China is a major trading partner, to the point that it is heavily reliant on its China trade. Central Asia is especially important for Xinjiang, accounting for 80% of all the region's international trade, particularly Kazakhstan, from which Xinjiang imports mineral fuel and which accounts for about half of all Xinjiang's trade. Notably, Xinjiang does not share a border with Uzbekistan and there is no direct road link between the two, and so the value of trade between the two is small. Imports from Uzbekistan include cotton and raw silk. Xinjiang itself is relatively undeveloped, yet its industrial economy features light industrial enterprises and labor-intensive manufacturing, which use energy and raw materials such as cotton and wool imported from Central Asia and process these into products such as clothing, footwear, and machinery for export. Thus, the economic ties between Central Asia and Xinjiang are tight.

With this complementarity of industrial structures, Central Asia is important to a fast-growing China for ensuring sufficient supplies of energy and natural resources, and conversely, China is important to Central Asia as an inexpensive source of essential consumer goods such as clothing and electrical appliances. Thus, the two regions need each other. However, since this complementarity of industrial structures is essentially vertical, the Central Asian republics risk becoming subordinate in the relationship, in a similar way to Japan's colonies in the prewar era.

As economic ties to China become stronger, the presence of China in Central Asia is growing; trade and investment with Kazakhstan in particular has risen dramatically in recent years. However, this trend has also given rise to increasing perceptions of China as a threat. The inflow of inexpensive Chinese textile products, machinery, and parts severely undermines the development of local industries dealing in similar products. When Chinese invest in the resources industry in Central Asia, they bring in large amounts of Chinese technology and personnel, and in the case of Kazakhstan, such projects have been criticized for being exclusively Chinese enclaves that are exploitative and do not lead to any significant technology transfer or creation of employment. The influx of Chinese farm workers and business people is also a source of friction. (Watanabe, 2012, pp.40-46)

3. Economic Problems of the Central Asia Region

There are several factors that are hindering economic development in Central Asia. The main ones are insufficient economic liberalization and regime shift, lack of infrastructure, over-reliance on resources, and a lack of diversity in its industrial structure, on top of the political instability due to dictatorial, authoritarian regimes, and the restrictions inherent in being the focus of geopolitical tensions between the U.S., China, and Russia. Here, we wish to look at two of these factors.

The first factor that is an issue for development in Central Asia is infrastructure, particularly the need to establish transportation routes over the Eurasian Land Bridge linking the EU to East Asia. The profitability of transportation routes is a problem due to the expense and time required for transport. If it is possible to transport goods at lower cost in less time by building and enhancing roads and railways, the role of overland transportation will grow.

To link East and West across Eurasia by sea takes approximately 60 days. Overland, however, via the Siberian Railway for example, the link can be made in much less time: about 20 days. In the case of crossing the "China Land Bridge" from Lianyungang through to Alashankou in Xinjiang, then passing through several Central Asian countries and Russia, and finally arriving in Europe, transshipment is necessary, due to the various customs procedures along the way and the incompatibility of Chinese and Russian railway track gauge. This drives up the cost in both time and money terms. In addition to costing more in time and money, inadequate roads also lead to damaged freight.

In Central Asia, overland transport is vital for linking together the landlocked countries of the region. Currently, 80% of freight transport is handled by rail, so railways are clearly an essential form of infrastructure. The Jingyihuo (Jinghe-Yining-Khorgos) Railway that passes through Khorgos in Xinjiang and connects with Kazakhstan is now operating, and the China-Kyrgyzstan-Uzbekistan Railway that links Kashgar, Kyrgyzstan, and Uzbekistan is also set to be completed soon. The designation of Khorgos and Kashgar as special development zones makes Central Asia an important trade region. To stimulate greater international trade in the coming years, there is a need to build high-speed roadways and railways, to simplify customs procedures, and to increase the efficiency of transshipments.

There is also a need to construct oil and natural gas pipelines. Building pipelines is ultimately cheaper and more secure than transporting oil and gas by rail or road. The development of more efficient and inexpensive transportation routes for energy resources is a major challenge for the New Silk Road.

With China's strong economic growth in the past a few decades, procuring sufficient energy became a significant problem for the country. In 1993, China began to import oil, and since 2000, oil imports have risen sharply. In 2009, China also became a net importer of coal, becoming the world's biggest consumer of energy after the U.S. In order to sustain economic development, it is necessary to ensure a stable supply of energy, and the procurement of any energy shortfalls from abroad needs to be dependable in terms of economic viability and distribution. Procurement from the Middle East comes with the risks inherent to sea transportation through the Strait of Hormuz and the Straits of Malacca and to political instability in the Middle East. Thus, from the point of view of the diversification and stability of energy supplies, the neighboring region of Central Asia is essential to China for enhancing energy security.

For China, the countries of Central Asia with their rich reserves of energy resources and the ability to trade with them directly without going through Russia are of great strategic significance. Currently, there is an oil pipeline connecting Kazakhstan with Alashankou in Xinjiang. In addition, a gas pipeline has been built that connects Khorgos in Xinjiang with natural gas-rich Turkmenistan and Uzbekistan.

The development of transportation routes is important not only in terms of connecting the giant consumer markets of East and West, but also to promote the economic development of the Central Asian republics at the heart of Eurasia. Improving access to the major centers of production and consumption in the East and West will boost economic prosperity in the regions along the connecting distribution routes. Positive impacts would be enjoyed by service industries such as hotels and restaurants, as well as manufacturing-related enterprises. Major cities along the distribution route could form production networks and coordinated enterprises of different specialization.

Next, it is necessary to overcome the lack of diversity in an industrial structure that relies on natural resources. The development of the abundant energy and natural resources of Central Asia has a vital role to play in the economic development not only of the Central Asian countries, but also that of Europe and East Asia. During the Soviet era, Central Asia was treated largely as a supplier of energy and mineral resources, agricultural products, and other raw materials, leading to a very skewed industrial structure and restricting the development of manufacturing industry. After independence too, it was almost inevitable that the structure of trade would continue to be characterized by the export of resources and the import of mass-market consumer goods.

Energy and mineral resources such as oil, natural gas, and rare-earth metals are essential export products, but the fact that they are internationally traded commodities makes their price vulnerable to substantial fluctuations. This is fine when prices go up, but since prices can also drop, be exposed to market speculation, and vary with the economic fortunes of particular countries, export earnings can be unstable. Also, since they are strategic commodities, they can easily get caught up in the machinations of international politics and security dramas. Agricultural products are similarly subject to price fluctuations and their production output is influenced by unpredictable factors such as weather and pest infestations.

When a country's economy and trade structure is dependent on primary exports, it is not possible to ensure a stable stream of revenue, because of the fluctuations of the international markets. In addition, the development of mineral resources does not provide much scope for expanding employment. In order to break out of this kind of industrial structure, it is necessary to cultivate a broad base of manufacturing and other supporting industries that will generate jobs. This requires the setup of economic development zones, the promotion of foreign investment, and attraction of export-oriented manufacturing enterprises. This kind of industrialization would put the Central Asian countries in competition with China, however, and being landlocked makes it hard to lure foreign investors. Thus, there are hurdles to achieving this kind of development.

In the case of Xinjiang, there is the question of what role exactly the region should play within the grand scheme of China. Due to the political imperative to preserve peace and security, the region has been earmarked for preferential development, and with an abundance of natural resources to fuel economic growth as well, there is a huge potential for economic development. The central government is aiming to create a network with Central Asia to secure energy supplies, but ethnic tensions between the Uyghurs and the huge influx of Han Chinese is worsening substantially as the disparity between rich and poor grows wider. The political issue of how to respond to this local instability and whether it can be eliminated casts a huge shadow on economic development.

IV. Central Asia's Renewed International Relations

After the collapse of the Soviet Union, the new republics of Central Asia had to establish international relations afresh. These relations changed dramatically once again following the September 11 terrorist attacks on America in 2001.

The independence of the Central Asian countries is not based on a strong sense of nationalism or ethnic identity, but rather on the political decisions made in the aftermath of the Soviet collapse (Uyama, 2010, p. 94). With their independence, the countries found themselves at a loss and facing all kinds of problems. Their economies collapsed dramatically: suddenly, border procedures and trade and human networks were broken; regional water supply and energy systems were weakened; industrial and agricultural relations were broken; large numbers of skilled Russians fled the country; aid from Russia dried up; and the Soviet system of administration disappeared. This resulted in poverty and weakened social security and stability, and the evolution of the countries was disrupted severely. The years from 1990 to 2001 were generally very troubled for the Central Asia republics. They had won their independence only to find themselves confronting economic stagnation and political instability. Furthermore, relations between the countries of Central Asia were very strained.

The Soviet Union's collapse presented China with both opportunities and challenges. As Russia became relatively withdrawn, tensions along the China-Soviet border eased. At the same time, five independent Central Asian republics arose, three of them sharing borders with China and thereby posing potential threats. On top of this, the revival of Islam as a political force in Central Asia could potentially spread to the ethnic groups of Xinjiang, and through the 1990s, the growing influence of Islamic fundamentalism fueled unrest in the Chinese region.

The borders between Central Asia and China started to open up in the late 1980s, facilitating greater trade and cultural exchanges, but also enabling the smuggling of drugs and arms, as well as criminality, including Islamic terrorism. Of particular concern to China was the spread of the Uyghur separatist movement. At the same time, trade and investment-related relations with China improved dramatically. As China's economy continued growing, its demand for energy increased, and in 1993, the country became a net importer of oil. This prompted China to deepen its relations with the resource-rich countries of Central Asia. Thus, for China, Central Asia offers great benefits while simultaneously posing a danger. Although China reaped great economic benefits, its anxieties concerning human rights and separatism in Xinjiang grew stronger.

1. Shanghai Cooperation Organization: Mechanism for Regional Stabilization?

After the fall of the Soviet empire in 1991, some of the newly independent Central Asian republics, Russia, and China gradually began cooperating on strategic political and economic initiatives. One such initiative was the formation of the Shanghai Cooperation Organization (SCO).

China's major concerns in the 1990s were securing its borders with the countries of Central Asia and the stability of the Xinjiang region. The SCO was established to accelerate economic modernization and build constructive relations with the Central Asian republics, to help promote trade between Xinjiang and Central Asia, and placate the opposition of ethnic minorities in Xinjiang. In 1996, this alliance was called the "Shanghai Five"; in 2001, it was more formally established as the SCO.

In April 1996, China, Russia, Kazakhstan, Kyrgyzstan, and Tajikistan concluded the "Treaty on Deepening Military Trust in Border Regions" at a meeting in Shanghai. The treaty was aimed principally at setting up demilitarized zones, building greater trust, and arms reductions. One political issue was that the newly independent states of Central Asia still needed to clearly demarcate their national territories, since their borders were not clearly defined under Soviet rule. The need to clearly define their boundaries with China to ensure border security was particularly urgent. Meetings of the Shanghai Five discussed a variety of security issues, such as ethnic separatism, religious extremism, and international terrorism. In June 2001, Uzbekistan was adopted as a new member of the group, which became more formally established under the name Shanghai Cooperation Organization. The name derives from the fact that the first meeting of the group was held in Shanghai.

The goals and mission stated in the charter of the SCO are broadly outlined below.
- To enhance mutual trust and good neighborly relations between member countries.
- To cooperate on maintaining regional peace, security, and stability, and to promote a

new democratic, just, and rational international political and economic order.
- To collaborate in opposing terrorism, separatism, and fundamentalism.
- To combat the illegal trade of drugs and arms, crime, and illegal immigration.
- To encourage political participation, trade, economic activity, self-defense, legal compliance, environmental protection, culture, science, technology, education, energy, transportation, and finance.
- To promote comprehensive and balanced economic growth and social and cultural development, to raise the standard of living and improve quality of life in the region.
- To cooperate on integration with the global economy.
- To promote human rights and basic freedoms.
- To maintain and promote relationships with other nations and international organizations worldwide.
- To prevent international disputes and provide peaceful solutions for them.
- To work together to find solutions to "21st century problems".

As this list shows, the SCO ostensibly deals with a broad range of concerns, but its main purpose is to cooperate on regional security. The SCO continues to grow more international, with a number of other nations now admitted as "observer countries": currently these include India, Iran, Mongolia, Pakistan, and Afghanistan.

There has been little interaction up to now between the Chinese region of Xinjiang and the former-Soviet countries of Central Asia, but over the first decade of the 21st century, their mutual dependence grew significantly. The bonds of interdependence relate to a variety of issues, including trade, security, and geopolitics, which affect both sides in similar ways. The relationship between Xinjiang and Central Asia is not an equal one: China is clearly the dominant partner economically, politically, and militarily, but that is not to say that it has the upper hand overwhelmingly. The Central Asian countries possess much of what China needs to sustain its economic growth. For this reason, China supplies substantial capital to Central Asia, in the form of infrastructure construction for example, thereby bringing great benefit to the local economies. This economic interdependence is increasingly important, as this relationship of economic cooperation serves to improve the economy of both sides and to promote mutual economic prosperity.

China's economic expansion into Central Asia is not just about economic development; it is also necessary for national security reasons. Furthermore, it is not just to help preserve its control over Xinjiang. Following the September 11 attacks of 2011, America began stationing troops in Central Asia. As a consequence, China was required to strengthen its presence in the region. The Chinese government is very conscious that the stability and prosperity of Central Asia ensures the stability and prosperity of Xinjiang. Although previously China's move into Central Asia was based primarily on a military logic, its attitude toward Central Asia is now mainly cooperative and economic in nature, with a strong emphasis on the stability of the entire region. (Mackerras and Clarke, 2009, pp.95-97)

The SCO was originally formed with a focus on regional security, but more recently its orientation has shifted to economic cooperation and it has become an important regional body. The logic is that in order to promote regional stability, the SCO must of course concern itself with maintaining security, but it must also promote regional trade, economic growth, and strive to raise people's standard of living.

The SCO is examining ways to promote trade and investment, and initiate large-scale economic cooperation projects. It is also considering the creation of an SCO development bank. In the coming years, the organization will be increasing collaboration on infrastructure construction and resource development, and it is looking to build rail and road networks and oil and gas pipelines. Furthermore, it is expected that the countries possessing natural resources will not merely export their commodities, but also develop oil and gas processing facilities and chemical industries. The hope is that the combination of Central Asia's resources and related industries and China's textile, apparel, and consumer electrical appliance industries will lead to the formation of a truly complementary economic relationship.

However, China's enthusiasm for shifting the character of the SCO away from security to economic cooperation is causing some concern to other member countries. China's proposal to establish a SCO development bank funded mainly by Chinese capital, to try and promote economic development in Central Asia, has drawn a wary reaction from Russia, which fears China's growing presence in the region. The other Central Asian member countries have also started to feel wary of China's posturing. China's economic aid has also come under criticism and fueled distrust, with suspicions that it is directed more at increasing Chinese profits than developing the economy of the recipient country. Thus, China is increasingly being seen as a threat.

2. U.S. Intervention in Central Asia and Unstable International Relations

Since the September 11 terrorist attacks of 2001, America has inserted itself into Central Asia to join fellow "great powers" China and Russia, thereby changing the international relations equation. The U.S. attitude toward Central Asia can be divided into two distinct phases: pre-911 and post-911. Pre-911, U.S. interest was lukewarm, due to Central Asia's remoteness and inaccessibility, as well as a lack of knowledge about the history and culture of the region. Post-911, the U.S. began to take a strong interest in the region, as it sought to combat terrorism, to promote the spread of democracy and economic liberalization, and to cooperate on regional peace.

When the U.S. began its invasion of Afghanistan to combat terrorism, China, Russia, and the countries of Central Asia expressed strong approval for its "war on terror". This was because of their shared desire to fight the "three evils of separatism, extremism, and terrorism", as embodied by the Uyghur movement in Xinjiang and certain Islamic sects in Central Asia. To facilitate its war on terror, the U.S. increased its involvement in the region considerably, for example, by setting up military bases in Central Asia. Within five months of the September 11 attacks, U.S. military bases had been set up in Uzbekistan and Kyrgyzstan, and in addition, Tajikistan granted permission for the U.S. to make use of some of its military facilities. The countries of Central Asia allowed the U.S. military to use their countries not just out of opposition to terrorism and fundamentalism, but also to contain the influence of China and Russia, and in anticipation of U.S. aid and the fees received for use of military facilities.

This was the first-ever military intervention by the U.S. in Central Asia. While China had faced the threat of the Soviets in the past, the potential of a U.S. threat on its western flank made the Chinese nervous. The growing political, military, and economic presence of the U.S. in Central Asia was a double-edged sword for Beijing. The U.S. war on terror would benefit Xinjiang and Central Asia, but a stronger relationship between the U.S. and Central Asia would disadvantage China. The initiation of the Iraq War by the U.S. in 2003 alarmed the leaders of Central Asia. America's involvement in Central Asia peaked at about the time of a series of so-called "color revolutions" that overthrew sitting governments around the world, including the "orange revolution" of 2004 in the Ukraine and the "tulip revolution" of 2005 in Kyrgyzstan. These events fueled a fear that the U.S. was not really promoting stability, but rather undermining it. There was a growing wariness that the challenge to order and stability in Central Asia was coming not just from Islamic extremism and international terrorists, but also from America's intervention in the guise of promoting "democracy and human rights". At the SCO meetings of 2005 and 2006, there was a distinct rise in anti-American sentiment, and calls began for the U.S. to withdraw its military presence from the region.

Viewing Central Asia as a region of instability within the Eurasian landmass, America involved itself in the region by supporting democratization and economic liberalization, by cooperating on anti-terrorism, and by stationing its military there. However, the question of energy was surely another factor, and so competition between the three great powers suddenly intensified. Eyeing the abundant oil deposits in Central Asia, the U.S. government and major U.S. oil corporations became involved in the region by launching American-funded energy resource development projects, as well as in other ways. This intervention weakened Russia's influence on the region. For example, the Americans began laying oil and gas pipelines that do not pass through Russian territory. Clearly, a geopolitical power struggle is taking place in Central Asia.

Nonetheless, China and Russia appear to remain Central Asia's main commercial partners in economic development. Russia has the advantage of facing only minimal linguistic and cultural barriers to the region, and since the Soviet era, it has preserved its role as a supplier of export markets, employment, education, and capital to Central Asia. China has its great economic power, and as it has grown, it has built a relationship of mutual dependency with Central Asia, born of its great thirst for energy. China's economic power is probably of positive net benefit to Central Asia. Chinese capital and specialist knowledge pours into Central Asia, feeding its economic development, which in turn promotes the development and security of Xinjiang, and by extension also the stability of China as a whole.

The Central Asia region is vitally important from a security perspective. Its possession of energy and mineral resource riches makes it the focus of a geopolitical power game between the three biggest global powers -America, China, and Russia- who each have their own designs on the region to do with political power, security, and economic benefit. The geopolitical importance of Central Asia in terms of energy and the war on terror tends to make its international relations unstable, but the question of how it can retain stability in the years ahead is closely tied to its economic development.

V. Conclusion

The countries of Central Asia, located on the fringes of the former Soviet Union under which they were ruled, gained their independence after the empire's collapse, whereas the region of Xinjiang is a vast territory on the far western flank of the great power China. Both are multicultural places, featuring a mix of Russian and Slavic culture, Chinese culture, and Turkic cultures; lands of prairies and deserts, with cities developed within the oases that dot the region; and lands of cultural variety shaped through the interaction of East and West by nomadic tribes. Their diversity masks a potential for rich development. Both Central Asia and Xinjiang face complex issues relating to their ethnic groups. They are also religiously similar, in that Islam is the major religion, and they each face anxieties about security due to religious extremism and a significant threat of chaos. They have great potential for development, due to their wealth of strategically important energy and natural resource commodities. However, as landlocked countries with multiple international borders, their development depends heavily on overland transport. Given its geopolitical significance, there are high hopes that Central Asia's economic development will bring about a New Silk Road, but numerous challenges must first be overcome.

The economic and industrial interrelationships between the countries of Central Asia are complementary, but the vertical division of specializations across the countries tends to inhibit development. For this reason, each country needs to diversify and upgrade its industrial structure to create a more horizontal division of industrial activity. In the coming years, the regions will use their massive reserves of natural resources as a weapon to promote the development of transportation routes; they will encourage greater political and economic exchange while attracting foreign investment; and they will push toward great economic cooperation and integration. Undoubtedly Central Asia has a huge potential for economic development and growth over the coming years.

References

Brzezinski, Zbigniew (2003), *The Grand Chessboard* (in Japanese), translated by Yamaoka, Y., Nihon Keizai Shimbun, Inc.

Chon Ajimu (Qong, Ajim) (2007), "Foreign Trade between Xinjiang Uyghur Autonomous Region and Central Asian Countries (in Japanese)", *Kumamoto Daigaku Shakai Bunka Kenkyu*, 5, 173-192.

CIA-The World Factbook (https//www.cia.gov/library/publications/the-world-factbook/)

Horie, Norio (2010), *Eurasian New Movements of Change: Russia, China and Central Asia* (in Japanese), Iwanami Shoten.

JETRO (2008), *Expanding Chinese Presence in Central Asia* (in Japanese), JETRO.

Mackerras, Colin and Michael Clarke (eds) (2009), *China, Xinjiang and Central Asia*, Routledge.

Shimoyashiro, Mamoru (2008), *Economic Graphic Explanations of Central Asia* (in Japanese), Toyo Shoten.

Uyama, Tomohiko (ed.) (2010), *60 Chapters of Central Asia* (in Japanese), Akashi Shoten.

Watanabe, Shino (2012), "Major Developments and Challenges in Sino-Central Asian Relations (in Japanese)," *Kaigai Jijyou* (*Journal of World Affairs*), 60 (9), 32-48.

Chapter 2

FORMING A BEADS-TYPE INDUSTRIAL CITY ALONG THE NEW SILK ROAD

I. Introduction

In recent years, the railway transportation route that crosses the Eurasian continent has been attracting much attention from home and abroad, as though recollecting the revival of the ancient Silk Road. In fact, the Trans-Asian Railway network plan proposed by ESCAP (The United Nations Economic and Social Commission for Asia and the Pacific) to construct traffic networks that cross the continent has been in place since the 1960s. This plan was for a railway network connecting Singapore to Istanbul, which was later to be extended to Europe and Africa. The plan describes many routes that connect the east and west of the Eurasian continent. Our research, however, focuses on a route corresponding to the northern corridor of the Trans-Asian Railway network plan, or what we consider to be the "New Silk Road." Among the northern corridor routes, with the support of the Asian Development Bank, the Second Eurasian Land Bridge (also known as the China route or the China Land Bridge) was opened to traffic between China's Lianyungang and Holland's Rotterdam in 1992. In addition, in October 2007, China and eight other countries in Central Asia reached an official agreement on a construction plan for a transit route connecting China's Hami to Turkey. In October 2008, scheduled container freight service began from China to Moscow.

This series of activities is closely related to viewpoints regarding the intercontinental distribution of goods and the economic development of China, Russia, and countries in Central Asia. For China, remarkable economic development has been achieved since the economic reforms of the 1980s; however, most economic activity has been concentrated in the eastern coastal area. As a result, problems of inter-regional disparity have become increasingly significant. To correct this inter-regional disparity, the Chinese government proposed the "Western China Major Development Plan" in 2000, and began to place greater emphasis on the role of the Second Eurasian Land Bridge. The central Asian countries through which it passes also have great interest in the route due to its implications for economic development and trade and are focusing on its role. Since Russia is also concentrating its effort on the development of the Far East, it uses the First Eurasian Land Bridge (also known as the Siberian Land Bridge); however, they are also paying special attention to the role of the Second Eurasian Land Bridge, since the first and second routes are in a competitive relationship in terms of the east-west transit route. Due to this relationship, Russia began infrastructure improvements such as electrification work to improve the competitiveness of the first route.

In addition to the countries along the railway line, Japan, Korea, and the European countries located at both the eastern and western ends of the Eurasian continent are interested in the Eurasian Land Bridge. These countries are focusing on the development of the transit route for resource development in Central Asia to penetrate the growing Chinese market and utilize China's abundant workforce.

However, the intentions for the development of the Eurasian Land Bridge differ among the countries that surround it. Nevertheless, since they hold the possibility of mutual benefit, the countries are cooperating for its development. Thus, economic interrelationships in the New Silk Road region along the Eurasian Land Bridge are becoming closer, the movement of people, material, and money is increasing, and the importance of this region continues to grow.

The interior of the Eurasian continent had been isolated from the economic development since the ancient Silk Road deteriorated. Now that the region is regaining attention with the New Silk Road, the question becomes whether economic development of this inland area is possible. If it is possible, then how would it come about? In response to these questions, in the current paper we posit the idea of a "Beads-type" development strategy and the formation of a Beads-type industrial city and discuss their plausibility and potential mechanisms for economic development.

II. Why a Beads-type Development Strategy?

1. Change of the Economic Center in the Trade Route and a Beads-type Development Strategy

When we reflect on the history of the interior of the Eurasian continent, we recognize that the overland Silk Road, which was constructed around 200 BCE, served as the center of east-west trade. Among China, Central Asia, and Europe, much merchandise (material) was traded including silk, porcelain, precious stones, pepper, and rugs; this promoted cultural exchange and the resultant transfer of technology. Also, oasis cities developed along the route as the ancient Silk Road became established as the center of trade. A period of prosperity in the interior of the Eurasian continent followed. Expressing these center cities in line with a Beads-type development strategy, we show that these cities can be viewed as a Beads-type city band along the ancient Silk Road. By 600 A.D., a marine Silk Road emerged and the land-based Silk Road was replaced as the age of great voyages emerged and cities along the land-based trade route began to decline. In addition, with the development of modern marine transport, new cities emerged and developed along the coast.

In the recent years, however, due to the development of land-based transit technology, and the rapid construction of transit infrastructure, competitiveness in the interior of the continent has increased. This also applies to the region through which the ancient Silk Road passed; in particular, since construction, expansion, and improvements in Central Asia's roads and railway infrastructure have been hastened, the possibility for cities along the ancient Silk Road to be redeveloped has arisen. Currently, the traffic route that connects the Eurasian continent does not connect China and the Middle East. Instead, it has been moving toward a direction of connecting China's coastal area, Japan, and Korea to Western European countries. That is to say, it is the New Silk Road.

For this area to achieve real economic development and regain its former prosperity, we believe it is necessary to apply a Beads-type Development Strategy. Currently, unique nucleated cities dot the ancient Silk Road within the interior of the Eurasian continent. We believe that if the economic cooperative relationship is deepened, if the potential for economic power can be shown, and if the necessary transit conditions that connect these nucleated cities are further improved, the formation of a Beads-type industrial area will no longer be simply a dream, but could possibly become a reality. According to the conventional view on economic development, the choices for a development strategy are either balanced growth according to Nurkse or unbalanced growth according to Hirshman. However, for the Beads-type Development Strategy that we propose, there is no need to adhere to the choice between conventional balanced and unbalanced growth. Rather, since we are in the era of globalization, with ever-increasing freedom of international trade, fueling rapid progress in transit technology and construction of the requisite infrastructures to facilitate international trade, we require a new development strategy. Specifically, the Beads-type Development Strategy explores the possibility of economic development within the relationship between industrial agglomeration and the formation of new focal points of economic growth.

2. Difference between the Beads-type Development Strategy and Conventional Development Strategy Model

The "Beads-type" Development Strategy is fundamentally different from the conventional development strategy, which primarily targets one country or one area. On the other hand, the Beads-type Development Strategy is unique in that it emphasizes on how to form a new growth base in an autonomous development process.

The T-shaped and Π-shaped development strategies are the conventional models applied to the development of China's coastal area. Essentially, since the founding of the People's Republic of China in 1949, China's economic development strategy has been focused on "balanced growth development." Since the 1950s, industrialization has been carried out to conform to the following three principles: degree of access between raw material production areas and consumption areas, correction of inter-regional disparities, and consideration of national defense and security.

In the 1960s, however, the foreign environment surrounding China changed dramatically against the backdrop of an escalated ideological dispute with the Soviet Union, and a confrontation with the U.S. that involved the Vietnam War. As a result, China's development strategy model shifted to being more inland oriented. At the end of 1978, after Deng Xiaoping proposed reforms and an open-door policy, China's development strategy converted from balanced to unbalanced growth. In 1988, the coastal area economic development strategy was introduced, whose main objective in promoting growth and development was to encourage trade between the coastal towns and village enterprises. The strategy was based on Deng Xiaoping's two broad perspectives and became the official national development strategy. By the end of the 1990s, the development cooperation strategy was launched. It encouraged a desire for efficiency and fairness and stressed the significance of each area's comparative advantage. In June 2000, in accordance with the 10th quinquennial plan, the Chinese government moved to the second broad perspective, wherein the T-shaped and Π-shaped strategies were developed, and China's Western Development in earnest. These strategies were intended to construct a harmonious society that facilitates development of the inland area while fostering rapid economic growth in the coastal area. In this way, China's development strategy followed a process of moving back and forth between the strategies of balanced and unbalanced growth.

The results of the T-shaped development strategy, announced after the 1990s, are shown in Figure 2-1. T-shaped means that the vertical part of the letter T indicates the coastal line and the horizontal part indicates the inland line. The strategic aim is to produce a wave of development from China's eastern coastal area to its western inland region and promote development in northeastern China. There are two factors that form the foundation of the T-shaped development strategy.

First, to resolve the economic disparity that developed between the East and West, political consideration is required. Second, the export-oriented economic development in the coastal region needs a strategic complement, since the backward linkage of effects toward the inland area -the coastal area's industrial induction strength, as it was- are weak. Since its industrial induction strength, the backward linkage effects toward the inland area are weak.

Shanghai's Pudong area, where the open coastal area and the Yangtze River (Chang Jiang River) cross, plays a central role in the T-shaped development strategy. Shanghai's Pudong area is not an offshore production area per se. Nevertheless, it receives preferential policy measures similar to those that an offshore production area would receive. According to the T-shaped development strategy, as the Yangtze River coastal cities open, economic spheres will be formed in the upper/middle/lower valleys, each with a large city as its core. These three economic spheres compose the downstream basin of the Yangtze River, with cities such as Shanghai, Suzhou, and Wuxi at the center. The middle basin of the Yangtze River comprises the cities of Hubei and Hunan, with Wuhan and Yichang at the center, and the upper basin of the Yangtze River included the cities of Sichuan province, such as Chongqing and Panzhihua.

Figure 2-1 The Image of the T-shaped Development

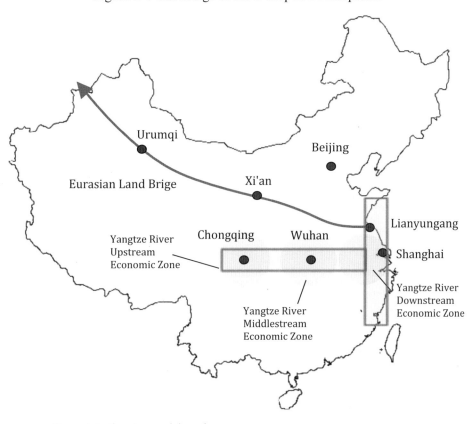

(Source) Authors' own elaboration

An enlarged version that adds the Eurasian Land Bridge to the coast of this T-shaped development strategy is called the Π-shaped development strategy. The Eurasian Land Bridge is a railroad route that connects Lianyungang and Xuzhou of Jiangsu, Zhengzhou of Henan, Xi'an of Shaanxi, Lanzhou of Gansu, and Urumqi of Xinjiang Uyghur Autonomous Region; furthermore, it connects to Rotterdam, Holland through central Asia. The objectives of these T-shaped and Π-shaped development strategies is to first increase the production capacity of fine industrial products within China and create domestic demand for industrial input goods through backward linkage effects. Switching from the import of industrial input goods to domestic production leads to the advancement of China's industrial structure and to the new development of China's inland area. This is how the development strategy that connects China's East and West through the coast, rivers, and railways was devised.

China is the object of the Π-shaped development strategy and the strategy attempts to utilize the Chinese railway area of the Eurasian Land Bridge in a Chinese version of a flying geese model. Shiyu Kan proposed a policy related to initial efforts to correct regional economic disparity, which states "For correcting the inter-regional disparity, promote the domestic version of FTA, flying geese, and ODA." Kan regarded China's inter-regional disparity to be mainly a reflection of the disparity between the eastern (the coastal) and mid-western (inland) areas and the urban and the farming areas. To correct this disparity, he proposed three policies: creation of a united domestic market (domestic version of FTA), division of labor based on a region's comparative advantage (a domestic version of the flying geese), and fiscal transfer from an economically advanced area to a relatively underdeveloped one through central government finance (a domestic version of ODA).

The essential problem with this idea is that, formerly, the flying geese strategy considered the country as an economic unit. Therefore, we cannot say it is necessarily beneficial to China. Kan identifies that along with foreign companies, eventually, China will also have to move their production base in pursuit of cheaper labor and land through foreign direct investment (FDI). Primarily, to maintain economic growth while correcting the inter-regional disparity, ailing industries in the eastern area must be moved to the mid-western area, rather than abroad (Kan, 2006, pp.65-66). However, Kan's assumptions may never materialize in reality. This is because, according to research by JICA (Japan International Cooperation Agency) more than 70% of the corporations that moved from the eastern to the western region targeted market development and not production. Results for the Factors Corporation, after its move from the eastern to the western area, are summarized in Table 2-1. These results show that private enterprises moving to the western area incur large risks. Also, we see cases in which ailing eastern industries benefit more by moving abroad than to the Midwest, counter to Kan's assumption.

Table 2-1 The Most Anxious Factors Eastern Firms Feel when They Advance into the Western Region

	The Most Affecting Factors Affecting for Firms	% of Firms Answered
1	Low Level of Urbanization, Insufficient Social Services and Lagged Infrastructure Improvement	47.41
2	Excessive Intervention of Local Government	43.70
3	Local Protectionism	39.26
4	Insufficient Financial Support, Lack of Capital	33.33
5	Exclusiveness of Local People, Difficult to Establish Sound Environment for Development	25.93
6	Inferior Natural Environment in the Western Region that Prevents Human Resources from Introducing from the Eastern Region	25.19
7	Lagged Reform of State Corporation, Non-establishment of Fair Competitive Environment in Many Sectors	15.56

(Source) JICA (2004) *Report on the Survey of Development Strategy of Middle-class Cities in the Western Region of China*, July, pp.V-38.

Although this type of corporate activity will not occur under the current planned economic system, it is a rational action under the market mechanism. A development strategy that relies on "the domestic version of the flying geese strategy," which means moving the coastal area's ailing industry to the inland area, is unreasonable to expect in a market economy. Therefore, we consider that the efficacy of this type of flying geese development strategy model will be questioned.

Our Beads-type Development Strategy, on the other hand, emphasizes on how to form a new growth base within the autonomous development process. Also, this development accommodates the country and the whole region in a global view. It is a strategy that aims for co-existence and co-prosperity by encouraging the formation of self-organizing cities in the New Silk Road area that crosses Western Europe, that is, from the west of the Eurasian continent to Japan and Korea in the east. Next we theoretically examine the approach to this strategy.

III. Possibility of Forming Beads-type Industrial Cities in the New Silk Road Region

In this section, we examine the theoretical possibility and the necessary conditions for the Beads-type Development Strategy. We generally characterize economic activity to be spatially concentrated. In particular, when we look at the spatial side of modern industries, we find that they are co-located, with cities at the center. This concept applies equally well to Western developed countries, which established a dominant economic position subsequent to the Industrial Revolution; Japan or Asia's newly industrializing economies (NIEs), which accomplished economic development after WWII; and more recently to the BRICs (Brazil, Russia, India, China), which is experiencing rapid economic growth. In all of these regions, and despite the era in which their industrial base developed and grew, we see that their manufacturing activities were performed with cities as their center. These characteristics are clarified in the many pioneering studies that belong to the discipline of Spatial Economics developed by Krugman *et al.* (see Krugman, 1991a, 1991b, 1995; Fujita *et al.*, 1999).

Krugman (1991a) used a two-region model and depended on Marshall's external economies to explain the spatial concentration of economic activities through the interaction of economies of scale and transportation costs. To explain this industrial agglomeration process according to Fujita (1996), as shown in Figure 2-2, individual companies minimize transportation costs by locating close to large-scale markets (many consumers and laborers).

At the same time, they benefit from being proximal to companies that supply a variety of goods. In addition, in an area where many companies are located, consumers (= laborers) can obtain various goods at a cheaper price; moreover, since many employment opportunities exist, they can earn a higher real income. Therefore, consumers (= laborers) will relocate

Figure 2-2 An Example of the Process of Industrial Agglomeration

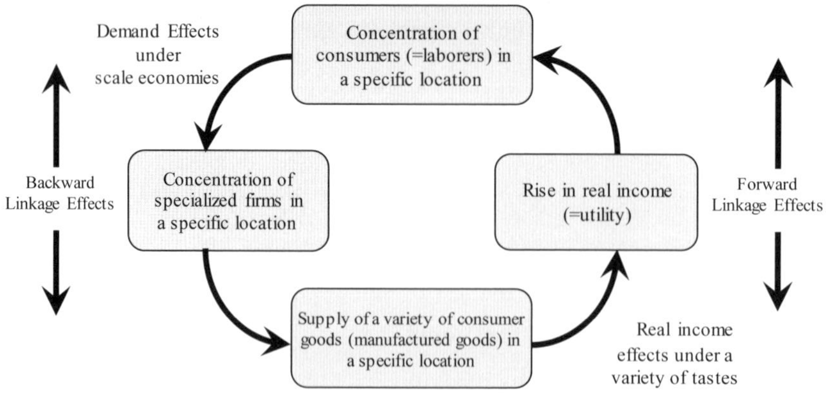

(Source) Fujita (1996)

there, resulting in the further expansion of the market of that area and increased relocation of companies. Thus, economic activities will be concentrated in a specific location through an endogenous yet cyclical accumulation process and large metropolitan areas will be formed.

The analytical result of Krugman (1991a) shows that industrial agglomeration occurs when transportation costs are sufficiently low, the market share of industrial goods are sufficiently high, and economies of scale exist in industrial production. In recent years, an enlarged form of this model has been devised. This is a two-country four-region model where simultaneous analyses of the international and domestic sides of the accumulation process of development are possible (see Monfort and Nicolini, 2000; Behrens *et al.*, 2003; Wu, 2007). Unlike the domestic side, for the international side, economic activities will not be concentrated in one country since the laborers' international movement is generally constrained. This is especially so for a modern society, where international output shows a tendency for dispersion with a decline in transportation costs, which are taken broadly to mean telecommunications and unrestricted capital flows. Modern industries that emerged in 18th century England have spread to the four corners of the world. Recently, it is noteworthy that output is moving to developing countries. This type of international dispersion of output does not conflict with the domestic concentration of output, but rather, we can consider that domestic and international output progress simultaneously. Wu (2007) explains this type of phenomenon by analyzing a homogeneous two-country four-region model with similar geographic conditions where "the international dispersion and the domestic concentration" increase simultaneously (see Figure 2-3).

T in Figure 2-3 represents transportation costs and τ represents the broad application of the cost of entry into international trade. The area below the critical line S1 represents the area

Figure 2-3 Analysis of Homogeneous Two-Country Four-Region Model

$\beta=0.70, \quad \mu=0.35, \quad \rho=0.75$

Critical Curve of Pattern 1:S1

Critical Curve of Pattern 5:B

Critical Curve of Pattern 3:S3

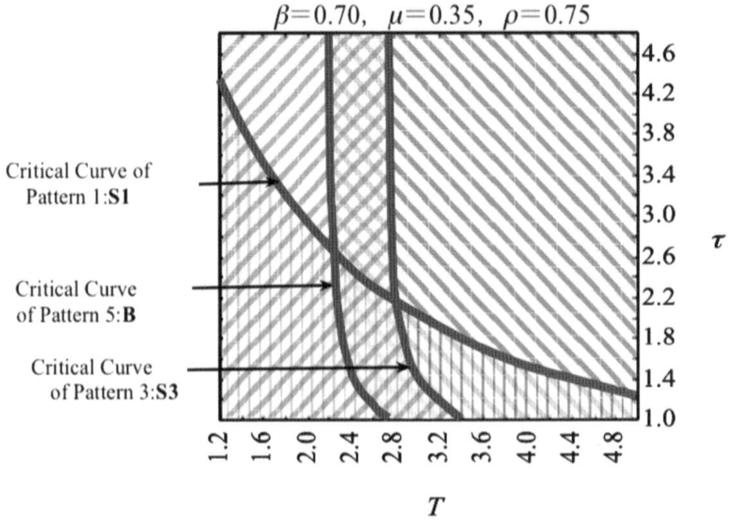

(Source) Wu (2007)

where the aggregated distribution of the industry to either of the areas of one country (pattern 1) is stabilized, the area to the right of the critical line B represents the area where the aggregated distribution of industry to all areas (pattern 5) is stabilized, and the area to the left of the critical line S3 represents the area where the distribution of industry's "international dispersion and domestic concentration" (pattern 3) is stabilized. If the early stage of industrial distribution is pattern 4, and if the transportation costs are low enough, industrial distribution changes to pattern 3. If the early stage of industrial distribution is pattern 1, transportation costs are relatively low; however, if the entry costs are relatively high, the industrial distribution can change to pattern 3. This analysis result suggests that the industrial distribution will change toward the distribution that "internationally disperses and domestically concentrates" in the long-term. In addition, it means that it is effective to implement temporal industry protection and the introduction of policy that helps developing countries catch up.

Although we say domestic concentration, when we examine the domestic conditions of current countries, we note that many economic activities are concentrated in coastal areas and that large cities are formed there. Wu (2000) used a heterogeneous two-country four-region model to show these characteristics. In this model, areas with relatively low foreign transportation costs are called "quasi border regions," and it is assumed that both countries will each have one quasi border region. Wu then divided pattern 3 into two cases and analyzed the stability conditions. Case 1 is where the manufacturing industry concentrates in an area distant from both countries' borders, and case 2 is where the manufacturing industry concentrates in an area

Figure 2-4 Heterogeneous Two-Country Four-Region Model

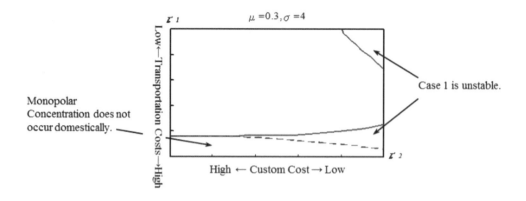

(Source) Wu (2000)

close to both countries' borders, as in a quasi border region. Results of the analysis can be seen in Figure 2-4, which shows that under the same entry cost conditions, case 2, when compared to case 1, stabilizes even under the condition of higher transportation costs. This suggests that an accumulation of manufacturing industries in quasi border regions is likely to occur more easily.

According to the above discussion on the theoretical suggestion related to the spatial distribution and the characteristics of economic activity, we consider the following for the possibility of Beads-type industrial cities forming autonomously in the New Silk Road region. First, if the competitiveness of transportation (convenience) is increased to some extent, foreign investment, which aims to natural resources and low cost labor available in the Eurasian continent inland area of the New Silk Road, will be accessed more easily than before. Once this type of investment begins, it will result in increased income in an area in the New Silk Road, domestic labor migration between areas as workers search for employment and higher wages, and increased urbanization. Furthermore, increased urbanization will require improvements in infrastructure, which will in turn lead to an improved investment climate. At the same time, efficiencies in transportation within this area will also increase along with an increase in transportation capacity, led by the increase in foreign investment activity. Thus, once many foreign companies begin to position themselves in this region, the possibility arises for the domestic companies to strengthen their competitiveness. Related industries will also gradually form, mutual cooperation in the New Silk Road area will strengthen, industries will slowly merge into the global economic system through means such as outsourcing, and trade will become more active. The result of this process will be that income in these areas will further increase and the scale of the consumer and intermediate goods markets will expand. Maturity of both markets will encourage foreign companies that aim for a market share to position themselves in the region, causing the increased growth of the city such that a metropolitan area will be gradually formed.

In reality, due to modernization and improvements in transportation networks such as highways and railroads in the New Silk Road area, transportation competitiveness in this area is increasing. Developed countries located at either the east or west end of the Eurasian continent are greatly attracted to invest in the inland countries of the New Silk Road area and perceive it as a potential market because of its low labor costs and natural resources. Strengthening the transportation competitiveness of the region even more will immediately attract further investment. We believe the Beads-type industrial cities at the New Silk Road will self-organize and form through this type of industrial agglomeration process.

IV. Policy Measures for the Beads-type Development Strategy

We now examine the policy measures that would facilitate the formation of Beads-type industrial cities within the New Silk Road area based on the theoretical mechanism of the Beads-type Development Strategy.

The China Land Bridge that connects Lianyungang, China and Rotterdam Holland was inaugurated in 1992. At the same time, the Π-shaped development strategy was devised by adding the second land route to the T-shaped development strategy.

This railroad plays a significant role for the Chinese government in its efforts to promote the development of its western region, since the China Land Bridge is an arterial railroad that connects China's coastal and inland areas. In addition, the China Land Bridge passes through Central Asia, which is rich in natural resources, and thus attracts attention as a resource trade route. In addition to the countries along the China Land Bridge, Japan, Korea, and advanced European nations located on both the east and west ends of the Eurasian continent show strong interest. These countries are interested in this route due to its potential for developing resource, securing Central Asian resources, penetrating the growing Chinese market, and utilizing the abundant yet cheap labor market.

At the same time, with the opening of the Eurasian Land Bridge, the importance of this area in terms of connecting the east and west of the Eurasian continent has increased and the environment of the international division of labor that surrounds Asia is showing unprecedented change. Figure 2-5 indicates the division of labor relationship among the developed nations that surround Asia.

In the past, this relationship has been a vertical one, where the developed nation exports industrial goods and the developing nation exports primary products. However, the division

Figure 2-5 An Image of International Division of Labor in Asia

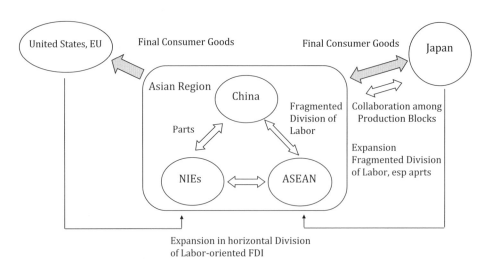

(Source) Adpated from METI, *Whitepaper on Trade, 2006*, p.87

of labor among nations in the Asian region, that is, between Asia and Japan and between Asia and Western countries, is already showing signs of a transition from a vertical relationship to a horizontal one. In the future, fragmentation of the division of labor relationship will deepen, and the flow of FDI toward the developing nations is expected to further expedite this tendency.

As mentioned above, the approach to the Beads-type Development Strategy is based on the theoretical analysis of Spatial Economics. Spatial distribution of output has a tendency to disperse internationally and concentrate domestically. Domestic industry concentrates on the quasi border areas and creates relatively stronger industrial agglomerations in areas with relatively cheaper international transportation costs. Therefore, once the competitiveness of the New Silk Road transportation increases, cities along the railway will have the same economic advantages as do cities located in quasi border areas. This will result in an accumulation of economic strength and the formation of "Beads." On the other hand, from a standpoint of economic development, how to benefit from the dynamism of the global economy and play a part in the international division of labor are key for the development of the western region of China and Central Asia, which lag behind in economic development. This is because the process of economic development is also a process that forms a new growth base in less developed regions.

The question arises as to what type of policy measure is necessary to form Beads-type industrial cities and lead the path toward autonomous economic development. To maintain the economic advantages that may accrue to the nucleated city along the New Silk Road, attracting a labor-intensive production department (a divided production group), reducing in international transportation costs, and forming of quasi border areas (new production bases) would be

Figure 2-6 An Image of "Beads-type" Development Strategy and its Policy Measures

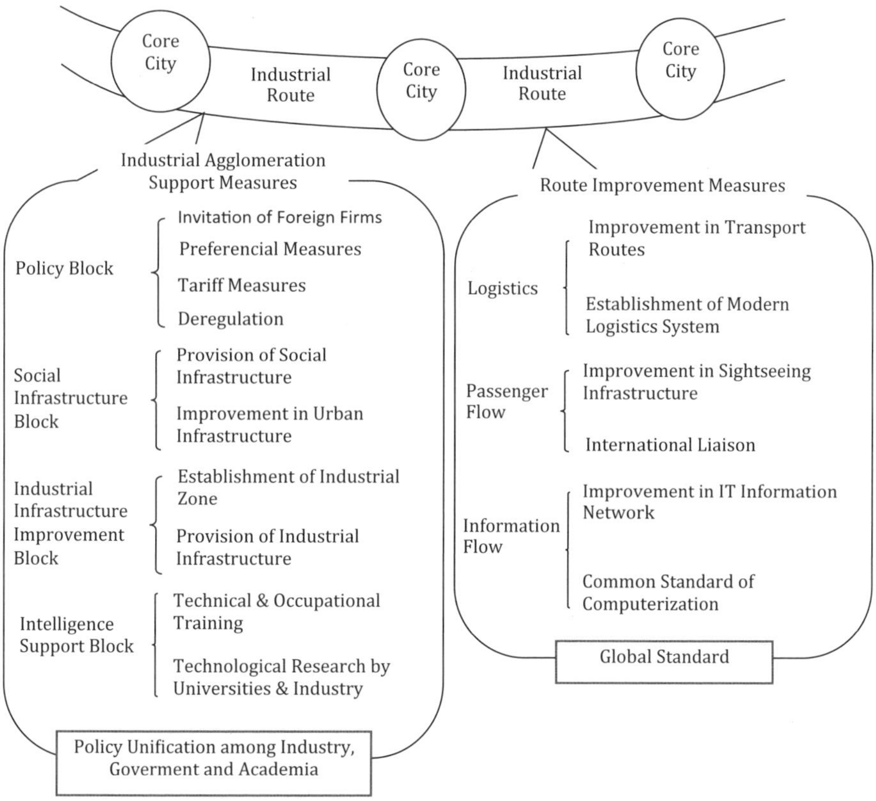

```
                Core                    Core                    Core
                City    Industrial      City    Industrial      City
                        Route                   Route
```

Industrial Agglomeration Support Measures / Route Improvement Measures

- **Policy Block**
  - Invitation of Foreign Firms
  - Preferencial Measures
  - Tariff Measures
  - Deregulation

- **Social Infrastructure Block**
  - Provision of Social Infrastructure
  - Improvement in Urban Infrastructure

- **Industrial Infrastructure Improvement Block**
  - Establishment of Industrial Zone
  - Provision of Industrial Infrastructure

- **Intelligence Support Block**
  - Technical & Occupational Training
  - Technological Research by Universities & Industry

Policy Unification among Industry, Goverment and Academia

- **Logistics**
  - Improvement in Transport Routes
  - Establishment of Modern Logistics System

- **Passenger Flow**
  - Improvement in Sightseeing Infrastructure
  - International Liaison

- **Information Flow**
  - Improvement in IT Information Network
  - Common Standard of Computerization

Global Standard

(Source) Authors' own elaboration

required. Therefore, government intervention or policy guidance is needed. That is to say, the role of the government will be to create new spatial factors. Figure 2-6 indicates the strategic image that differs from the T-shaped or Π-shaped development strategy. This strategic image explains how to form an industrial agglomeration core. Thus, a strategy supporting industrial agglomeration requires a policy that unites an industry, government, and academia. More specifically, the policy system should correspond to each of the policies indicated in Figure 2-6 and fit into the four policies of the policy block, which include the social infrastructure block, the improvement of industrial infrastructure block, and the intelligent support block. To advance the process of industrial agglomeration, we must adopt a temporal industry protection policy in addition to a foreign capital induction plan. Also, since the risks in investing in the inland area are high, it is necessary to devise improvement measures for risk factors, such as low urbanization standards, insufficient social services, and delays in infrastructure improvements. In addition, to aim for continuous economic development a policy for intellectual support must also be implemented simultaneously. Specifically, support for occupational training and industry-academia collaboration will be essential.

To implement autonomous economic development, it is extremely important that distribution runs smoothly on the New Silk Road. However, in addition to the flow of materials that is important, it is necessary to treat the three "flows" as a batch. In addition to the flow of materials, there is the flow of travelers (the movement of people) and that of information (the movement of information). Unlike the existing development strategy that is orientated toward the improvement of infrastructure carried out in China's major western development, the route maintenance we emphasize here is based on global standards. The question arises as to how to implement the three flows of materials, travelers, and information smoothly. As such, we consider it a "unification of the three flows" and believe that the real role of infrastructure improvement must be to facilitate these three flows. Consequently, infrastructure improvements of the New Silk Road at a global standard are required. This will definitely be insufficient for one country to initiate and international cooperation by each related countries is crucial.

V. Prospect of Economic Development in the New Silk Road Region

As stated above, if we introduce policies that construct a new growth base by leveraging the effects of industrial agglomeration under the present market mechanism, even the relatively underdeveloped inland of the continent can benefit from the present global economic dynamism. We also expect that an autonomous economic development process can be implemented even in inland China or Central Asia. A conceptual diagram of the economic development surrounding

Figure 2-7 Coexistence and Co-prosperity in the New Silk Road Region

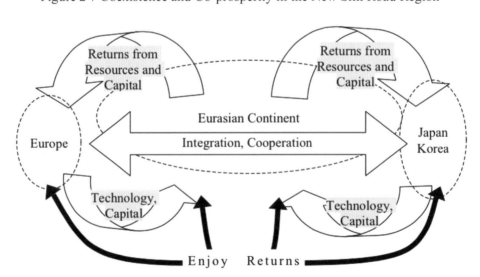

(Source) Authors' own elaboration

these areas is depicted in Figure 2-7.

Essentially, integrated economic activity in the region may be achieved by (i) introducing Japan's or Korea's system of capital and technology in eastern Asia and those of developed European countries of the western end of the Eurasian continent (ii) implementing economic development in the New Silk Road region (iii) returning the resources and income to the developed nations at both ends of the continent (iv) redirecting the flow of investment and

Figure 2-8 A Satellite Image of the Current New Silk Road

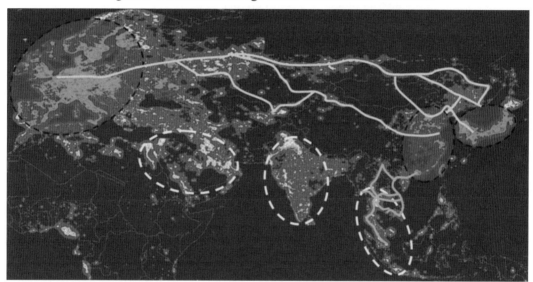

(Source) Authors' own elaboration

Figure 2-9 A Satellite Image of the Future New Silk Road

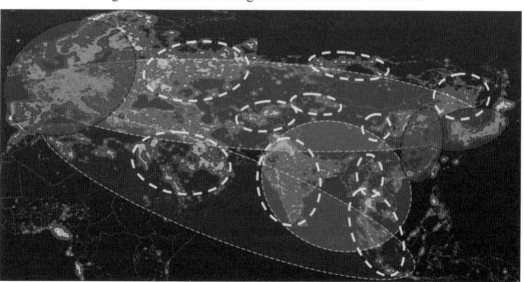

(Source) Authors' own elaboration

technology through the New Silk Road area, and (v) strengthening cooperation among regions by implementing these economic integration activities, such that both countries in the New Silk Road region and throughout the entire Eurasian continent will have a share in the profits. Figure 2-8 shows a satellite image of the earth at night. The highlighted areas are those with vigorous economic activity. That is, they indicate the international spatial distribution of industries (industrial production bases). Other areas, circled with the yellow-dotted lines, are also areas with vigorous industrial activity.

They show that industrial production bases are dispersed in several areas in the world. In particular, the areas indicated in red show extremely vigorous economic activity in the region's developed nations, where the Eurasian Land Bridge connects the east and west of the Eurasian Continent.

However, this transportation route is not adequately performing under the present circumstances and, as a result, the New Silk Road region is unable to achieve its full potential for economic development. Therefore, if countries and cities along the New Silk Road continue to develop according to our Beads-type strategy, the east and west ends of the continent will be connected by industrial areas as shown in Figure 2-9, and several nucleated cities will develop as industrial agglomeration bases within that belt of industrial areas. It is possible to implement autonomous economic development even in the inland of a continent. Doing so will lead to the alleviation inter-regional disparities. In the future, through the Beads-type Development Strategy, the role of the over-land transportation route will be equally important to that of the marine route to support trade between the East and West. Our Beads-type Development Strategy represents a promising new strategy that has the potential to replace conventional development strategy.

References

Behrens K., C. Gaigne, G. I. P. Ottaviano and J. F. Thisse (2003), "Interregional and international trade: Seventy years after Ohlin," *Centre for Economic Policy Research Discussion Paper*, No.4065.

Fujita, M., P. Krugman, and A. J. Venables (1999), *The Spatial Economy: Cities, Regions, and International Trade*, Cambridge: MIT Press.

Fujita, Masahisa (1996), "Self-Organization of Spatial Economic System and its Development," in Michihiro Oyama, *Current Issues in Modern Economics 1996* (in Japanese), Toyo Keizai Shinposha.

Honda, Mitsuo, Yiliang Wu, Yugun Riku, Naohiko Ijiri and Tadahiro Tsuji (2007), *Industrial Agglomeration and a New International Division of Labor: a New Analytical Viewpoint of the Globalizing Chinese Economy* (in Japanese), Bunshindo.

JICA (2004), *Report on the Survey of Development Strategy of Middle-class Cities in the Western Region of*

China (in Japanese), July.

Kan, Shiyu (2006), *China's Economic Structure Reform* (in Japanese), Nihon Keizai Shimbun, Inc.

Krugman, P. (1991a), "Increasing Returns and Economic Geography," *Journal of Political Economy*, 99 (3), 483-499.

Krugman, P. (1991b), *Geography and Trade*, Cambridge: MIT Press.

Krugman, P. (1995), *Development, Geography, and Economic Theory*, Cambridge: MIT Press.

Ministry of Economy, Trade and Industry (METI) (2006), *Whitepaper on Trade*.

Monfort P. and R. Nicolini (2000), "Regional Convergence and International Integration," *Journal of Urban Economics*, 48 (2), 286-306.

Wu, Yiliang (2000), "Limited Labor Mobility and Industry Accumulation: Relevancy of Industry Location Facing Borderline (in Japanese)," *Keizaishushi*, 70 (1), 55-69.

Wu, Yiliang (2007), "International Dispersion and Domestic Concentration: An Analysis on a Two-Country Four-Region Model of Industrial Agglomeration," in Mitsuo Honda *et al.*, *Op. cit.*, 1-37.

Chapter 3

Dynamic Catch-Up and the Possibility for New Regional Economic Development

I. Introduction

Since the second half of the 1990s, a new international division of labor has appeared, and with the formation of global economic dynamism, new possibilities have appeared for emerging countries to catch up. This is referred to as "dynamic catch-up."[1] Dynamic catch-up differs from the existing flying-geese pattern pillared by the international transmission effects of industrial transfer. Dynamic catch-up is a process by which new self-organizational growth centers are formed by adopting global economic dynamism, through acting on their own to develop an environment and access the globalization of economic activities, without passively waiting for industrial transfer from developed countries.

In this paper, we analyze a new catch-up process that is observed in emerging countries, with the appearance of a new international division of labor. The latter stems from the trade of parts and intermediate goods arising from the globalization of corporate production activities, as mutual dependencies grow deeper in regional economies, such as with the progress of negotiations for free trade agreements (FTAs) and economic partnership agreements (EPAs).

Dynamic catch-up is a hypothetical concept that mainly draws from the experience of emerging countries in East Asia. It describes a process to form self-organizational growth centers through endogenous and cyclic agglomeration effects based on market theory and can also be applied to other emerging country economies. In this paper, we elucidate the dynamic catch-up process and examine the possibility for new development in inland regions, particularly regions along the New Silk Road.

---

[1] Dynamic catch-up is a concept proposed by Yugun Riku and Tadahiro Tsuji (2011).

II. Globalization of Corporate Production Activities and Emergence of a New Internalization Division of Labor

1. Globalization of Corporate Production Activities and Changes in the International Division of Labor Structure

In the period from the 1970s through the first half of the 1990s, a pattern was often observed among various countries centering on Asian newly industrialized economies (NIEs) that had adopted export-oriented industrialization strategies. These countries imported intermediate goods and capital goods from industrialized Japan, which they processed into final goods for export to the United States and European markets. As shown in Figure 3-1, this international division of labor structure is taken to be a conventional trilateral trade structure. Under such a trade and international division of labor structure, low-wage labor resources do not always confer a competitive advantage. In the East Asia region, it was not possible to engage in local production of exportable products without the transfer of Japanese technology, but catching up to Japanese manufacturing technology is difficult to achieve. Teaching assembly and processing skills to employees and getting them to acquire quality control know-how requires tremendous effort and simultaneously depends on the ability and education level of local employees. A very long period of education and training is needed in order to efficiently assemble the plans, designs, parts, and components of Japanese products, with the result that low wages did not necessarily translate into a national advantage.

Figure 3-1 Conventional Trilateral Trade Structure

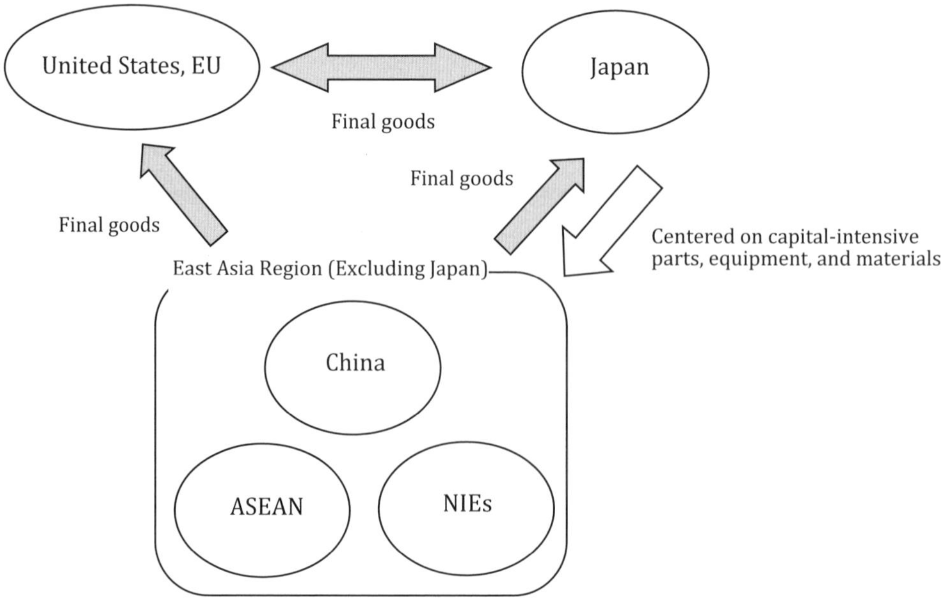

(Source) Revised and prepared from page 99 of Riku (2010)

Product development and the stage of initial model prototyping is becoming an integral design process involving the mutual interaction of parts and components. To achieve mass production, it is necessary to devise positioning methods between parts and develop well-thought-out designs that facilitate assembly. In order to thoroughly satisfy multiple goals such as reduced weight, compact size, energy efficiency, reduced environmental impact, and safety, the integral design must cover the smallest details (Fujimoto, 2004).

Due to the difficulty of achieving overseas transfer of this kind of manufacturing technology, Japanese companies situated their R&D, product design, and manufacturing processes in Japan and sought to export their products, not going as far as to divide labor between production processes. As the industrial structure and export structure of the Japanese economy grew increasingly sophisticated, the Japanese economy became dependent on importing labor-intensive goods because of a relatively strong competitiveness in intermediate goods and capital goods, so that industries that had lost their competitiveness shifted abroad. Furthermore, the impact of yen appreciation since the Plaza Accord further accelerated the trend to shift abroad.

Production centers were introduced in nearby Asian countries through direct investment centering on the overseas shift of comparative disadvantage industries. Countries that accepted the direct investment increased their exports, so that a flying-geese pattern of economic development was observed within the region. In terms of trade structure, a trilateral structure developed in which East Asian emerging countries mainly imported intermediate goods and capital goods from Japan, which they processed into final goods for export abroad such as to the United States.

Since the second half of the 1990s, changes arose in the trade and division of labor structure in the Asia region. Unprecedented changes have appeared in the division of labor between developed and developing countries in Asia, changing to a horizontal division of labor that differs from the existing vertical division of labor in which developed countries export industrial products and developing countries export primary commodities. In this paper, we take this to be a fragmentation-type multitiered trilateral trade structure, as shown in Figure 3-2.

In terms of international division of labor, an unprecedented international production and distribution network extending across developed countries and developing countries is being developed by multinational companies or through direct investment. This is leading to the introduction of a new international division of labor at the fine production process level that differs from the conventional horizontal division of labor or vertical division of labor.

Multinational companies are playing a critical role in the new international division of labor. Changes have appeared in the location choices of companies, and there are instances in which companies are dispersing their locations by production process according to the production process level, instead of locating a single industry or sector as a group in a certain country or region as occurred until now. However, analysis of international trade by itself is not sufficient to determine why such structural changes have occurred, and a micro-level approach

Figure 3-2 Fragmentation-Type Multitiered Trilateral Trade Structure

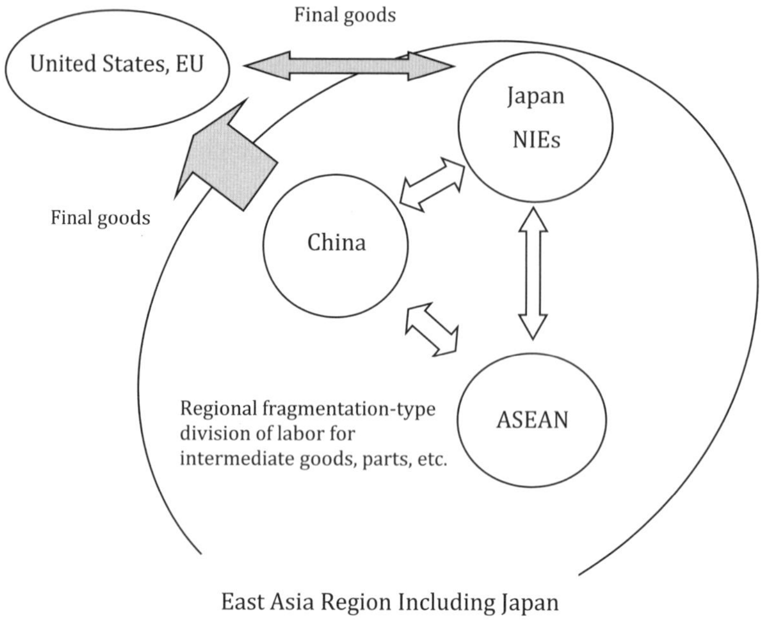

[Figure 3-2: Diagram showing trade flows. United States, EU exchanges final goods with Japan/NIEs. Final goods flow from China to United States, EU. Within the East Asia Region Including Japan, there is regional fragmentation-type division of labor for intermediate goods, parts, etc. among China, Japan/NIEs, and ASEAN.]

East Asia Region Including Japan

(Source) Revised and prepared from page 99 of Riku (2010)

that examines corporate behavior is needed. Rapid innovation of production technologies and modularization of product architectures since the 1990s have brought about a change in the situation in which a country's low-wage labor resources had not necessarily led to a competitive advantage. The advent of modularized product architectures also led to a focus on markets in emerging countries, from the perspective of low-wage labor resources in addition to the potential for market growth.

According to Yasumuro (2012), if interfaces are prescribed as international standards, such as specifications (protocols) covering module performance and information relay between modules, in principle it is possible for a parts manufacturing company from any country to be involved in production. If the number of module producers increases, the chances for capturing innovation can be expected to increase accordingly, preventing the monopolization of parts suppliers, bringing prices down, and leading to performance leaps in assembled products. Opening up design concepts in this way leads to rapid growth of network-type companies, whereas vertically integrated companies that are self-sufficient lose their competitiveness. Accordingly, innovations in production technologies enable markets in low-wage emerging countries to at once seize an advantage as a production location. Furthermore, for module assembly-type production, it is no longer necessary to master the skills required for integral production.

In terms of module production, production processes that require greater concentration of capital and technology are distributed between Europe, United States, Japan, Taiwan, and Korea. Multinational companies from these countries oversee product development, with Taiwan, Korea, and Southern China serving as the main bases for production. Meanwhile, labor-intensive modular-type assembly and production is being introduced through contract manufacturing centered in southern China, which has given rise to business models in the form of Electronics Manufacturing Service (EMS), Original Design Manufacturer (ODM), and Specialty store retailer of Private label Apparel (SPA). Business models that incorporate contract manufacturing for multinational companies have given rise to functional differentiation whereby R&D, product design, module production, and marketing is conducted in developed countries, while assembly, processing, and delivery are conducted in markets in emerging countries.

As economic globalization has advanced, so too has the segmentation of production processes, which is to say production fragmentation triggered by factors such as investment by Japanese companies in Asia. As a result, Asia is establishing a position as the world's manufacturing hub, while a production network is simultaneously being formed within the region. The percentage of intraregional trade has grown to exceed that of the NAFTA, so that economic integration is in fact progressing at a rapid pace. Stronger regional economic cooperation is expected to further cement the new international division of labor that we refer to in this paper, which is to say a fragmentation-type multitiered division of labor. The changes in the international division of labor since the second half of the 1990s will also change the catch-up of emerging countries in the East Asia region into a process that differs from the conventional flying-geese pattern.

2. Demise of the Flying-Geese Pattern of Catch-Up

In East Asia from the 1970s through the first half of the 1990s, it was often the pattern for emerging countries to import intermediate goods and capital goods from Japan, which they processed into final goods for export to the United States. Japan's trade structure was to import primary commodities and export manufacturing goods, but since Japan had an industrial structure that was not very dependent on importing labor-intensive goods from abroad, Japan's ability to absorb final products manufactured in Asia was weak. That is, Japan's trade with East Asian countries mainly centered on supplying intermediate goods and capital goods needed for production and export in Asian countries. East Asian emerging countries used these goods to carry out manufacturing and processing for export to the United States and European markets.

Under this division of labor structure, Japan's direct investment in the East Asia region progressed in sequence from Japan→NIEs→ASEAN→coastal China, in order of differences in the stage of development. As Japan's domestic industrial structure became increasingly diverse and sophisticated, Japan took the lead in industrial transfer while fulfilling its role as a leader of industrial development. At the same time, the export-oriented industrialization of Asian NIEs has traced the same kind of process that occurred in Japan, so that direct investment from Japan and NIEs is introducing production centers in nearby emerging countries, which has led to increased exports in countries receiving the direct investment. The international transmission effects from industrial transfer have progressively penetrated from Japan to NIEs, NIEs to ASEAN, and ASEAN to China, leading to the advent of a flying-geese catch-up pattern in the East Asian region. The theory of the flying-geese pattern of economic development by Kojima (2003) develops a model from the experiences of East Asia during this era.

The flying-geese model assumes that foreign direct investment from investing countries is conducted in sequence beginning from comparative disadvantage industries. That is, the model supposes that comparative disadvantage industries in investing countries engage in industrial transfer presuming differences in the development stage, and that these industries either have a comparative advantage or potentially have a comparative advantage in the country receiving the investment. The investing country leads the decision on which type of industries will transfer abroad, which is passively caught by the country receiving the foreign direct investment. Accordingly, the flying-geese pattern is a type of passive catch-up process for emerging countries.

Globalization of economic activities, liberalization of trade, and technological progress are facilitating the spatial movement of goods and services, making it possible to subdivide production processes between corporate locations. As a result, changes have appeared in the existing trade pattern comprising inter-industry trade between developed countries and developing countries. The changes in the division of labor structure in East Asia since the second half of the 1990s should be taken to represent a new form of division of labor that is related to the location choices and production behaviors of multinational companies. This new division of labor is neither a conventional vertical distribution of labor nor an EU-type horizontal division of labor.

The division of labor structure of Asia and primarily East Asia will change from a conventional trilateral structure to a fragmentation-type multitiered trilateral division of labor structure, which can no longer be explained by existing theories for inter-industry trade and intra-industry trade. Additionally, the era of the flying-geese model of the East Asian economy led by Japan is meeting its demise as mutual dependencies grow deeper in East Asia. Our analysis in this paper concludes that the flying-geese pattern of catching up in emerging countries will change to a dynamic catch-up. In the next section, we will elucidate the dynamic catch-up process for forming new growth centers through access to globalization of economic activities.

III. Dynamic Catch-Up Model

1. Globalization of Corporate Production Activities

The changes in the division of labor structure in East Asia represent a new form of division of labor relating to the location choice and production behaviors of multinational companies. This new division of labor is neither a conventional vertical distribution of labor nor an EU-type horizontal division of labor. The changes were made possible by the modularization of products and modularization of manufacturing method architectures. According to Sanchez (1995, 1999), multinational companies that are confronted with a dynamic competitive environment can adopt modular designs for products and services, which gives rise to strategic flexibility making it possible to seize a competitive advantage, while at the same time giving rise to a new marketing dynamism.

As the basic location strategies of multinational companies, the following two approaches are necessary: (i) the pursuit of efficiencies through concentration of value-creating activities, specifically through integration and concentration of production, procurement, R&D and other activities in a specific geographic location, and (ii) securing flexibility by dispersing these various activities, specifically through cross-border sourcing and adjusting production to adapt to economic changes and changes in market conditions. In that sense, in many industries today it is becoming critical for multinational companies to increase their flexibility by strategically adopting modular designs for products and services, in addition to having strategic flexibility.

Morokami (2012) elucidated that by adopting modular designs, it is often possible for companies to significantly expand their boundaries beyond national borders and rapidly increase their product variations at a low cost. Standardizing the interface between the constituent parts of products enables economies of substitution and furthermore enables embedded adjustments to function under common design rules, even as corporate boundaries expand significantly. This makes it possible to efficiently execute an international division of labor as well as international development on a parts-specific basis (Morokami, 2012, pp.96-97).

The behavior of multinational companies has brought about the global dispersion of locations, with the result that it has given rise to a new international division of labor. In this paper, we take this globalization of corporate production activities to be fragmentation from the perspective of international division of labor. According to Cheng and Kierzkowski (2001), fragmentation is the breaking down of production activities that were previously conducted in one location into multiple production blocks, dispersing them to locations that offer location conditions that are suited to the respective production activities. Since multinational companies oversee the subdivision of production processes spanning across multiple countries, fragmentation is in essence the international dispersion of production centers resulting from the globalization of corporate production activities.

The strategic adoption of modular designs for products and services eliminates the conventional need for multinational companies to aggregate production processes, so that they can subdivide production processes taking into account the technical characteristics of each process, and disperse them to countries that can produce them at the lowest cost. Accordingly, even if a given industry is capital intensive when viewed as a whole, the production processes are finely divided and dispersed to locations in both developed countries and developing countries rather than locating all production activities for that industry in developed countries, with developing countries mainly engaging in production activities for labor-intensive production processes. In that sense, fragmentation is a type of intra-industry vertical division of labor.

As vertical intra-industry trade through fragmentation involving the subdivision of production processes becomes increasingly specialized, it becomes possible to secure trade profits between countries that have different endowments of production factors and to secure profits on a scale that gives rise to concentration of production. The service link cost that ties together production blocks in dispersed locations must be sufficiently low, which affects whether it is possible to lower the overall production cost through fragmentation. The service link cost encompasses constituent factors such as telecommunications costs, transportation costs (external transportation costs), and customs clearance costs. Since these constituent elements encompass elements that have economies of scale, reducing the service link cost contributes significantly to dispersal of the location of production activities by companies, so that globalization of corporate production activities also greatly influences the formation of industrial agglomeration.

2. Formation of New Growth Centers and Industrial Agglomeration

Krugman (1995) expounded on the effectiveness of the modern version of the big push theory, by incorporating the approach of industrial agglomeration into economic development issues. The argument by Krugman (1995) is dependent on the Murphy-Shleifer-Vishny model (Murphy, Shleifer and Vishny, 1989). Under the big push theory reconsidered from a spatial economic perspective, initial conditions and historical chance play a critical role in industrial location. Krugman elucidated that government intervention in industrial location has a great influence on the process by which industrial agglomeration is formed in a given region, and economic development process is a process by which new growth centers are formed in less-developed regions. Additionally, Wu (2007)[2] elucidated the trend for the spatial distribution of production activities to be dispersed internationally and concentrated domestically, so that domestic industry is concentrated in the quasi-border area while giving rise to industrial agglomeration in the border area region where external transportation costs are relatively lower.

We believe that the advent of an industrial agglomeration theory that is called a new spatial

---

[2] Published in Mitsuo Honda *et al*. (2007).

economics will reveal new paths for the catch-up direction of developing counties. That is, three factors need to be included for consideration of how to form new growth centers: spatial agglomeration effect of industry, dispersed location choices for production processes, and endowment of elements. When countries begin catching up, the characteristics that appear in the spatial distribution of industry depend on differences in technology, endowment of production elements, and initial conditions such as the initial distribution of industry.

These initial conditions have an influence on the formation of industrial agglomeration patterns (whether it is a labor-intensive production sector or a capital-intensive production sector). In developing countries that have relatively abundant labor compared with capital, having a sustainable labor force supply helps external economies work in interaction with internal economies of scale. This gives an incentive to dispersed location choices by companies at the production process-specific level and further strengthens the agglomeration of industry, and by such a process gives rise to agglomeration so that new growth centers are progressively formed.

When considered in this way, the changes occurring today in the division of labor structure in East Asia truly represent a composite process of international dispersion (fragmentation) of production centers from the globalization of production activities by multinational companies, and domestic formation (agglomeration) of new growth centers from developing countries catching up.

3. Formation of Infrastructure Network

Another essential factor in the formation of a new international division of labor is the infrastructure foundation. The formation of an infrastructure network has an impact on the total cost of international trade and direct investment. The formation of this infrastructure network needs to be considered from both the policy infrastructure and logistical infrastructure in regard to infrastructure foundation.

In regard to policy infrastructure, Asian countries have in recent years been vying to enter into FTAs and EPAs. FTAs in the East Asia region are structured with ASEAN as a hub, with regional negotiations being advanced between the ASEAN+6 nations (Japan, Korea, China, India, Australia, and New Zealand) that are dialogue partners in the area centering around ASEAN. The ASEAN Free Trade Area (AFTA) and bilateral agreements such as FTAs and EPAs that Japan, China, and Korea have entered into with respective ASEAN countries have formed a network that connects East Asia or the entire Asian region. This vitalization of intra-regional economic partnerships is lowering the barriers to international trade and direct investment, so that a fragmentation type division of labor is widely occurring in Asia, which differs from the conventional division of labor and is bringing about changes in the international division of labor.

As agglomeration of economic activities enlarges, production costs decrease, which confers profits from industrial agglomeration so that the agglomeration force increases the more that markets are globalized through FTAs. The move toward regional economic integration in East Asia based on the concept of open regionalism is in line with the characteristics of the international division of labor in East Asia.

Next, we examine the development of a logistics network as another critical element relating to the formation of a new international division of labor. In the East Asia region where a new international division of labor is forming, there are growing logistics needs between production centers that have been introduced in East Asian countries. Furthermore, emerging countries in East Asia are actively focusing their efforts on developing a logistics infrastructure capable of supporting the needs of users, in order to make their own countries more appealing as agglomeration centers. For example, the development of a logistics infrastructure network such as highways, railways, and sea routes linking China-ASEAN, ASEAN intra-regional countries, ASEAN countries-India, and China-India matches Asian economic dynamism. The formation of an infrastructure foundation through the development of a seamless economy and logistics network in East Asia is a critical contributing factor supporting the Asianization of the Asian economy. We believe that actively contributing to formation of infrastructure foundation in Asian emerging economies will lead these countries to successfully catch up.

4. Dynamic Catch-Up Model

We believe that the experience of East Asia is not only exclusive to East Asia, but reveals new possibilities for developing countries to catch up through the experience of East Asia. In this paper, we developed a more generalized model of the mechanism for how developing countries can access the globalization of economic activities to catch global economic dynamism, as shown in Figure 3-3.

In the dynamic catch-up model shown in Figure 3-3, three factors relate to global economic dynamism and the mechanism for formation of a new international division of labor: industrial agglomeration, globalization of corporate economic activities, and infrastructure foundation. The formation of an infrastructure foundation through the development of a seamless economy and logistics network gives an incentive for the globalization of corporate economic activities, while the international dispersion of production centers from the globalization of corporate economic activities has a great influence on the formation of industrial agglomeration. Additionally, a stronger infrastructure foundation increases the industrial agglomeration force, and as agglomeration of economic activities enlarges, production costs decrease, which confers profits from industrial agglomeration. Furthermore, lower production costs act as an inducement for corporate expansion into countries, to further vitalize the globalization of corporate economic activities.

Figure 3-3 Dynamic Catch-Up Model

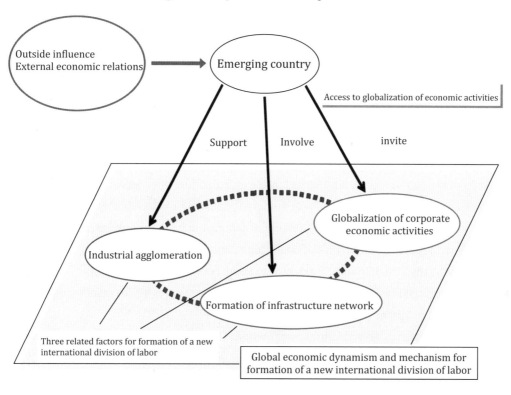

(Source) Prepared by the author

The dynamic catch-up model is a new approach to take the place of the flying-geese model pillared by the international transmission effects of industrial transfer. This model focuses on how the emerging countries can access the globalization of economic activities to form new growth centers, under global economic dynamism and the mechanism for formation of a new international division of labor. When countries begin catching up, the characteristics that appear in the spatial distribution of industry depend on differences in technology, endowment of production elements, and initial conditions such as the initial distribution of the industry. These initial conditions have an influence on the formation of industrial agglomeration patterns (whether it is a labor-intensive production sector or a capital-intensive production sector).

More concentrated use of abundantly endowed elements gives rise to comparative advantages and helps external economies work in interaction with internal economies of scale, which gives further incentive to dispersed location choices by companies. In this way, industrial agglomeration further increases the agglomeration force that comes with dispersed location choices for production centers arising from the globalization of corporate production activities. If agglomeration occurs through such a process, new growth centers are progressively formed so that emerging countries face global economic dynamism and the mechanism for formation of a new international division of labor, which will lead to the formation of new growth centers if emerging countries can access the globalization of economic activities while utilizing their comparative advantages.

In this way, global economic dynamism and a new international division of labor are formed through the interaction of these three factors, so that how emerging countries or developing countries access the globalization of economic activities is key to successfully catching up. These three factors are mutually related, with the governments of emerging countries or developing countries having a certain role in the background. At the same time, external influences (such as international affairs) also have a certain influence on the governments of developing countries in adopting global economic dynamism.

Accordingly, amid new trends marked by the globalization of economic activities, adoption of market economies, introduction of a new international division of labor, and in particular the introduction of a fragmentation-type division of labor, it is becoming necessary to undertake new efforts in the catch-up strategies of emerging countries or developing countries, as typified by the following three main points. First, how to adopt economic dynamism (that is, fragmentation) is critical in relation to regional economic development and is key to creating an economic advantage as a hub city or core city.

Second, in order to give rise to new growth centers by utilizing the effects of industrial agglomeration under market mechanisms, it is necessary to develop infrastructure under international standards and strengthen international partnership. Third, it is necessary to achieve regional economy integration so that countries can utilize their comparative advantages, such as their labor force, capital, or technology, and undertake efforts to realize stronger interregional partnership while profiting together.

As a result, emerging countries or developing countries that have incorporated capital and technology from developed countries can realize advantages such as from their own labor force. By share the created profits to the developed countries that directly invested in the emerging country or developing country, profits are shared between developed countries and developing countries.

IV. Conclusion

The dynamic catch-up model is a generalized model of the experience of emerging countries in East Asia, but the catch-up process described by the model can also be applied to regions along the New Silk Road, in particular western China and Central Asian countries that are situated inland. As suggested by the modern version of the big push theory by Krugman (1995), the economic development process is also a process by which new growth centers are formed in less-developed regions. In the case of the New Silk Road, western China and Central Asian countries are inland, where transportation is less convenient than in coastal areas. If the convenience were to progressively improve with the development of land routes, overland transportation can be expected to be made more competitive because of the relatively lower external transportation costs, so that companies that are highly suited for these regions will relocate there.

Through dynamic catch-up, the three related factors of industry agglomeration, globalization of corporate economic activities, and formation of an infrastructure network that relate to a new international division of labor have a cyclic effect in strengthening the industrial agglomeration force and creating a process of endogenous and cyclic agglomeration. If regions along the New Silk Road were to start such autonomous industrial agglomeration, it would enable these regions to play a role in the international division of labor so that self-organizational growth centers are formed. This opens up possibilities for new development in inland countries and regions that were until now denied the possibility of autonomous development.

Amid the new trends of the global economy, in regions along the New Silk Road, successfully achieving real economic development from new possibilities for dynamic catch-up requires that countries utilize their comparative advantages, such as their labor force, capital, and technology through the Beads-type Development Strategy, i.e., regional economy integration, and undertake strategic efforts to realize stronger interregional partnership while sharing profits.

References

Bartlett, C. and S. Ghoshal (1989), *Managing Across Borders: The Transnational Solution* (in Japanese), Harvard Business School Press.

Cheng, L. K. and H. Kierzkowski (2001), *Global Production and Trade in East Asia*, Kluwer Academic Publishers.

Honda, Mitsuo, Yiliang Wu, Yugun Riku, Naohiko Ijiri and Tadahiro Tsuji (2007), *Industrial Agglomeration and a New International Division of Labor: a New Analytical Viewpoint of the Globalizing Chinese Economy* (in Japanese), Bunshindo.

Kojima, Kiyoshi (2003), *Flying Geese Pattern of Economic Development* Vol.1 (in Japanese), Bunshindo.

Krugman, P. (1995), *Development, Geography, and Economic Theory*, Cambridge: MIT Press.

Fujimoto, Takahiro (2004), *The Philosophy of Japanese Manufacturing* (in Japanese), Nihon Keizai Shimbun, Inc.

Morokami, Shigeto (2004), "The Background and Opportunities of Global Marketing," in Shigeto Morokami and Takeshi Fujisawa, *Global Marketing* (in Japanese), Chuokeizaisha.

Morokami, Shigeto (2012), "The Business Platform of MNE and Emerging Market Exploitation," in Academy of Multinational Enterprises, *Multinational Enterprises and Emerging Marketing* (in Japanese), Bunshindo.

Murphy, R., A. Shleifer and R. Vishny (1989), "Industrialization and the Big Push," *Journal of Political Economy*, 97, 1003-1026.

Nemoto, Takashi and Shigeto Morokami (1996), *Coordination Mechanism of Global Management* (in Japanese), Bunshindo.

Porter, M. (ed.) (1980), *Competitive Strategy*, Free Press, New York.

Porter, M. (ed.) (1986), *Global Marketing Management*, 4th edition, John Wiley & Sons Inc.

Riku, Yugun (2010), "A Study of the Deepening International Division of Labor in Asian and Regional Economic Development (in Japanese)," *Kiyo*, Distance Learning Division Nihon University, 23.

Riku, Yugun and Tadahiro Tsuji (2011), "A Study on the Application of East Asian Emerging Countries' Experiences to Economic Development of Central Asia," *JAFTAB*, Japan Academy of Trade and Business, 48.

Sanchez, R. (1995), "Strategic Flexibility," *Strategic Management Journal*, 16.

Sanchez, R. (1999), "Modular Architectures in the Marketing Process," *Journal of Marketing*, 63.

Tabata, Shohei (2012), "Multinational Enterprises and Product Development," in Takeshi Fujisawa (ed.), *Global, Marketing and Innovation 2012* (in Japanese), Dobunkan.

Teece, D. J. (2007), "Explicating Dynamic Capabilities:The Nature and Micro-foundations of (Sustainable) Enterprise Performance," *Strategic Management Journal*, 28 (13), 1319-1350.

Yasumuro, Kenichi (2012), "The Business Model of Global Marketing Enterprises," in Takeshi Fujisawa (ed.), *Global, Marketing and Innovation 2012* (in Japanese), Dobunkan.

Chapter 4

EU Trade Policy towards Central Asia States:
Implications for China and Japan

The purpose of this article is to make clear the aims of EU Trade Policy towards Central Asia and the feature of trade relation between EU and Central Asia. And as a conclusion the implications for China and Japan, and the prospect of New Silk Road economic area are to be shown.

I. Aims of EU Trade Policy towards Central Asia

1. The Aims of EU Trade Policy

The EU Trade Policy has been at the turning point in these years as the situation of world economy and the order of world trade have changed largely on the one hand and the European integration has undergone the inexperienced challenges on the other. Developed economies, not only EU but also USA and Japan, are facing both internal economic difficulties and external competitions. Presences of these economies in the world have declined compared with those of developing or emerging economies.

But EU has been straggling in order to keep prosperity and stability in European economic area. On July 2013 Croatia has joined EU as 28th member. Within a decade or so the enlargement of EU, i.e. the widening of European market, will complete, at the same time European market will reached the point of saturation and maturity, therefore EU must find wider market outside EU. However other developed economies and emerging economies have the similar intentions as EU that they want to take dynamic economic development of developing countries, especially Asian countries, into their own economic revitalization. EU has been involved in the great competition game whether it likes it or not willy-nilly.

After the mid-2000s EU, i.e. European Commission, decided to encounter such a hard situation positively as is shown by the following policy papers; "*Global Europe Competing in the World, A Contribution to the EU's Growth and Jobs Strategy* " (European Commission, External Trade, 2006), "*Global Europe EU performance in the global economy* " (European Commission, Directorate General for Trade, 2008) and "*Trade, Growth and World Affairs: Trade Policy as a Core Component of the EU's 2020 Strategy*" (European Commission, External Trade, 2010).

In the background of these papers power shift on the global level is in progress. EU took up Brazil, Russia, India and China (BRICs) as economic strategic partners to strengthen economic relations with them. Of course EU respects the role of WTO, has taken "WTO first" policy, but at the same time EU have recognized success of multilateral trade negotiation DDA would be unlikely, therefore switched to bilateral negotiations with major potential markets especially in Asia. In fact EU has concluded bilateral FTA with Korea in 2011, and negotiations with India, Malaysia, Vietnam, Thailand, Singapore and Japan are in progress, further EU is preparing for opening negotiation with Brunei, Indonesia and Philippines. But EU has not decided to start negotiation of FTA with China because EU doesn't regard China as market-economy country, and only negotiates Investment Agreement. However as there have already been China-ASEAN FTA, Japan-ASEAN FTA and are several projects concerning FTA, other regional trade agreements such as Japan-Korea-China FTA, especially TPP, in the near future EU may change its trade policy to China. It depends on the regional and global situation in flux.

To meet such a change the EU has reformed its organizations and policies underpinned by Lisbon Treaty, of which main features are further Europeanization of trade policy; to speak with one strong voice, democratization of the process of decision making; to strengthen the role of European Parliament; to coordinate trade policy with other external policies, i.e. foreign policy, development policy, environmental policy and energy policy (European Commission, 2011). In short EU needs holistic and coordinated policy to correspond to the newly emerging global situation. Alterations are as follows.

Firstly Parliament's powers have increased significantly, i.e. it is now co-legislator with the Council on trade matters: All basic EU trade legislation must pass through the Parliament before being adopted or amended by the Council; All trade agreements must be approved by Parliament to be ratifies; Status of trade negotiations - the Commission must transmit documents and report regularly on this to the European Parliament. We need to think Parliament to be a delegate from European citizens.

Secondly The Lisbon Treaty creates a more solid basis for the EU to adopt autonomous acts on trade in services and commercial aspects of intellectual property. Trade in cultural/audiovisual, educational and social/health services are now an EU power, subject, in certain cases, to specific voting rules. Foreign direct investment is now an EU power under trade policy, i.e. the EU can both conclude international agreement and adopt autonomous measures on FDI.

Thirdly qualified majority voting becomes the general rule in Council for all aspects of trade policy. Unanimity is required only in the following specific circumstances: where commitments on cultural/audiovisual services risk undermining the EU's cultural and linguistic diversity; where commitments on social, educational or health services risk seriously disturbing the national organization of these services and impeding member governments' ability to deliver them; where unanimity is required for the adoption of internal rules.

The aims of recent reforms are to progress European Integration. As far as trade policy goes the EU desires strengthening the bargaining and negotiating power, opening the markets of emerging economies and sharing the growth and diversifying energy suppliers to decrease the extent of over-dependence on Russia.

We are going to investigate EU Trade Policy toward Central Asia from the point of view as described above.

2. The EU Central Asia Strategy

The growing importance of Central Asia for the EU has been reflected in the "New EU Central Asia Strategy "adopted by the European Council (22 June 2007).

The Strategy aims at enhancing the EU's relations with the region as a whole and each of its particular countries. It sets priorities for cooperation in six main areas: democracy and human rights, education, trade and investment, energy and transport, the environment and combating common threats and challenges. I'll take up trade and investment, and energy from the viewpoint of EU's economic strategy towards Central Asia.

In the area of trade and investment, the EU strategy focuses on accession of the entire Central Asian region to the World Trade Organization. It also aims to help Central Asian countries take greater advantage of the EU's GSP (Generalized System of Preferences). EU introduces Central Asian Countries into global economy and growth. Concerning WTO membership, Kyrgyzstan acceded to the WTO in 1998. Turkmenistan hasn't applied for WTO membership. Tajikistan and Uzbekistan applied in 2001 and 1994 respectively, but their accession negotiations are still at the initial stages. Kazakhstan's accession process is significantly more advanced and the EU and Kazakhstan are making efforts to conclude a bilateral agreement on accession in the near future.

In the sphere of bilateral agreement, i.e. Partnership and Cooperation Agreement (PCA), the EU's bilateral trade relations with Kazakhstan, Kyrgyzstan and Uzbekistan are provided for by PCA with each country. The PCA with Tajikistan and Turkmenistan have not been ratified. In the area of trade the PCAs are non-preferential agreements, the parties grant each other most-favored nation (MFN) treatment with respect to tariffs and quantitative restrictions are prohibited in bilateral trade.

In the sphere of energy and transport, strengthening Energy Strategy both in acquiring and transporting energy resources is absolutely necessary for EU. As is shown in Figure 4-1, Table 4-1 and Figure 4-2, about 60% of the gross inland consumption of fuels by EU members are petroleum and gas (Figure 4-1), and EU has been over-dependent on importing fuels (Table 4-1). And most of fuels have been imported from Russia, Middle East and North Africa excluding Norway so far (Figure 4-2). We must make a mental note that Kazakhstan's import share was 6%, which has gradually increased in these years. Share of oil out of all EU's import from Kazakhstan amounts to over 90%, and the sum of oil import (Mio €) have increased in 9,741, 14,296, 20,933, 22,574, from 2009 to 2012 (Eurostat Comext). For the EU, Central Asian countries are sources of significant energy imports either substituting Russia and Middle East

Figure 4-1 EU-27 Gross Inland Consumption-Energy Mix (%)

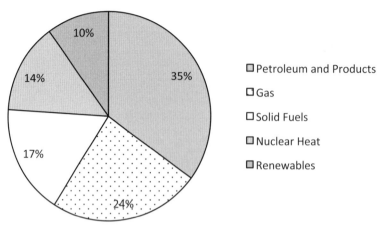

(Source) European Commission, EU Energy in figures, *Statistical Pocketbook 2013*, p.20

Table 4-1 EU's Import Dependency on Fuels (%)

	2005	2007	2009	2010	2011
All Fuels	52.4	53.1	53.8	52.6	53.8
Solid Fuels	39.2	41.2	41.1	39.4	41.4
Petroleum Fuels	82.2	82.6	83.2	84.1	84.9
Natural Gas	57.7	60.3	64.3	62.4	67.0

(Source) European Commission, EU Energy in figures, *Statistical Pocketbook 2013*.

or diversifying import sources.

In such a situation, on December 2009 Lisbon Treaty has come into force to progress and strengthen EU's external policy for the sake of globalizing role and presence of EU. Lisbon Treaty could give a basis not only for the attempt to maintain its eminence of being an important actor in global affairs, but also for the EU Strategy for the Central Asian countries that are rich in resources. As Lala pointed out, the Strategy of 2007 has reinvigorated the importance of Central Asia as the EU grapples with the issues of energy diversification. And EU is a credible alternative for the Central Asia states that remain cautious as China slowly and steadily replaces Russia as the preeminent power in the region. Partnership between EU and Central Asian states needs to be accelerated post-Lisbon Treaty as this is the interest of both the regions (Lala, 2012).

Figure 4-2 EU-27 Imports by Country of Origin, 2011

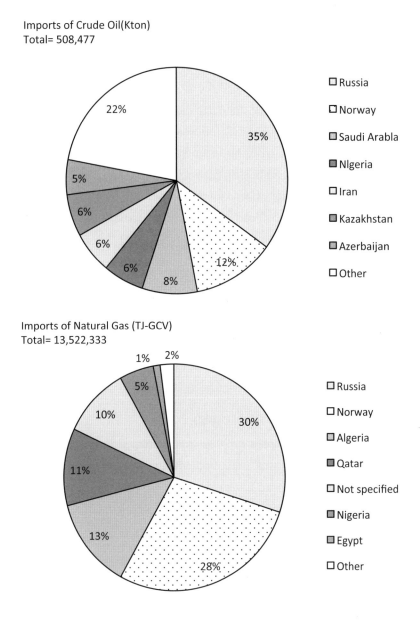

(Source) European Commission, EU Energy in figures, *Statistical Pocketbook 2013*, p.24

However as authoritarian trends have been prevailing in Central Asia, EU as normative power have put a stress on development aid from the long view of constructing civil society instead of trade and investment so far. And Lisbon Treaty has push such a policy forward. The office of the High Representative and the EEAS (The European Union External Action Service) should push for greater visibility of EU's development assistance in Central Asia. In fact as EU development aid is a cornerstone of the broader European engagement in the region, there are a variety of development aid instruments and mechanisms. In the past aid for this region was delivered through the Technical Assistance to the Commonwealth of Independent States (TACIS) programme, which in 2007 was replaced by a broader regional instrument, the Development Cooperation Instrument (DCI). DCI delivered aid to developing countries and has a broad range of objectives, including poverty reduction, governance and assistance in post-crisis situations to fragile states. Out of the EU programmes and instruments applied to Central Asia, only DCI provides multi-annual indicative programming, which in 2007-10 amounted to €314 million and in 2011-13 to €321 million (Tsertsvadze and Boonstra, 2013, p.6).

In Central Asia, DCI is complemented by several thematic instruments and programmes. The Instrument for Stability (IfS) addresses global security and development challenges, especially in emerging crises and post-crisis countries. The European Instrument for Democracy and Human Right (EIDHR) provides support to civil society through democracy and human rights-oriented projects. The Non-States Actors and Local Authorities in Development (NSA-LA) aims to support local participation in development and improve governance. The Food Security programme seeks to assist states with extreme poverty levels, while the EU Food Facility programme supports countries that are severely affected by increased food prices. Additionally, Central Asia benefits from an Instrument for a Nuclear Safety Co-operation Instrument (NSCI), primarily targeted at Kyrgyzstan, Tajikistan and Uzbekistan (Tsertsvadze and Boonstra, 2013, p.7).

3. Evaluation of the EU Central Asia Strategy

The EU's Central Asian Strategy adopted in 2007 was evaluated in "Progress Report on the implication of the EU Strategy for Central Asia, Implementation Review and outline for Future Orientations", prepared by the European External Action Service and European Commission service in 2012. In this report, it is said, "The strategy has proven itself to be valid and much progress has been made in achieving what the EU set out to do in 2007", "All priority areas of the strategy remain important", "At the same time the region is facing increasing challenges, notably as regards developments in Afghanistan, and security issues have come to fore in relations with the EU. There is thus scope for adjusting the focus of EU actions and to target EU efforts more narrowly in the framework of the priorities set out in the strategy" (European External Action Service and European Commission, 2012).

This Progress Report was finalized in the Council Working Party on Eastern and Central Asia, and Council issued "Council conclusions on Central Asia" in which same evaluation was shown (Council of The European Union).

Against such an evaluation, critics was thrown in "EU Central Asia Policy: Steady as She Goes" by Boonstra, researcher of EU-Central Asia relation (Boonstra, 2012). She says, "This was a missed opportunity because the world has dramatically changed over the last five years, including Europe and Central Asia; that should have led to a rethinking of the strategy. The EU is in crisis as a result of the ever deepening economic and debt crisis, while Central Asia is far less stable than it was a few years ago." In other words European and Central Asia circumstances have changed over the last five years and the Strategy's impact remains low. And security concerns over the future of Afghanistan and Central Asia's internal stability are increasingly highlighted as a priority compared to energy security interests. The EU's security approach to Central Asia is largely based on soft security activities that include development aid and promotion of values but lacks a clear narrative of what Europe seeks to achieve. She concluded that a clearer security narrative is necessary to outline the most urgent threat to EU interest.

She stresses on the security aspect and pointed the EU is not a hard security actor in the region. And said that though the main external powers China, Russia and the United States understand that Central Asia offers little opportunity or economic gain and a high potential for security problems. The EU currently plays a second role on a geopolitical level that includes hard security interests and capabilities, and is probably well advised to keep it that way (Boonstra, 2012, pp.4-5).

We'll see the economic performance of Central Asian countries and development of the economic relation between EU and Central Asian states in the next section.

II. Features of Economic Relation

1. Central Asian Economic Structures

Thanks to the rising price of Oil and Gas, Kazakhstan and Turkmenistan could attain good performance, that can be witnessed both by the change of GDP growth rate, and by increase of GDP share of industrial sector and decrease of that of agricultural sector (Table 4-2, 4-3). These two states could realized industrialization steadily for 20 years, thus middle class people have increased as is shown by GDP per capita $ (Table 4-3). It is over 10,000 for Kazakhstan and over 5,000 for Turkmenistan, that are comparable with ASEAN states, i.e. Malaysia and Thailand respectively. But other three states, especially Kyrgyzstan and Tajikistan that are the poorest in five, have not taken-off toward industrialization.

However we can know from the exported commodities that recent good performance has been mainly led by rising price of natural resources and foreign investment to the resource-related industries and construction of infrastructure. So it may be key for these states whether they will able to progress the domestic industrial modernization or sophistication. For that purposes they must introduce market-based economy and competition, and reform the existing economic regime. However when we see the Worldwide Governance indicators (Table 4-3), the way to such a direction would be far away. Worldwide Governance indicators average is that of six indicators

Table 4-2 Central Asian GDP Growth Rates, 2001-2013

country \ year	2001	2002	2003	2004	2005	2006	2007	2008	2009	2010	2011	2012	2013
Kazakhstan	13.5	9.8	9.3	9.6	9.7	10,7	8.9	3.2	1.2	7.3	7.5	5.0	5.6
Kyrgyzstan	5.3	0.0	7.0	7.0	-0.2	3.1	8.2	7.6	2.9	-0.5	5.7	-0.9	6.5
Tajikistan	10.2	9.1	10.2	10.6	6.7	7.0	7.8	7.9	3.9	6.5	7.4	7.5	7.1
Turkmenistan	20.4	15.8	17.1	14.7	13.0	11.4	11.6	10.5	6.1	9.2	14.7	11.1	10.0
Uzbekistan	4.1	4.0	4.2	7.7	7.0	7.3	9.5	9.0	8.1	8.5	8.3	8.2	7.7
Avarage	10.8	8.6	8.9	9.8	9.1	9.8	9.2	5.0	3.0	7.3	n.a.	6.4	6.7

(Source) 2001-2008; Emerson, Michael, Jos Boonstra, Nafisa Hasanova, Marlene Laruelle and Sébastien Peyrouse (2010), *Into Eurasia: Monitoring the EU's Central Asia Strategy*. Report of the EUCAM Project, Center for European Policy Studies CEPS, Brussels and Fundación para las Relaciones Internacionales y el Diálogo Exterior FRIDE, Madrid. p.18, 2009-2013; EBRD, 2012 and 2013 date are forecasts.

Table4-3 Central Asian Economic Structures

country	Population thousands (2012)	GDP million $ (2012)	GDP per capita $ (2012)	GDP by sector %					Export by commodities	Worldwide Governance indicators Ave.-2.5 to 2.5
					(1990)	(1999)	(2004)	(2009)		
Kazakhstan	16,700	200,642	12,021	Agri.	27	10	7	6	Oil, Minerals Iron and Steel	-0.59
				Indus.	45	30	39	40		
				Serv.	29	60	53	53		
Kyrgyzstan	5,600	6,197	1,109	Agri.	35	44	39	29	Gold Cotton Textiles	-0.83
				Indus.	36	22	23	19		
				Serv.	29	35	38	51		
Uzbekistan	29,600	51,622	1,753	Agri.	33	31	35	20	Gold Cotton Fertilizers	-1.29
				Indus.	33	27	22	33		
				Serv.	34	42	43	47		
Tajikistan	7,800	7,263	912	Agri.	27	6	24	22	Aluminum Electricity Cotton	-1.10
				Indus.	34	30	21	24		
				Serv.	39	65	55	54		
Turkmenistan	5,250 (2011)	33,466	5,961	Agri.	32	25	21	12	Gas Cotton Crude oil	-1.41
				Indus.	30	42	45	54		
				Serv.	38	34	34	34		

(Source) JETRO, 2013.04.23, World Trade Organization, *Trade Profiles 2013*
World Bank, *World Development Report 2000/2001, 2006, 2007, 2012, 2014*
Turkmenistan, figures of 2004 are substituted by 2005

reflecting broad dimensions of governance (voice and accountability; political stability and absence of violence; government effectiveness; regulatory quality; rule of law; control of corruption) as defined by the Worldwide Governance Indicators project. For example, the worst 3 in 2013 are Somalia; -2.30, Afghanistan; -1.75 and Congo Dem. Rep.; -1.64 (World Bank, *World Development Report 2014*). For the endogenous development good governance is *sine qua non*.

2. Trade Structure: Which States They Trade with

For Central Asian states, Russia, China and EU have been the big and main three trade partners Table 4-4 so far, and such a situation will not change in the near future.

Table4-4 Share of Russia, China and EU in Central Asian Countries' Imports, Exports and Total Trade (2008, 2012) and Their Rank

country	import		export		total	
	2008	2012	2008	2012	2008	2012
Kazakhstan	Russia: 36% b (1st)	Russia: 31.4% (1st)	EU: 45.9% (1st)	EU: 39.9% (1st)	EU: 34.4% (1st)	EU: 31.6% (1st)
	China: 24.3%(2nd)	China: 26.5% (2nd)	China: 14.3% (2nd)	China: 20.5% (2nd)	Russia: 23.4% (2nd)	China: 23.0% (2nd)
	EU: 21% (3rd)	EU: 19.9% (3rd)	Russia: 12.3% (3rd)	Russia: 9.7% (3rd)	China: 18.9% (3rd)	Russia: 18.7% (3rd)
Kyrgyzstan	China: 70.5% (1st)	China: 55.8% (1st)	Russia: 29.6% (1st)	Russia: 13.5% (3st)	China: 62.3% (1st)	China: 50.3% (1st)
	Russia: 13.9:%(2nd)	Russia: 17.6%(2nd)	China: 7.6% (5th)	China: 6.5% (4th)	Russia: 15.9% (2nd)	Russia: 17.2% (2nd)
	EU: 4.1% (3rd)	EU: 5.7% (4th)	EU: 2.5% (8th)	EU: 2.9%(8th)	EU: 3.9% (4th)	EU: 5.4% (4th)
Uzbekistan	Russia: 27.6% (1st)	Russia: 20.6% (1st)	Russia: 25.3% (1st)	China: 17.9% (1st)	Russia: 26.7% (1st)	Russia: 18.1% (1st)
	EU: 17.9% (2nd)	China: 16.5% (2nd)	EU: 11% (2nd)	Russia: 12.5% (4th)	EU: 15.2% (2nd)	China: 16.9% (2nd)
	China: 16.3% (3rd)	EU: 14.0% (4th)	China: 6.1% (6th)	EU: 2.8% (9th)	China: 12.2% (3rd)	EU: 10.5% (5th)
Tajikistan	China: 26% (1st)	China: 39.9% (1st)	EU: 24.7% (1st)	China: 9.5%(2nd)	Russia: 22.6% (1st)	China: 34.5% (1st)
	Russia: 24.5%(2nd)	Russia: 15.3%(2nd)	Russia: 15.7% (2nd)	EU: 8.1% (3rd)	China: 20.8% (2nd)	Russia: 13.53 (2nd)
	EU: 6.4% (5th)	EU: 4.6% (5th)	China: 1.7% (9th)	Russia: 4.3% (7th)	EU: 10.3% (3rd)	EU: 5.2% (5th)
Turkmenistan	Russia: 16.6% (1st)	China: 18.2% (1st)	EU: 25.8% (2nd)	China: 62.9% (1st)	EU: 22.5% (2nd)	China: 41.8% (1st)
	EU: 15.7% (2nd)	EU: 17.3% (2nd)	Russia: 0.9% (11th)	EU: 6.8% (2nd)	Russia: 7.2% (5th)	EU: 11.8% (2nd)
	China: 14.7% (3rd)	Russia: 11.7% (4th)	China: 0.3% (16th)	Russia: 1.4% (8th)	China : 6.0% (7th)	Russia: 6.3% (4th)

(Source) http://ec.europa.eu/trade/trade-statistics/ Oct. 2009 and Jul.2013

IMF, *Direction of Trade Statistics.*

Originally as Central Asian states had been members of USSR, it's natural for them Russia to be a main partner. And as EU is so big, rich, neighboring, and matured market that it is attractive for Central Asian countries to deal with EU members. But recently instead of Russia and EU, China has been strengthening its economic presence in Central Asia both through economic assistance, trade and investment, and through its activities for the security and political purposes in Shanghai Cooperation Organisation (SCO). China is eager to make sure of importing natural resources and exporting a bewildering variety of goods to Central Asian market. For the time being, China will be more aggressive than before.

3. EU Central Asia Trade

After issuing *European Union and Central Asia Strategy for a New Partnership* in 2007, have the economic relations between EU and Central Asian states changed or not ?

On the one hand EU is a very big, developed and sophisticated economic area comparable to U.S., but on the other hand Central Asian states are developing or underdeveloped countries in general even though Central Asia is very large area geographically, and the sizes of population and GDP are small, high-value-added industries haven't developed yet and wouldn't develop in the near future. Especially Kyrgyzstan and Tajikistan are poor and least developed countries as we saw (Table 4-3).

Nonetheless the EU is now the main trading partner of Central Asia, accounting for almost a third of its overall external trade. However, total turnover of the EU's trade with Central Asia remains low and the five countries are insignificant trade partners for the EU. Even Kazakhstan, the EU's largest trade partner in Central Asia by far, accounting for almost 88% of the EU's overall trade with the region, occupies the 26th position and represents only 0.9% of the EU's overall trade with the world (2012). Central Asian states are marginal for EU in trade. So we can point out the imbalance or asymmetry in trade relations between two areas (Table 4-5). It's no wonder when we consider the economic size of each countries of Central Asia. That's why regional integration in this area should be recommended, and the commitment by EU must be promoted (Pomfret, 2011, p.143).

Central Asian exports to the EU remain concentrated in a few commodities (Table4-6), especially crude oil, gas (these are the same as "mineral products"), metals and cotton. "Products of the chemical and allied industries" by Kyrgyzstan and Uzbekistan are thought to be mercury-related products and GTL (Gas to Liquids) - related products respectively. EU exports to Central Asia are dominated mainly by machinery, vehicle and transport equipment. Such products accounted for more than half of EU exports in the region. We can see in this relation the traditional or typical pattern of North-South trade, and can characterize such a condition as Vertical Division of Labor, or inter-industrial trade.

Table4-5 Imbalances in Trade Relations between EU and Central Asian States

country	year	Position of state as EU trading partner (import, export)	Position of the EU as trading partner (import, export)
Kazakhstan	2007	29th (22nd, 36th)	1st (2nd, 1st)
	2010	30th (20th, 38th)	1st (3rd, 1st)
	2012	26th (16th, 37th)	1st (3rd, 1st)
Kyrgyzstan	2007	147th (163rd, 133rd)	4th (3rd, 8th)
	2010	129th (116th, 131st)	5th (4th, 9th)
	2012	133rd (144th, 122nd)	4th (4th, 8th)
Uzbekistan	2007	79th (69th, 93rd)	2nd (2nd, 1st)
	2010	83rd (92nd, 72nd)	4th (2nd, 5th)
	2012	91st (111st, 77th)	5th (4th, 9th)
Tajikistan	2007	142nd (116th, 151st)	3rd (6th, 1st)
	2010	148th (144th, 143rd)	5th (4th, 6th)
	2012	142nd (118th, 146th)	5th (5th, 3rd)
Turkmenistan	2007	120th (106th, 122nd)	3rd (1st, 3rd)
	2010	96th (95th, 94th)	3rd (3rd, 2nd)
	2012	83rd (82nd, 74th)	2nd (2nd, 2nd)

(Source) http://ec.europa.eu/trade/trade-statistics/

Table4-6 Exports and Imports of Central Asian Countries 2012

country	Exported products to EU (%) 2012		Imported products from EU (%) 2012	
Kazakhstan	Mineral products	(92.5)	Machinery and mechanical appliances	(35.2)
	Base metals and articles of base metal	(1.8)	Vehicles, aircraft, vessels, transport equipment	(16.1)
	Products of the chemical and allied industries	(1.6)	Products of the chemical and allied industries	(15.2)
Kyrgyzstan	Products of the chemical and allied industries	(40.7)	Vehicles, aircraft, vessels, transport equipment	(26.5)
	Base metals and articles of base metal	(32.2)	Machinery and mechanical appliances	(16.7)
	Vegetable products	(15.1)	Mineral products	(16.6)
Uzbekistan	Products of the chemical and allied industries	(50.7)	Machinery and mechanical appliances	(32.7)
	Textile and textile articles	(16.0)	Products of the chemical and allied industries	(22.8)
	Pearls and precious stones	(13.1)	Vehicles, aircraft, vessels, transport equipment	(10.4)
Tajikistan	Base metals and articles of base metal	(79.6)	Vehicles, aircraft, vessels, transport equipment	(30.4)
	Textile and textile articles	(19.6)	Machinery and mechanical appliances	(19.6)
	Pearls and precious stones	(0.3)	Products of the chemical and allied industries	(12.7)
Turkmenistan	Mineral products	(91.9)	Machinery and mechanical appliances	(43.1)
	Textile and textile articles	(4.6)	Pearls and precious stones	(17.0)
	Machinery and mechanical appliances	(1.8)	Vehicles, aircraft, vessels, transport equipment	(9.7)

(Source) European Commission, DG Trade, Statics

4. Evaluation

What are the implications after surveying economic relations between EU and Central Asian states? According to Pomfret's analysis, the EU strategy for promotion of economic development and trade focuses on promoting multilateral trade, improving regional infrastructure and supporting development of market economy structure. The diversity of the Central Asian economies after a decade and a half of transition from central planning and their ongoing dependence on a few commodities whose prices are determined in world markets limits the scope for EU action at a regional level. He suggested that rather than both supporting WTO membership and enhancing the usage of EU Generalized System of Preferences scheme, much more important is assistance to help the Central Asia countries' to diversify their exports through technical and financial assistance for education, improved business environment, financial sector development Central Asian countries boost any non-traditional exports. Also he stressed that the EU can help Central Asia by living up to its commitment to promote regional cooperation of European dimension, e.g. the programme of restricting the drag trade or supporting initiatives to develop trade corridors such as the E40 Tashkent-Berlin road.

He concluded that prospects for significant change in economic policies in the near future are limited because the entrenched political regimes have little incentive to sponsor major reforms. Fundamental across Central Asia is the question of whether an autocratic and repressive political regime is consistent with a flourishing market-based economy (Pomfret, 2011, pp.142-144). From such a point of view, the role of EU as a normative power is in the long run more necessary and important than the role of China and Russia being pragmatic to Central Asian states.

We can say it's difficult for Central Asian states to be a "Next Market" in near future.

5. Recent Trends

In Oct. 2013, Japanese authentic newspaper, The Nikkei reported about recent Central Asian situations, titled "Central Asia, New Economic Area" (Nikkei, 21st, 22nd and 23rd, Oct. 2013, originally in Japanese). According to the articles, in Central Asia there has been a three-way race between China, Russia and Turkey in these years. China seeking for natural resources, Russia trying to keep its traditional influence and Turkey with similar language and ethnicity investing to infrastructures positively. On the one hand, countries with rich oil or gas have developed smoothly, e.g. GDP per capita of Kazakhstan became bigger than that of Malaysia and GDP per capita of Turkmenistan bigger than that of Thailand and Philippines, and many enterprises from developed countries tend to concentrate on these countries, but on the other hand, countries with little or limited resources, i.e. Tajikistan and Kyrgyzstan have been staying underdeveloped.

So external disparities between these countries are the most alarming cause for anxiety from the viewpoint of regional integration of Central Asia. At the same time, domestic disparities can also cause a serious problem because they could relate to the authoritarian regime and introduce Islamic extreme movement from Afghanistan. That is the reason why the priority areas of EU strategy remain human rights, rule of law, good governance and democratization. EU is really a normative power.

After considering EU-Central Asia economic relations, we come to recognize that Central Asia remains marginal in EU world trade partners, but EU must keep good relation with Central Asian states for the sake of diversification of importing oil and gas, moreover to keep stability and to prevent illegal trafficking in this area is necessary for the sound economic growth and democratization in the long run. We can call the last point to be the Geostrategy. Furthermore there could exist a possibility of forming New Silk Road economic area as we'll see in the last part.

III. Conclusion: Implications for China and Japan, Prospect for New Silk Road

We can conclude as follows: first, the main aims of EU Trade Policy towards Central Asian countries are diversifying energy import and Geostrategy, next, feature of trade relation between EU and Central Asian countries is imbalanced, asymmetry, and vertical, and last, it's difficult for Central Asian states to be a "Next Market" in near future. Based on the above let us consider a couple of issues lastly.

(1) Implication for China

As we saw in above chapters, Central Asia is an important source of raw materials and also a growing market for China. However the intension of China is not limited to economy. Chinese government aims at stabilizing the neighborhood of Xinjiang province. The Third Plenary Session (sān zhōng quán huì) of Chinese Communist Party was held in Beijing from 9 to 12 Nov. 2013. Just before the Session, several protest movements occurred by possibly Muslim Uyghur minority from the Xinjiang province. Central Asian countries, especially Kazakhstan, Kyrgyzstan and Tajikistan, are neighboring to the Xinjiang province. Thanks to democratic EU as normative power, EU have never had a heart-to-heart talk with authoritarian governments in Central Asia before, thus China can strengthen the bilateral and regional relation with Central Asian authoritarian states through trade, investment and assistance regardless of issues of human rights, rule of law, good governance and democracy implicitly. In conjunction with the declining influence of Russia, China and Central Asian states are making closer and mutually advantageous relations (Zasztowt, 2012).

(2) Implication for Japan

Confronted with a growing Chinese presence and the preservation of a declining but strong Russian influence, Japan has had difficulty in establishing its place in Central Asia. Japan has spent much in the form of credits, subsidies for specific projects, and technical cooperation, to bolster the development of the Central Asian states. Despite this substantial aid, Japan remains rather invisible as a partner, that illustrates the difficulties involved in projecting soft power in a region where precepts of spheres of influence and geopolitical rivalry are dominant. In 1997 Japan's new "Eurasian diplomacy " and in 2004 "Central Asia Japan" dialogue have started. In 2013, Japan and 3 states Kirgyz, Tajikistan and Uzbekistan have agreed on border control against Afghanistan. These were designed to shift from bilateral relation to a multilateral dialogue on complex subjects such as economic cooperation, the joint management of energy resources, trade development through regional transport, the fight against terrorism and drag trafficking. While Japan struggles to establish a significant role in the region alongside Russia and China, Japanese investment has been quite diversified. Major Japanese companies have invested substantial sums in strategic domains such as access to hydrocarbons, the construction of refineries, and uranium. Indeed, Kazakhstan is major partners in Japanese nuclear domain (Emerson *et al.*, 2010, pp.49-50, Ministry of Foreign Affairs, Japan, http://www.mofa.go.jp/mofaj/area/europe/caj/index.html). Central Asia will remain potential partner and Japan shoud play a role of soft power.

(3) Prospect for the formation of New Silk Road Economic Area

Currently China-European trade is confined to the see route or, to a minor extent, Trans-Siberian Railway or air transport, but there are prospects for new linkages between Europe and China. Central Asia has increasingly become a transport hub. The current revitalization of the Silk Road and development of a continental transport corridor running from China's east coast to Europe are expected to bring massive gains to the landlocked countries of Central Asia as well as for China and Europe. At present sea journey China to Europe takes 20 to 40 days, while the new links could cut transport time to eleven days. The trans-regional trade and transport system could be one of the most positive factors for the Central Asian states and one in which cooperation between China, Central Asia and Europe is very likely and profitable for all actors. Of course this would need a more stable and economically sound Central Asia that has been able to control the rampant corruption and narcotrade (Swanström, 2011, p.8, pp.65-69). Road development plans in Silk Road area are proceeded now by Asian Development Bank, Japan International Cooperation Agency (JICA) and China. And the construction of two railways between China and Kazakhstan were completed (Nikkei, 22nd Oct.2013). If these roads and railways through Central Asian states with stable and sound economy would lead to Europe, New Silk Road economic area and literally Eurasian could emerge.

References

Boonstra, Jos (2012), "EU Central Asia Policy: Steady as She Goes," *Central Asia Policy Brief*, 4, 1-5.

Council of the European Union, General Secretariat (2007), European Union and Central Asia Strategy for a New Partnership (New EU Central Asia Strategy).

Council of the European Union, General Secretariat (2010), Joint Progress Report by the Council and the European Commission to the European Council on the implementation of the EU Strategy for Central Asia, 11402/10, Brussels.

Council of The European Union (2012), Council Conclusions on Central Asia, 3179th Foreign Affairs Council Meeting, Luxembourg, 25 June 2012.

Delcour, Laure (2011), *Shaping the Post-Soviet Space EU Policies and Approaches to Region-Building*, Ashgate.

European Community (2007), Regional Strategy Paper for Assistance to Central Asia for the period 2007-2013.

European Commission (2011), Policy Making, What did the Lisbon Treaty Change? Factsheet 14 June 2011.

European Commission, External Relations Directorate General, Directorate Eastern Europe, Southern Caucasus, Central Asia Republics (2010), Central Asia DCI Indicative Programme 2011-2013.

European External Action Service and European Commission (2012), Progress Report on the implication of the EU Strategy for Central Asia, Implementation Review and outline for Future Orientations (June, 2012).

Emerson, Michael, Jos Boonstra, Nafisa Hasanova, Marlene Laruelle and Sébastien Peyrouse (2010), *Into Eurasia: Monitoring the EU's Central Asia Strategy*, Report of the EUCAM Project, Center for European Policy Studies CEPS, Brussels and Fundación para las Relaciones Internacionales y el Diálogo Exterior FRIDE, Madrid.

Lala, Rajeev (2012), European Union Central Asia relations after the Lisbon Treaty, Downloaded at http://www.academia.edu/1453159/European_Union_-_Central_Asia_relations_after_the_Lisbon_Treaty.

Peyrouse, Sébastien (2009), Business and Trade Relationships between the EU and Central Asia, EUCAM, Working Paper 01.

Pomfret, Richard (2011), "Economic Development and Trade" in Alexander Warkotsch (ed.), *The Eurorean Union and Central Asia*, Routledge, 132-147.

Swanström, Niklas (2011), China and Greater Central Asia: New Frontiers? SILK ROAD PAPER December 2011, Central Asia and Caucasus Institute & Silk Road Studies Program A Joint Transatlantic Research and Policy Center.

Tsertsvadze, Tika and Jos Boonstra (2013), Mapping EU development aid to Central Asia, EUCAM Factsheet 1, July 2013.

Warkotsch, Alexander (ed.) (2011), *The European Union and Central Asia*, Routledge.

Zasztowt, Konrad (2012), "China's Policy Towards Central Asian SCO States", *BULLETIN*, 72 (405), Politish Institute of International Affairs, 772-773.

http://eurodialogue.org/eu-central-asia-strategy/10

http://ec.europa.eu/trade/

http://www.mofa.go.jp/mofaj/area/europe/caj/index.html

Chapter 5

MEASURING THE TRANSPORTATION COMPETITIVENESS OF THE NEW SILK ROAD

I. Introduction

In recent years, economic development in the regions located along the New Silk Road has drawn much interest from around the world. There are two main reasons for this. The first is the fact that the economic development of the vast landlocked countries and regions of central Eurasia presents great promise and opportunity. It is hoped that this development will greatly benefit the more than 3 billion estimated to inhabit this huge area. The second reason is that the development of the natural resources of the region will also benefit many other countries around the world. However, in order to reliably develop the economies that lie along the New Silk Road, it is absolutely essential to improve the competitiveness of commercial transportation services through the region. At the same time, the construction of the new infrastructure needed to enhance overland transportation competitiveness will itself help to drive economic development along the New Silk Road.

A series of studies by the New Silk Road Research Group at Nihon University[1] has identified the conditions necessary for the industrial development of the regions along the New Silk Road. It is hoped that making overland transportation along the New Silk Road more competitive will provide opportunities for further development of existing major cities along the routes, as well as stimulate the rise of new cities in border areas, thereby leading to the formation of an economic belt like a string of beads.

The New Silk Road's overland economic competitiveness does not yet seem to be sufficiently understood. For one thing, not enough is known about the current state of east-west commercial transportation along the New Silk Road; for another, there is a lack of understanding about the competitiveness of overland transportation on the New Silk Road. The former problem is due to our not knowing how east-west distribution is being conducted along the New Silk Road. The latter problem has to do with the fact that not enough theoretical research has been conducted to precisely define what transportation competitiveness means and how to measure it. Furthermore, if the latter problem is not sufficiently well understood, it is not possible to accurately understand the former problem or to formulate effective measures to promote greater transportation competitiveness on the New Silk Road.

---

[1] Refer to Wu (2007, 2009, 2011, 2012), Tsuji (2009), Riku (2009).

In this chapter, we set out to try and measure the transportation competitiveness of the New Silk Road, based on a theoretical explication of our understanding of overland transportation competitiveness in the region. In addition, we analyze the current state of east-west commercial transportation on the New Silk Road and identify measures to improve the competitiveness of transportation.

In the following section, we explain what we mean by transportation competitiveness and propose a novel method for measuring it. In Section III, we attempt to measure the transportation competitiveness of the New Silk Road using Chinese trade data. Finally, in Section IV, we offer an overview of the current state of commercial transportation on the New Silk Road and put forward measures to promote greater transportation competitiveness.

II. Transportation Competitiveness

1. Scope of Competitiveness on the New Silk Road

Transportation competitiveness of the New Silk Road does not merely refer to reducing the costs of transportation or increasing transportation efficiency. Undoubtedly, in terms of cost and efficiency, transportation on the New Silk Road today is much better than in the pre-modern era, when it was typically handled by caravans of camels. However, it cannot be said that the caravans of the past were definitely a less competitive form of transportation. The old caravans once handled almost all east-west commercial transportation along the Silk Road, making journeys across the Eurasian continent over a long period of time. They enjoyed a strong transportation competitiveness that could not be matched by sea transportation. Conversely, even if transportation along the New Silk Road today is far more cost effective and efficient than in the old days, we cannot conclude that it is as highly competitive as in the past. Thus, in order to understand what transportation competitiveness on the New Silk Road means precisely, we need to first be aware of all alternative means of transportation and all possible routes. Then we need to compare all the alternative means and routes based on cost and efficiency to decide which are the most competitive. In this sense, transportation competitiveness of the New Silk Road is a concept that shows the relative magnitude of transportation cost and efficiency when we compare it with alternative competing transportation means and routes. Thus, when we talk about the transportation competitiveness of the New Silk Road, we must first clearly identify its competitors.

There are currently three main commercial transportation routes for east-west trade across the Eurasian continent. The first is by sea; the second is the Trans-Siberian Railway that crosses Russia; and the third one is the rail transportation route that we are calling the New Silk Road, which extends from the eastern coastal region of China and connects to the West via the European railway network after crossing China, Kazakhstan, and other countries.

Alternative routes exist, but the only real competitors to the New Silk Road are the sea route and Trans-Siberian Railway.[2] From the viewpoint of developing the landlocked region at the heart of Eurasia, the competition between the New Silk Road and the Trans-Siberian Railway is distinctly different in nature from that between the New Silk Road and sea transportation. The New Silk Road and Trans-Siberian Railway share the same mode of transport (rail) and both use overland routes to cross Eurasia. The competition between these two alternatives is good for promoting railway transportation efficiency. That is, technological advances and management innovations on one of these routes will tend to be adopted on the other, so that ultimately the efficiency of both will improve. This kind of competition will prove beneficial to the development of the landlocked countries of central Eurasia. On the other hand, the question of competition between the New Silk Road and sea transportation is a crucial one that has serious implications for the ultimate success or failure of the development of these landlocked countries. Or put another way, answering the question of how the New Silk Road can compete with sea transportation to once again become the main transportation route for east-west commercial traffic across Eurasia is the key to the success of the region's development. For this reason, it is logical to focus on sea transportation as the main competitor to the New Silk Road. What remains is to compare the cost and efficiency of transportation of these two modes of transportation.

2. Principles and Method for Measuring Transportation Competitiveness

Trying to compare the New Silk Road and sea transportation in terms of cost and efficiency of transportation is a relatively difficult problem. Since these are two different modes of transportation, cost and time will vary significantly, even if the departure and destination points are the same, and conclusions will differ according to which points are used. In addition, these are both intermodal forms of transportation to some extent, making it impossible to make a pure comparison. Furthermore, it is difficult to obtain useful data on transportation times and costs, and whatever information is available is hard to interpret. For this reason, in this chapter, we propose an original measurement method that does not rely on transportation time and cost data. This method will allow us to ascertain the transportation competitiveness of the New Silk Road. We will first explain the method for measuring transportation competitiveness by using a simple model.

Figure 5-1 shows a schematic of a single overland transportation route connecting two

---

[2] In the modern society, air transportation plays an important role. It, however, is not as highly competitive as in overland and sea transportation. Since limits caused by geographical factors are not as big as in other means of transportation, the competitiveness of air transportation along the New Silk Road is not extremely less competitive than in other regions. Because of these reasons, discussion about air transportation is omitted.

Figure 5-1

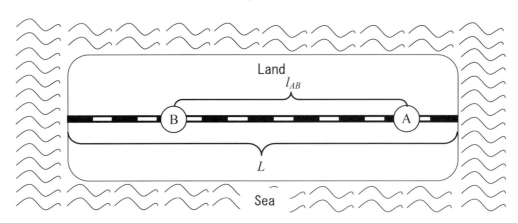

endpoints at the far left and far right, separated by a distance L. There is also a sea transportation route that joins the two endpoints. Let us consider the transportation between two arbitrary points A and B. The distance between A and B is l_{AB} (where $l_{AB} \leq L$). In this case, there are two possible routes for transporting a given freight between A and B. The first route uses the direct overland route to the destination. The other intermodal route involves delivering the freight overland to the nearest sea port and then transporting it by sea to the sea port on the opposite side, before the final leg of overland transport to the destination. We will refer to the former as Route 1 and to the latter as Route 2. We also assume that a rational shipping agent decides which route to take by comparing a composite cost index for each of the transportation routes. For simplicity, the cost index T_{1AB} is assumed to be an increasing function of the transportation distance l_{AB},

$$T_{1AB} = f(l_{AB}), \tag{1}$$

since the cost and time of overland transport increases with increasing transportation distance. In addition, if we take the composite cost index for sea transportation between the two endpoints at east and west to be tsea, then the composite index for Route 2, T_{2AB}, can be expressed as follows:

$$T_{2AB} = f(L - l_{AB}) + t_{sea}. \tag{2}$$

In Eq. (2), L is a constant, and so T_{2AB} depends only on l_{AB} and t_{sea}. Notice that T_{2AB} is a decreasing function of l_{AB} and an increasing function of t_{sea}.

If $T_{1AB} < T_{2AB}$, then Route 1 is selected for transportation between A and B. Conversely, if $T_{1AB} > T_{2AB}$, then Route 2 is selected. The value l^* at which the index values are equal (i.e., $T_{1l^*} = T_{2l^*}$) represents the boundary value where the rational route selection changes from one option to the other. In particular, if the distance between A and B does not exceed l^*, then Route 1 is selected; if it exceeds l^*, then Route 2 is selected.

For example, if the distance from A to X in Figure 5-2 equals l^* then $T_{1AX} = f(l^*) = T_{2AX} = f(L - l^*) + t_{sea}$. Then for $l_{AB} < l^*$, $T_{1AB} = f(l_{AB}) < f(l^*) = T_{1AX}$, and since $T_{2AB} = f(L - l_{AB}) + t_{sea}$

Measuring the Transportation Competitiveness of the New Silk Road 79

$> f(L - l^*) + t_{sea} = T_{2AX}$, we can deduce that $T_{1AB} < T_{2AB}$. Alternatively, for $l_{AC} > l^*$, $T_{1AC} = f(l_{AC})$ $> f(l^*) = T_{1AX}$ and $T_{2AC} = f(L - l_{AC}) + t_{sea} > f(L - l^*) + t_{sea} = T_{2AX}$, which implies that $T_{1AC} > T_{2AC}$. Therefore, between A and B Route 1 is chosen, and between A and C Route 2 is chosen.

Figure 5-2

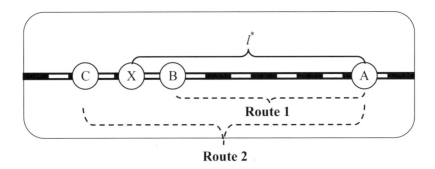

This distance l^*, which we will refer to as the "break-even distance" for overland transport, can be used as an indicator for expressing the competitiveness of overland transport. Thus, as an example, for a given value of tsea, the value of l^* should increase when there is an improvement in overland transportation technology. Conversely, for a given value of tsea, if the value of l^* increases, we can reasonably assume that overland transportation technology has improved, and more precisely, even in the case where the value of tsea decreases, if the value of l^* increases, then we can assume that overland transportation technology has improved more rapidly than sea transportation technology. Therefore, the improvement in the competitiveness of overland transport can be measured by looking at the increase in the value of l^*. The advantage of using this break-even distance l^* as an indicator of competitiveness is that it allows us to measure competitiveness without relying on information about the expense and time required for the two routes, by simply looking at the transportation choices made for imports and exports. This method also neatly reflects any relative changes in overland and sea transportation technology.

Furthermore, if we assume uniform overland transportation conditions along a route, it is easy to prove that $l^* > L/2$ is always true through proof by contradiction. For example, if $l_{AB} = L/2$, then from the above argument $T_{1AB} \geq T_{2AB}$ should be true. However, $T_{1AB} = f(L/2)$ and so $T_{2AB} = f(L - L/2) + t_{sea} = f(L/2) + t_{sea} > f(L/2)$, which implies that $T_{1AB} < T_{2AB}$, which is a contradiction. Since this leads to a contradictory result, $l^* \leq L/2$ never holds.

Finally, taking into account the current state of the New Silk Road, we assume that $l^* \leq L$. When $L \geq l^* > L/2$, we find the following. As shown in Figure 5-3, taking A1 and A2 as the endpoints, we move toward the center and define the two points X1 and X2 that are at the same distance from their respective endpoints, namely, l^*. Thus, the distance between X1 and X2 is

Figure 5-3

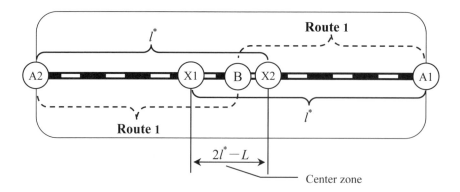

$2l^* - L$. The region of overlap between X1 and X2 is referred to as the center zone. If $L \geq l^* > L/2$, then a center zone definitely exists. Also, since the distance between any point within this region and any other point is always less than l^*, the rational choice for transportation between the two points can only be Route 1. On the other hand, for points outside this center zone, Route 2 may also be a rational transportation choice. In other words, the center zone defines all points where Route 1 is the only rational choice for transportation. Thus, if we can make empirical observations to determine where these points start and end, then we can deduce the value of l^*. If the competitiveness of overland transportation rises, then the value of l^* increases and the center zone, as defined here, expands.

III. Transport Competitiveness of the New Silk Road

1. Measuring Transportation Competitiveness Using Trade Statistics

If we try to measure the competitiveness of transportation on the New Silk Road using the concept developed in the previous section, then we must face another problem: we may not necessarily be able to obtain information about what routes are used for transportation between various points. To resolve this problem, we chose to adopt a specific method of measurement that utilizes the gravity equation, a well-known formula in the field of international trade theory. The gravity equation was first employed by Tinbergen (1962) and later developed considerably through both theory and demonstration.[3] In its most basic form, the gravity equation is as follows:

$$\text{Trade value}_{AB} = \alpha (GDP_A \cdot GDP_B) / Distance_{AB}. \tag{3}$$

---

[3] For the theoretical studies, refer to Eaton and Kortum (2002), Deardorff (1998), Helpman (1987), Chaney (2008). For empirical studies, refer to Bernard *et al.* (2007).

Trade value$_{AB}$ expresses the value of exports or imports in terms of GDP_A and GDP_B, the scale of economic activity at points A and B, respectively, and *Distance*$_{AB}$, the distance between A and B, where α is a constant. However, in its basic form, Eq. (3) cannot be applied, because *Distance*$_{AB}$ is not actually necessarily inversely proportional to *Trade value*$_{AB}$ and because any precise information cannot be necessarily obtained. In addition, it may not be possible to acquire precise information about transportation distance. Therefore, we consider a modified form of Eq. (3):

$$\text{Trade value}_{AB} = \alpha(GDP_A \cdot GDP_B)/T_{AB}, \tag{4}$$

where T_{AB} is a composite cost index for transportation between A and B. This can be further rewritten as

$$T_{AB} = \alpha(GDP_A \cdot GDP_B)/\text{Trade value}_{AB}. \tag{5}$$

Since data on GDP and trade value can be obtained quite easily, this equation can be used to estimate T_{AB}. Also, by calculating the value of T_{AB} for various pairs of points along the New Silk Road, we can make rational decisions about transportation routes according to distance. If a positive correlation between T_{AB} and L_{AB} is observed, then Route 1 would be chosen for transportation between A and B. If the converse is found, then Route 2 would be chosen (See Figure 5-4). Based on this information, it becomes possible to estimate the value of the break-even distance l^* for overland transportation.

Figure 5-4 shows total transportation cost T plotted versus one point along the length L of the overland transportation route across the continent with the other point taken as fixed. In the figure, point B is located adjacent to points B1 and B2, which are to the east and west of B, respectively. If the distance between A and B is equal to the break-even distance l^* for overland transport, then T_{AB} must be a local maximum cost value. To the east of B, where Mode 1 is the preferred choice for transportation, T_{Aj} is positively correlated with distance, whereas to the

Figure 5-4

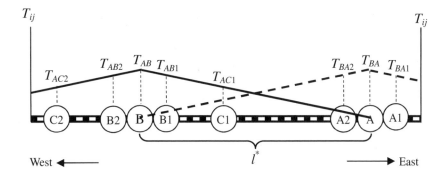

west of B, Mode 2 is the transportation choice and T_{Aj} is negatively correlated with distance. It follows that the relations $T_{AC1} < T_{AB1} < T_{AB}$ and $T_{AB} > T_{AB2} > T_{AC2}$ should hold. Accordingly, if we compare the total transportation cost at A for various points to the west of A, we might find, for example, that $T_{AC1} < T_{AB1} < T_{AB}$ and that $T_{AB} > T_{AB2} > T_{AC2}$. From this we can deduce that the distance between A and B represents the break-even distance for overland transportation. In this case, we should also find that for two points A1 and A2 adjacent to A, relations $T_{BA1} < T_{BA}$ and $T_{BA2} < T_{BA}$ should hold. (Note also that $T_{AB} = T_{BA}$.)

2. Measuring the Transportation Competitiveness of the New Silk Road

Here, we consider a rail route stretching from the Chinese port of Lianyungang, on the far east of the Eurasian landmass, to the Dutch port of Rotterdam, on the western side of the continent, as well as to points further west, to include countries that can be reached by rail from Rotterdam. This defines our limits for possible overland transportation. We are going to analyze what specific route to use for transportation between such points. Traveling west from China, the countries along the route to be considered are Kazakhstan, Russia, Belarus, Poland, Germany, the Netherlands, Belgium, France, Spain, and finally Portugal, which we take as our western terminus. The Chinese territory extends from Jiangsu on the east coast to (moving westward) the provinces of Henan, Shaanxi, Gansu, and Xinjiang Uyghur Autonomous Region on the western border. Along the route, two countries, Kazakhstan and Belarus, and the Chinese provinces/regions of Henan, Shaanxi, Gansu, and Xinjiang are all landlocked, whereas all other countries and regions have sea ports. Of particular importance are the Dutch port of Rotterdam, the Belgian port of Antwerp, and the German port of Hamburg -the three busiest ports in Europe[4]- and the Chinese port of Lianyungang in Jiangsu province, an important gateway to the sea for China.[5] These ports can also be considered to deal mainly in intermodal transportation. Under these assumptions, we set out to use external trade data for different areas in China along the overland route to try to measure total transportation costs. Note that since Russia's border with China is very long, overland transportation between localities in China and Russia may not necessarily be transported over this route. (Refer to the measurement results for Russia.)

First, as the essential criteria for our measurement, we examined the GDP and trade of various Chinese regions along the overland route. GDP values (Table 5-1) show that apart from Xinjiang, GDP and foreign trade increase from west to east: Jiangsu on the east coast had the highest values, followed by, in descending order, Henan Province, Shaanxi Province, Xinjiang (Xinjiang Uyghur Autonomous Region), and Gansu. In terms of total foreign trade value

---

[4] Refer to César Ducruet and Theo Notteboom (2012).

[5] Data of the 2009 container volumes show that 9,743 TEU goes to Rotterdam, 7,309 to Antwerp, and 3,020,000 TEU to Hamburg (*Containerisation International Yearbook*, Informa UK Ltd).

Table 5-1 GDP (hundred million RMB)

	2000	2005	2006	2007	2008	2009	2010
Jiangsu	8582.73	18305.66	21742.05	26018.48	30981.98	34457.30	41425.48
Henan	5137.66	10587.42	12362.79	15012.46	18018.53	19480.46	23092.36
Shaanxi	1660.92	3675.66	4743.61	5757.29	7314.58	8169.80	10123.48
Gansu	983.36	1933.98	2276.70	2702.40	3166.82	3387.56	4120.75
Xinjiang	1364.36	2604.19	3045.26	3523.16	4183.21	4277.05	5437.47

(Source) *China Statistical Yearbook*

Table 5-2   Total Trade (Exports + Imports) (million USD)

	2000	2005	2006	2007	2008	2009	2010
Jiangsu	49194.37	238475.21	299041.18	372247.46	430467.00	365931.94	498782.58
Henan	3123.89	9065.80	10982.15	14206.76	19888.60	15068.24	20015.29
Shaanxi	2387.54	6149.31	6922.39	8235.94	10455.86	8673.00	11703.66
Gansu	691.55	2986.92	4439.69	5874.07	6562.53	4484.60	7388.09
Xinjiang	2586.10	8303.18	10210.89	15443.39	24975.47	16125.35	21363.30

(Source) *China Statistical Yearbook*

(see Table 5-2), similarly, Jiangsu ranking highest and Gansu lowest. Interestingly, however, since 2007, Xinjiang in the far west has ranked second to Jiangsu in terms of total foreign trade value, despite ranking second to last in terms of GDP. Another interesting observation is that the disparity in foreign trade between regions far exceeds the disparity in GDP.

Based on data for the foreign trade value of the different regions with various partner countries (see Table 5-3), we see that Xinjiang's highest level of trade is with the Central Asian nation of Kazakhstan, followed by Russia and Germany. Shaanxi's and Jiangsu's main foreign trading partners are Germany, the Netherlands, Belgium, and France, whereas their trade with Kazakhstan and Russia is not very large.[6] Table 5-4 shows which region of China the various countries trade with most. For example, Kazakhstan trades mainly with neighboring Xinjiang, the value of this trade accounting for almost half (48.82%) of its total trade with China. Apart from Kazakhstan, however, all countries trade more with faraway Jiangsu than with any of the inland regions. Furthermore, when we compare the trade value of the Netherlands, Belgium, France, Spain, and Portugal with the Chinese regions, we note that trade value is inversely proportional to distance.

---

[6] An analysis on the Gansu Province is excluded because data are not available.

Table 5-3 Total Trade (Exports + Imports) of Chinese Regions with Different Countries (2009, million USD)

	Xinjiang	Shaanxi	Henan	Jiangsu	China
Kazakhstan	689,751	1,316	n/a	n/a	1,412,913
Russia	30,911	8,006	31,951	266,051	3,875,155
Belarus	507	145	n/a	n/a	80,997
Poland	1,251	4,798	n/a	204,174	899,290
Germany	25,584	83,212	60,942	1,761,035	10,563,581
Netherlands	1,173	18,283	n/a	1,075,538	4,180,605
Belgium	793	23,336	n/a	226,718	1,671,959
France	2,898	12,248	n/a	463,526	3,445,624
Spain	470	6,620	n/a	241,252	1,835,537
Portugal	335	430	n/a	43,274	240,438

(Sources) *China Statistical Yearbook*, statistical yearbooks of Chinese provinces/autonomous regions

Table 5-4 Share of China's Total Trade (Exports + Imports) with Different Countries by Region (2009, %)

	Xinjiang	Shaanxi	Henan	Jiangsu
Kazakhstan	48.82	0.09	n/a	n/a
Russia	0.80	0.21	0.82	6.87
Belarus	0.63	0.18	n/a	n/a
Poland	0.14	0.53	n/a	22.70
Germany	0.24	0.79	0.58	16.67
Netherlands	0.03	0.44	n/a	25.73
Belgium	0.05	1.40	n/a	13.56
France	0.08	0.36	n/a	13.45
Spain	0.03	0.36	n/a	13.14
Portugal	0.14	0.18	n/a	18.00

(Sources) Same as Table 5-3

Next, we consider measuring the total transportation cost between the various regions of China and their international trading partners. We can use the following equation:

$$T_{ij} = \ln(GDP_i) + \ln(GDP_j) - \ln(Trade\ value_{ij}), \qquad (6)$$

where i represents the particular region of China and j represents the particular foreign trading partner country.[7] T_{ij} is thus the total transportation cost between region i and country j.

---

[7] The GDP data for the counterpart is obtained from IMF's *World Economic Outlook*.

Table 5-5 Results of Calculations Based on Export Trade Value of Chinese Regions for 2009

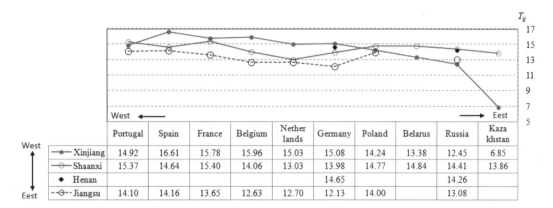

		Portugal	Spain	France	Belgium	Netherlands	Germany	Poland	Belarus	Russia	Kazakhstan
	Xinjiang	14.92	16.61	15.78	15.96	15.03	15.08	14.24	13.38	12.45	6.85
	Shaanxi	15.37	14.64	15.40	14.06	13.03	13.98	14.77	14.84	14.41	13.86
	Henan						14.65			14.26	
	Jiangsu	14.10	14.16	13.65	12.63	12.70	12.13	14.00		13.08	

Table 5-5 shows the results of calculations performed using export trade value. Each row lists the total transportation cost of exports from a Chinese region to the various countries along our route, and thus each column allows comparison of the total transportation cost for imports between Chinese regions for a partner country. We will use this table to make some deductions about transportation routes for each of these Chinese regions.

(1) Xinjiang

The region of Xinjiang in the far west of China borders Kazakhstan and is more favorably positioned than other regions of China for overland transportation to Europe. On the other hand, it is the most disadvantaged for intermodal transportation. Comparing horizontally from right to left in Table 5-5, the total transportation cost to neighboring Kazakhstan is strikingly low, and up through Germany, the cost correlates positively with distance. Moving further west from Germany, although transportation cost continues to increase, it no longer correlates positively with distance. From this, we can surmise that overland transportation from Xinjiang can be used as far as Germany. However, Table 5-5 also shows that for countries from Kazakhstan to Poland, the total transportation cost from Xinjiang is less than that from Shaanxi further east. If intermodal transportation were used from Xinjiang to these countries, the total cost would not be lower than that for Shaanxi. On the other hand, the total transportation cost from Xinjiang to Germany is higher than for any of the other Chinese regions. If intermodal transportation were used from Xinjiang to Germany, the total transportation cost would have to be higher than for the other Chinese regions. It follows that overland transportation should be the main choice at least for countries up to Poland. From Xinjiang to Germany, overland and intermodal transport are probably of similar cost, and so we could say that Germany marks the approximate break-even distance for overland transportation from Xinjiang. For exports to countries further west than Germany, intermodal transportation is more likely to be more economical than overland transportation. This explains why the total transportation cost from

Xinjiang to the Netherlands is less than that to Germany.

(2) Shaanxi

Comparing vertically in Table 5-5, we note that the total transportation cost from the Chinese regions to Russia is highest for Shaanxi. In the case of overland transportation to Russia, the total cost from Shaanxi would obviously be higher than from Xinjiang. If intermodal transportation is used from Shaanxi, the total cost would be higher than from Henan or Jiangsu. So both possibilities may be similarly viable. If intermodal transportation to Russia were used, the total cost should be higher than to Belarus, but the data show that the total transportation cost to Belarus is in fact higher. For this reason, we can assume that exports from Shaanxi to Russia are mainly transported overland. Since either transportation mode might be used to Belarus, we can conclude that the distance from Shaanxi to Belarus is close to the break-even distance for overland transportation. Comparing horizontally, we see that between Belarus and further west as far as the Netherlands, the total transportation cost is negatively correlated with distance, whereas further west (excluding Spain), it is positively correlated. This observation suggests that exports from Shaanxi to countries west of the Netherlands are most likely transported intermodally via a major Dutch port.

(3) Henan

Since our limited data only show that the total transportation cost to Russia is higher than the cost to Germany, it is difficult to make any definite decision about transportation mode.

(4) Jiangsu

Comparing horizontally in Table 5-5, we see that total transportation cost is lowest to Germany. As we move either east or west from Germany, transportation cost tends to increase (excluding Russia). Comparing vertically, we see that transportation to Germany costs less from Jiangsu than any of the other Chinese regions. We can assume from this that trade between Jiangsu and Europe is mainly handled by intermodal transportation through the major ports of Germany, the Netherlands, or Spain. However, it is difficult to draw any conclusions about the best mode of transportation to Russia.

From the above analysis, we can estimate the break-even distance l^* for overland transportation for exports from China. The estimated values are the distance from Xinjiang to Germany, and the distance from Shaanxi to Belarus. Both estimates put the break-even distance for transportation on the New Silk Road at about 7,500 km. Since this estimate represents more than half of the 10,900 km length of the China Land Bridge between Lianyungang to Rotterdam, it is a theoretically valid value.

Next, we calculated total transportation costs based on the value of imports for the Chinese

Table 5-6 Results of Calculations Based on Import Trade Value of Chinese Regions for 2009

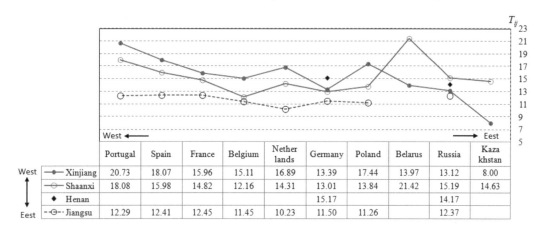

regions. The results are shown in Table 5-6. Analyzing the results in the same way as above, we can surmise that the break-even distance for overland transport for these imports corresponds to the distance from Xinjiang to Poland or the distance from Shaanxi to Belarus. This matches quite closely with the results obtained using export values.

The above analysis demonstrates that the transportation competitiveness of the New Silk Road can be measured using quite limited trade data, as carried out above for the year 2009. More detailed data about the cities along the route would make the measurements more precise; that is, the transition in transportation costs could be identified more clearly. However, a note of caution needs to be expressed here: the break-even distance for overland transportation as measured in this study is only an indicator, i.e., a yardstick, for the transportation competitiveness of the New Silk Road. It does not mean that all transportation for distances exceeding this break-even distance is handled by intermodal transportation; nor does it mean that overland transportation is always used for distances less than this value. Undeniably, however, identifying the break-even distance makes it possible to roughly select the best transportation route. In addition, if the break-even distance for overland transportation is 7,500 km, then the whole of Kazakhstan and the length of Xinjiang (a distance of approximately 4,000 km) becomes our center zone (as explained above). The lack of precision in the measurements presented in this study is due to the lack of detailed data, but we were nonetheless able to loosely surmise the break-even distance for overland transportation. In the next section, we outline the current state of transportation on the New Silk Road and explore how transportation competitiveness has changed up until quite recently.

IV. Current State of Transportation on the New Silk Road and Potential Improvements

1. Changes and Problems with Transportation Competitiveness on the New Silk Road

In Section II, we discussed the transportation competitiveness of the New Silk Road and outlined a way to ascertain the cost or efficiency of transportation in comparison with sea transportation. Transportation cost and transportation efficiency depend principally on the monetary expense and time required for the transportation. Improving the transportation competitiveness of the New Silk Road essentially means making overland transportation along the route faster and less expensive than sea transportation. Accordingly, the challenge of increasing the competitiveness of the New Silk Road is finding ways to lower the cost and increase the speed of transportation. Here, we want to begin by examining the changes in transportation competitiveness on the New Silk Road with reference on its current state.

In 1992, a 10,900 km-long railroad linking the port of Lianyungang in China with the port of Rotterdam in the Netherlands commenced operation. This route is shorter than the Trans-Siberian Railway (11,600 km from Nakhodka in Russia to Germany). Because part of the route runs along the ancient Silk Road trade route, it is also known as the New Silk Road.[8] Since the New Silk Road began operating, amounts of commercial traffic on the route have generally been increasing (Figure 5-5). The volume of rail freight handled at Alashankou, a railroad gateway in far western China inside the border with Kazakhstan, shows that traffic totaled 16.58 million tons in 2012 and 17.75 million tons in 2013.

This kind of increase in freight traffic certainly reflects is an indication of an improvement in the transportation competitiveness of the New Silk Road. This can be confirmed in another way. In Section III the break-even distance for overland transportation on the New Silk Road was roughly calculated to be about 7,500 km. This indicates that the transportation conditions in the Chinese regions of Gansu, Shaanxi, and Henan are relatively disadvantageous for foreign trade. As can be noted from the foreign-trade dependency values listed in Table 5-7, Gansu, Shaanxi, and Henan are less dependent on foreign trade than Jiangsu and Xinjiang. Table 5-8 shows that these regions also account for a significantly lower proportion of China's total foreign trade (import and exports) than Jiangsu and Xinjiang. However, the substantial change occurring between 2000 and 2010 indicates that the transportation competitiveness of the New Silk Road improved over this period. Looking at Gansu, Shaanxi, and Henan in Table 5-7, the increase in the foreign trade dependency of the westernmost of these regions, Gansu, is particularly striking. Similarly, Table 5-8 shows that although the proportion of China's total foreign

---

[8] In order to differentiate it from the Siberian Land Bridge, it is also called as the China Land Bridge or the Second Eurasian Land Bridge.

Figure 5-5 Rail Freight Traffic at Alashankou

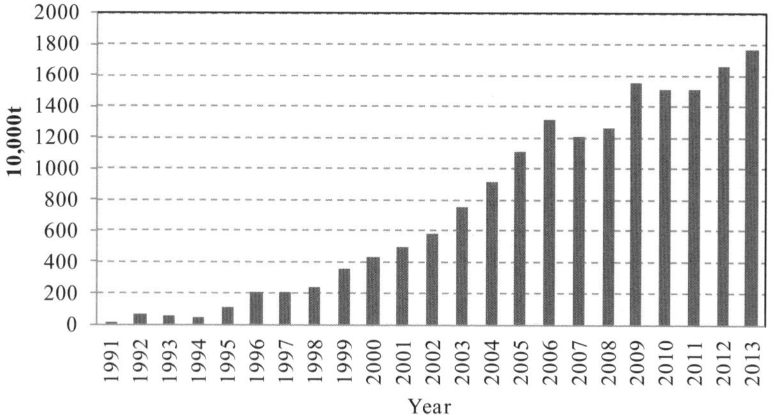

[Bar chart showing rail freight traffic in units of 10,000t from 1991 to 2013, with values rising from near 0 in 1991 to approximately 1750 in 2013.]

(Source) Up through 2009, Wu (2011); after 2009, Alashankou Port Management Committee website: http://tgb.alsk.gov.cn/
(Note) 1t=1000kg

Table 5-7 Total Trade (Exports + Imports) Value as a Proportion of GDP (%)

	2000	2009	2010
Jiangsu	4.40	7.74	9.29
Henan	0.47	0.56	0.67
Shaanxi	1.10	0.77	0.89
Gansu	0.54	0.96	1.38
Xinjiang	1.46	2.75	3.03

(Source) Same as Table 5-3

trade was remained constant for Henan and decreased for Shaanxi, in Gansu it increased. Together, these suggest that the transportation conditions for foreign trade in Gansu improved. If this improvement derived from routes east of Gansu, we would expect to see Shaanxi and Henan reaping the benefits of this improvement even sooner than Gansu, but Tables 5-7 and 5-8 show that this is not the case. Thus, we can conclude that the improvement in the transportation conditions for foreign trade at Gansu are due to an increase in transportation competitiveness on the New Silk Road to the west of the region. This also fits with the observed expansion of Xinjiang's foreign trade.

However, the increase in demand for transportation resulting from the improved competitiveness of the New Silk Road has given rise to new problems. Two very serious

Table 5-8 Share of Total China Trade (Exports + Imports) Value by Region (%)

	2000	2009	2010
Jiangsu	10.37	16.58	16.77
Henan	0.66	0.68	0.67
Shaanxi	0.50	0.39	0.39
Gansu	0.15	0.20	0.25
Xinjiang	0.55	0.73	0.72

(Source) Same as Table 5-3

problems are inhibiting transportation in the region. The first relates to the fact that the New Silk Road passes through many different countries with differences in rail track gauges along the way.[9] This necessitates transshipment and complex customs procedures, which tend to make effective transportation times longer than expected. The other problem is that current transportation and transshipment capacity cannot keep up with demand. On top of this, there tends to be an excess or deficiency of containers due to the imbalance between west and eastbound traffic, and there is also a great deal of wasted transportation of empty containers. These problems have come to the fore in the past few years with the phenomenon of freight congestion, which has become the norm for this route. Usually, freight congestion occurs during the peak period for transportation, which is summer, but in 2011 congestion had already appeared by spring. At the end of October 2011, there were about 8,000 TEUs of accumulated freight at the port of Lianyungang; over 6,000 TEUs at Qingdao (port of Huangdao), and about 800 TEUs at Tianjin Xingang.[10] At the end of October 2012, there were approximately 2,000 FEUs of accumulated freight at Lianyungang, 4,000 FEUs at Qingdao, while at the main railway stations between Urumqi and Alashankou, the freight congestion was reported to be 2,200 FEUs.[11] At the end of 2012, when a new railway started operating at Khorgos, located just inside China's border with Kazakhstan, a portion of rail freight was diverted to Khorgos,[12] thereby greatly easing freight congestion at Alashankou. Of course, this measure alone cannot solve the problems, but it should be considered a comprehensive countermeasure.

---

[9] The rail gauge is 1,435 mm in almost all countries in China and Europe, whereas it is 1,520 mm in the former Soviet republics such as Russia and Central Asian countries.

[10] Based on a Chinese source (http://www.landbridgenet.com/wenku/2013-03-03/4952.html).

[11] Shibamoto Eiichi "Kazakhstan: An emerging new border route to China (in Japanese)," *JETRO Censor*, JETRO Overseas Research Office, 2013.

[12] The freight traffic in rail transportation at Khorgos amounts to 1.51 million tons between January and November 2013. It is reported that it amounts to 1.61 million tons for the first year after the start of operation.

2. Measures to Increase Transportation Competitiveness on the New Silk Road

Before considering measures to improve the transportation competitiveness of the New Silk Road there are three points that need to be kept in mind. The first is that the purpose of improving transportation competitiveness is strictly to promote the economic development of the landlocked, inland regions that lie along the New Silk Road. To achieve this goal, making transportation more competitive is absolutely essential. In view of this, measures to improve transportation competitiveness on the New Silk Road need to be seen as part of a series of initiatives concerned with promoting economic development of the landlocked regions along the route.

The second point is that while improving transportation competitiveness stimulates economic development, the converse is also true: economic development tends to promote greater transportation competitiveness. There is a two-way cause-and-effect relationship between the two. More competitive transportation leads to greater industrial capability and integration, which in turn promotes the economic development of existing major cities along the route. In this development process, the economic ties between the countries and regions along the route become closer, leading to greater trade, which then drives transportation demand and efficiency higher, resulting in greater industrial capacity and capability. Through this process, the main existing cities along the route grow bigger, while at the same time new cities gradually arise around the borders between countries, resulting hopefully in the formation of an economic belt like a string of beads. Thus, when developing new transport infrastructure to improve transportation competitiveness, it is necessary to proceed incrementally, formulating long-term plans, and to take into account the economic conditions of all the countries and regions concerned. These long-term plans also need to give due consideration to the future impact of proposed infrastructure development on the distribution of urban settlements.

The third point is that since the New Silk Road constitutes an international transportation infrastructure, construction projects must have the cooperation of all the affected countries along the route. Furthermore, this kind of international cooperation cannot be achieved unless all the concerned countries are able to benefit from the project. In this way, establishing international cooperation and ensuring that benefits are shared by all countries are always mutually dependent considerations: if just one of these elements is lacking all will be lost.

If the above cautions are kept in mind, we can proceed to consider ways to increase the transportation competitiveness of the New Silk Road, focusing primarily on reducing the expense and time of transportation. The effective cost of transportation generally consists of the expense of maintaining transportation infrastructure systems and the expense of operating the systems. The cost of maintaining infrastructure has steadily fallen in recent times as technology has advanced. Therefore, to reduce infrastructure maintenance costs, it is important to actively adopt and utilize advanced technology. It is also important to realize that particularly for developing countries and regions, actively adopting and digesting the latest technology serves to promote greater industrial sophistication and capability. On the question of reducing the cost of operating transportation systems, it is essential to make use of competition. A prerequisite for this is that the development and maintenance of transportation systems and their operation are independent, and that systems are put in place to preserve fair competition, in order to prevent monopolistic operation.

Next, on the matter of reducing transportation time, there are two main problems that need to be solved. The first is the need to reduce the time taken for procedures required every time an international border is crossed. The other problem is freight congestion. The first problem can be solved through international consensus, by working to conclude international accords to simplify procedures. The second problem can be solved by developing infrastructure capable of coping with the demand for transportation.

The above two points are interrelated to a large extent. For example, a lack of infrastructure leads to freight congestion, thereby driving up transportation time, and a lack of international cooperation will slow down the progress of infrastructure development. Furthermore, if all the countries concerned cannot coordinate on sharing the benefits, or if they fail to establish relationships of trust, it is not possible to achieve international cooperation. For these reasons, measures to improve the competitiveness of transportation on the New Silk Road must address all these problems comprehensively and simultaneously, rather than tackling them individually.

While in Kazakhstan during his visit to Central Asia in September 2013, Chinese president Xi Jinping proposed joint construction of a "Silk Road Economic Belt". This was not a new idea, because in the course of the New Silk Road's development to date, the need to bolster international cooperation to ensure joint benefit was already well recognized. Although the "Silk Road Economic Belt" proposal is not yet accompanied by any concrete plans, it is in line with the general effort to promote the development and urbanization of China's central western frontier regions. In terms of initiatives directly associated with improving the competitiveness of transportation on the New Silk Road, the proposal would involve plans to expand direct international rail services to Europe and to set up new transportation routes. Direct international rail services to Europe operate from various ports, including Lianyungang and Tianjin (including port of Tianjin Xingang) along the coast, and recently new regular services have started operating from the inland locations of Chongqing, Chengdu, Zhengzhou, Xi'an, and Urumqi. All these rail services pass through either Alashankou or Khorgos, then cross Kazakhstan, Russia, and other countries, before finally terminating at major cities or ports in Germany or the Netherlands. Customs procedures on these routes have been simplified, substantially reducing transportation time. If an international treaty to facilitate more-efficient international rail freight transportation can be concluded in the coming years, then the transportation competitiveness of the New Silk Road will undoubtedly improve even further.

For two main reasons, this kind of improvement in the competitiveness of transportation will lead to greater freight traffic in the long term. One is that freight volume will increase as some of the transportation now handled by sea is switched over to overland transportation on the New Silk Road. The other reason is that more competitive transportation will lead to rapid growth of the major cities along the route, leading to closer economic relations between these cities, thereby driving up trade volume. In view of this projected long-term growth in transportation demand, the handling capacity of existing routes will become inadequate: the current rail freight handling capacity at Alashankou is only 20 million tons per year and that at Khorgos is 35 million tons. For this reason, it is necessary to develop new routes. Of the new routes currently being planned, the most notable are three high-speed motorways/railways that will facilitate the development of economic corridors. One runs from Kashgar in China through to Kyrgyzstan and Uzbekistan, one is from Kashgar to Pakistan, and another is from Yunnan in China to Myanmar, Bangladesh, and India. The China-Myanmar-Bangladesh-India economic corridor arose from a joint proposal by China and India in May 2013, and work on the project seems to be advancing steadily with the active support of all the countries concerned. Construction work on the China-Pakistan economic corridor project has been delayed due to terrorism and other security threats. The China-Kyrgyzstan-Uzbekistan railway project was originally agreed on by the three countries in 1997, but for various reasons, including the domestic situation in Kyrgyzstan and funding problems, progress has stalled several times. More recently, Kyrgyzstan has proposed the development of a different rail route, linking Russia, Kazakhstan, Kyrgyzstan, and Tajikistan. For Kyrgyzstan, both routes should be considered necessary, as they complement each other, rather than one of the two routes being a substitute for the other. Due to problems of funding, however, Kyrgyzstan must make a political decision about which of the two projects should get priority. Naturally, if conditions allow, it is conceivable that both projects are implemented simultaneously.

In order to implement measures to reduce transportation time and plan new routes, the benefits of economic development must be evenly balanced between the countries involved, and the countries must be able to cooperate effectively. In recent years China and Kazakhstan have enjoyed a very strong collaborative relationship that has clearly produced very positive outcomes. If the success of this cooperation effort inspires other countries and leads to broader international cooperation in the region, then the transportation competitiveness of the New Silk Road is likely to go on improving. This can only help to further accelerate economic development across the whole of Eurasia.

References

Anderson, James E. and Eric van Wincoop (2003), "Gravity with Gravitas: A Solution to the Border Puzzle," *American Economic Review*, 93 (1), 170-192.

Bernard, Andrew B., J. Bradford Jensen, Stephen J. Redding, and Peter K. Schott (2007), "Firms in International Trade," *Journal of Economic Perspectives*, 21 (3), 105-130.

César Ducruet, Theo Notteboom (2012), "Developing Liner Service Networks in Container Shipping", in D. W. Song and P. Panayides, *Maritime Logistics: A Complete Guide to Effective Shipping and Port Management*, 77-100.

Chaney, Thomas (2008), "Distorted Gravity: The Intensive and Extensive Margins of International Trade," *American Economic Review*, 98 (4), 1707-1721.

Deardorff, Alan V. (1998), "Determinants of Bilateral Trade: Does Gravity Work in a Neoclassical World?" in J. A. Frankel (ed.), *The Regionalization of the World Economy*, Chicago: The University of Chicago Press, Or Alan V. Deardorff (1995), "Determinants of Bilateral Trade: Does Gravity Work in a Neoclassical World?," *NBER Working Paper*, No. 5377.

Eaton, Jonathan, and Samuel S. Kortum (2002), "Technology, Geography, and Trade," *Econometrica*, 70 (5), 1741-1779.

Helpman, Elhanan (1987), "Imperfect Competition and International Trade: Evidence from Fourteen Industrial Countries." *Journal of the Japanese and International Economies*, 1 (1), 62-81.

Riku, Yugun (2009), "Regional Economic Development in the New Silk Road and the 'Beads-Type' Development Strategy (in Japanese)," *Kiyo*, 39, 165-180.

Shibamoto, Eiichi (2013) "Kazakhstan: An Emerging New Border Route to China (in Japanese)," *JETRO Censor*, JETRO Overseas Research Office.

Tsuji, Tadahiro (2009), "The Potential for Economic Development in the New Silk Road Regional through a 'Bead-Type' Development Strategy (in Japanese)," *Kiyo*, 39, 181-193.

Tinbergen, Jan (1962) "An Analysis of World Trade Flows," in Jan Tinbergen (ed.), *Shaping the World Economy*, New York: Twentieth Century Fund.

Wu, Yiliang (2007), "International Dispersion and Domestic Concentration: An Analysis on a Two-Country Four-Region Model of Industrial Agglomeration," in Mitsuo Honda *et al.*, *Industrial Agglomeration and a New International Division of Labor: a New Analytical Viewpoint of the Globalizing Chinese Economy* (in Japanese), Bunshindo, 1-37.

Wu, Yiliang (2009), "'Beads-Type' Cities Formation and its Process along the New Silk Road (in Japanese)," *Kiyo*, 39, 149-164.

Wu, Yiliang (2011), "Will Khorgos Become the Shenzhen of Western China? (in Japanese)," *Kiyo*, 41, 73-95.

Wu, Yiliang (2012), "The Role of Japan in the New Silk Road Area Development (in Japanese)," *Keizaishushi*, 82 (1), 57-75.

Chapter 6

ECONOMIC DEVELOPMENT IN CENTRAL ASIA AND INFRASTRUCTURE

I. Introduction

Central Asian countries are landlocked nations spanning the Eurasian continent, where autonomous growth based on conventional development strategies (strategies generally developed on a single country basis) has been impossible. East Asian countries, which border the open sea, have enjoyed economic dynamism and come to symbolize "Asian Growth" by proactively manufacturing industrial products for export to developed markets. By contrast, even if Central Asian countries try to export industrial products, they face problems in terms of access to these markets. They cannot even import raw materials for production of industrial goods. In this sense, these regions could be called areas of "Asian Stagnation."

However, the Beads-type Development Strategy, which has already been mentioned, reveals that it is possible to form industrial city groups even in the inland region of the New Silk Road Area. This is achieved through the agglomeration and dispersion of economic activity, generating economic might from industrial agglomeration in areas with relatively low foreign transport costs. The bead-model industrial city groups formed in this way are not limited to developing the economy in just one country; rather they extend geographically across multiple countries. In this sense, in order to form the new growth centers, or "Beads" with autonomous development processes in the New Silk Road Area, it is important to have conditions that allow the centers to cooperate with one other. To this end, infrastructure is an essential foundation.

Therefore, in this chapter, we will focus our study on infrastructure and discuss whether necessary conditions exist in the New Silk Road Area to allow for the Beads-type Development Strategy.

II. The Current State of Integration with the Global Economy

The collapse of the Soviet Union brought huge changes to international trade and logistics in the Central Asian countries. These changes were so dramatic that economic ties among the former Soviet republics were severed in the immediate aftermath of the empire's collapse. However, each individual country subsequently became engaged in international trade and re-integrated into the global economy as a result. Accordingly, we would like to look at the current state of the Central Asian countries' integration into the world's economy.

First, we will approach this from the perspective of international trade. In general, the economic chaos caused by the collapse of the Soviet Union meant that trade volumes plummeted among the former republics, including those of Central Asia.[1] From Table 6-1, we can see that trade volumes fell immediately after the collapse of the empire in the midst of confusion. However, trade subsequently recovered. In particular, a rapid expansion in trade volumes since 2000 demonstrates that the CIS (Commonwealth of Independent States) countries have been completely rehabilitated into the global economy.

Table 6-2 shows the CIS countries' commodity trade export markets. According to the table, nearly half of the total is accounted for by exports to the EU, which is geographically close. Of the remainder, it is noticeable that while commodity exports to North America showed a relative fall in importance, those to Asia showed a relative increase.

Table 6-1 Merchandise Exports of CIS Countries
(million of US dollars at current prices)

	1990	1993	1996	2000	2005	2010	2011
Exports	400,600	89,791	119,098	144,904	299,481	491,162	662,788
Imports	412,924	76,001	84,027	69,588	148,503	315,314	413,726
Balance	-12,324	13,790	35,071	75,316	150,978	175,848	249,062

(Source) Adapted from Broadman, 2005, pp.64-65; World Bank Database.

Table 6-2 Destination of Merchandise Exports of CIS Countries (%)

	CIS	EU(27)	North America	Asia	Other
1993	21.0	46.2	9.4	14.7	8.7
1996	47.7	32.5	5.2	8.6	6.0
2000	19.7	43.7	7.0	13.7	15.9
2005	17.7	46.9	7.0	12.0	16.4
2010	18.9	45.0	5.7	14.9	15.5
2012	18.5	45.8	4.6	15.7	15.4

Note: Figures in 1993 and 1996 refer to those of EU(15), NAFTA and East Asia.
(Source) Adapted from Broadman, 2005, p.72; World Trade Organization Database.

---

[1] However, in view of the unique way that trade volumes were calculated in the Soviet era, some hold the opinion that the collapse of the Soviet Union did not necessarily lead to a sharp decline in trade volumes among the former republics (Broadman, 2005, p.64). Under this opinion, the trade volumes among the former republics have not decreased significantly when evaluated at a fixed exchange rate.

Table 6-3 shows changes in the nature of the items traded. We can see significant changes in the items traded by the former Soviet Union countries before and after its collapse. This phenomenon is called "centralization of trade goods." Looking at the example of Kazakhstan, in terms of the factor intensity of export goods, there has been a significant increase in natural resources on the one hand, while labor (both skilled and unskilled) and capital intensity have greatly declined on the other. Import goods show the reverse, with a substantial reduction in natural resources and significant increases in labor and capital intensity. This shows a tendency for goods related to natural resources to form the core of Kazakhstan's export goods, while products requiring high levels of labor and capital intensity are at the center of the country's imports. Prior to the collapse, the country traded a wide variety of goods, but after the collapse, the trend was one of centralization.

Table 6-3   Percentage Changes in Factor Intensity of Merchandise Trade between 1996 and 2003 (Kazakhstan)

	Natural Resource	Unskilled Labor	Capital	Skilled Labor
Exports	19	-76	-69	-20
Imports	-35	33	30	9

(Source) Adapted from Broadman, 2005, pp.85 and 87

Next, we will consider the institutional framework that would encourage the former Soviet republics to engage in international trade. These states have already signed, or are party to, various trade pacts and distribution agreements. First, after their independence, the former Soviet states formed the CIS under the Minsk Agreement in 1991. Originally, this agreement examined the construction of a common economic zone to promote cooperation in the transport and communications sector, using tariff policies. In practice, however, the participants were more interested in politics; they sought national sovereignty and mutual non-aggression, rather than economic cooperation (Libman, 2011, p.5). Thereafter, the CIS signed a free trade agreement in 1994 to eliminate tariffs and economic restrictions among member states. This agreement achieved very little in reality. As a matter of fact, the member states adopted protective measures that went against economic liberalization during the Russian financial crisis of 1998. In 1995, Russia and Belarus formed a Customs Union (with the Kyrgyz Republic joining the following year). This, too, was a Customs Union in name only and was disbanded in 1999.

Thus, one agreement after another was concluded on economic liberalization, amounting to nothing but rhetoric from start to finish. However, the start of the 21st century saw the beginning of a real initiative. This took the form of the Eurasian Economic Community (EurAsEc), founded in October, 2000. EurAsEc was established under the signatures of the leaders of five countries (Belarus, Russia, Kazakhstan, Kyrgyz Republic, and Tajikistan). The heads of state, ministers, and other high-ranking officials participated in various institutions, including the Interstate Council, the Community's executive body. EurAsEc is the successor to the Customs Union established in 1995. One of its primary objectives was to integrate (i) tariff and non-tariff measures, (ii) foreign exchange controls, (iii) customs administration, and (iv) transport systems and services. It was decided at the regularly scheduled heads of state summits to establish a Customs Union area by means of a two-stage process. Stage 1 would include the three nations of Belarus, Russia and Kazakhstan; and Stage 2 would include participation by the remaining countries once they were ready.

Ten years after its formation (as of July 2010), its track record was not particularly outstanding, especially in comparison with the EU (European Union) and NAFTA (North American Free Trade Agreement). Certainly, within EurAsEc member countries, (i) the majority of products are traded on the principle of free trade, (ii) the first three countries have introduced uniform tariffs for imports (with some exceptions), and (iii) a Joint Customs Code has been introduced. In addition, (iv) initiatives are currently underway for the harmonization of standards (certification of standards) pertaining to technical matters, sanitation matters, and the quarantine of plant life. (v) However, there are significant limits to the Customs Union; more than 400 sensitive items are excluded unified tariffs. For example, the import duties on cars are higher in Russia than in Belarus or Kazakhstan. Moreover, (vi) Russia is in a weak position in terms of its customs procedures. According to one study on the simplicity of tariffs, Russia ranked 140th of 183 countries surveyed (RBTH, 2010).

Despite the slow progress of EurAsEc, a trilateral Customs Union was established within EurAsEc among Belarus, Russia and Kazakhstan by 2011, with the Customs Union Commission acting as the executive body in charge of its administration. The objectives of the Customs Union were (i) the establishment of a common customs zone; (ii) the introduction of a common customs tariff code; (iii) the adoption of a common trade system vis-a-vis third countries; (iv) the introduction of common tariff/non-tariff regulatory measures; (v) the abolition of customs clearance procedures for commodity trades between member states and transference of tariff controls (rights) to an external board. It seems that as a result of these measures, (i) trade among the three nations increased; (ii) the cost of goods decreased; and (iii) the three countries came to account for more than 80% of the CIS's GDP (RIA Novosti, 2010).

Subsequently, the pace of economic integration accelerated among Belarus, Russia, and Kazakhstan. In October, 2011, the CIS Free Trade Zone Agreement was signed by the CIS member states (with the exception of Azerbaijan, Uzbekistan, and Turkmenistan). Also in October, 2011, the presidents of Belarus, Russia and Kazakhstan signed the Declaration on Eurasian Economic Integration, which provided a roadmap for economic integration aimed at the establishment of a Eurasian Economic Union. In December of the same year, the Eurasian Economic Commission was set up as a supranational organization of the Eurasian Economic

Union, absorbing the previous Customs Union Commission.

In January 2012, the Common Economic Space officially came into effect in the EurAsEc. This resulted in the free movement of people, goods, and money (capital) among the three countries. With the Customs Union formed in 2011 positioned as the first phase, the free economic zone of Belarus, Russia, and Kazakhstan saw the start of a new phase.

In January 2012, Russian President Dmitry Medvedev stated that he expected the Eurasian Economic Union to come into effect by 2015, with the unification of various policies, including those on the macro-economy, taxes, currency, trade, and tariffs (RIA Novosti, 2012a). In July of the same year, it was revealed that Medvedev, who was prime minister of Russia at that time, held talks with Kazakhstan's president, Nursultan Nazarbayev, on the need for a single currency (RIA Novosti, 2012b).

III. The Necessity for Trade and Transport Facilitation (TTF) in the Economic Development of Inland Areas

As already mentioned, the countries of Central Asia have shown a proactive attitude in their involvement in the global economy by participating in the framework of economic cooperation between the former Soviet republics on a multitude of levels. However, the fact that the countries are landlocked is, economically speaking, a handicap to development. Furthermore, the Central Asian nations, located far from the world's major markets, cannot be physically connected to the U.S. or European. So how are these drawbacks for the landlocked Central Asian countries to be overcome? One plausible method is Trade and Transport Facilitation (TTF), which could shrink the economic distance.[2]

In order to achieve TTF, it is very important to build cooperative relationships among each of the countries concerned and realize regional economic cooperation. However, there are factors that inhibit the construction of such regional economic cooperation. Such factors are (i) corruption related to customs clearance and border crossings, (ii) inefficient customs clearance operations (the number of days to clear customs, the customs clearance system etc.), (iii) poor transportation services (carriers, transport systems etc.), (iv) underdeveloped physical infrastructure (road, rail etc.), and (v) security issues (international relations with neighboring countries etc.). (Molnar, 2003, pp.9-10) These inhibiting factors have delayed the construction of basic infrastructure and, as a result, have led to increased distribution costs.

---

[2] There is also a study by APEC claiming that TTF brings almost twice the benefits of tariff reductions. According to this study, TTF resulted in a 0.25% rise in real GDP (equivalent to US $ 46 billion at 1997 prices); while trade increases due to tariff reductions remained at 0.16% of real GDP (Molnar, 2003, p.39).

IV. The Current Status and Problems of TTF in Central Asian Countries

1. TTF: Hard Factors

We will consider the current status and problems of TTF in Central Asian countries. First, we will examine the "hard" factors (status of transport infrastructure development) connected with TTF. Poor conditions in infrastructure in terms of road and rail are among the main obstacles to the facilitation of trade and distribution. Although there is a tentative network of roads and railway throughout the area, it is poorly developed, and consequently the quality of the transport network in Central Asian countries is dreadful (Molnar, 2003, p.31).

Looking at the status of development in the rail and road transportation networks (see ADB, 2006, pp.10-12), we find that on one hand there is a significant trend in passenger transport using the roads, despite the overwhelmingly long distances of the road network compared with the rail network. On the other hand, it is the railways that transport most of the freight (with the exception of the Kyrgyz Republic). If we consider Kazakhstan's main railway, it has a total length of 14,600 km, of which 37% is double track, and only 28% electric. In Uzbekistan, the main railway is 4,000 km in total length, with 150 km double-tracked and 10% electric. Meanwhile, the combined total length of the road network for four of the Central Asian states (excluding Turkmenistan) is 59,430 km. Of this, 19,600 km is thought to be used for international distribution, but most of this is two-lane roadway and the estimated travelling speed is 100 km per hour. Moreover, these cannot be said to be high-standard roads, with only a short length of those in Uzbekistan meeting the criteria of first grade roads in international terms. Instead, by international standards, the majority of routes comprise third-grade roads or worse (ADB, 2006, p.58).

Given such circumstances, we would like to highlight the problems faced by the transport infrastructure in Central Asian countries. Underlying the problem is the historical fact that in the former Soviet Union, which included the nations of Central Asia, the transport network was constructed with Soviet industrial and military needs in mind. For example, (i) despite the fact that each republic had a border, in Soviet times these borders were ignored in the construction of the transport network; (ii) in the Soviet era, priority was given to the construction of railways and pipelines to transport natural resources to specific industrial plants; (iii) the road network was designed to link the capital of each republic to Moscow, and therefore; (iv) rail and road networks were not laid out to provide direct domestic links within each republic; and it is worth mentioning the fact that since independence, it has been necessary to cross national borders for domestic travel within a country because the rail and road networks themselves cross these borders. In addition, (v) different gauge track is used in the railway that links the east and west of the Eurasian continent. Most of Europe, China, and the Korean Peninsula uses standard gauge track (1435 mm), whereas Russia and Central Asian countries use a different gauge (1520 mm). This has the drawback of requiring cargo to be transshipped when crossing borders. Therefore, although the transport network covers a wide area, it cannot necessarily meet present-day distribution needs.

In response to these conditions, international organizations have discussed various projects to improve physical infrastructure that still remains undeveloped. One such initiative is the Asian Development Bank's (ADB) Central Asia Regional Economic Cooperation (CAREC) project. This is a joint project with the European Bank for Reconstruction and Development (EBRD), the International Monetary Fund (IMF), the United Nations Development Programme, the World Bank, and the Islamic Development Bank. It aims to improve the distribution of transit cargo by lowering transportation costs in Central Asia and to overcome external diseconomies. The ADB signed a Regional Transport Sector Roadmap in 2005 with the nations concerned to construct an efficient, integrated transport system in accordance with the roadmap. The roadmap features five areas of emphasis: (i) harmonization and simplification of cross-border transport procedures; (ii) harmonization of transportation regulations between CAREC's member states; (iii) construction of an international distribution network connecting production bases with markets; (iv) reconstruction and modernization of the railways; (v) improvements in transport sector management (ADB, 2006, p.53). As part of this plan, there are feasibility studies underway on the rail network development of the Dushanbe-Kyrgyz Corridor Project, the road development project between Bishkek-Torugart, and the construction of a road to link Oybek and Pungan.

In 1993, the TRACECA (Transport Corridor Europe-Caucasus-Asia) project was announced in Europe. This is an infrastructure development project promoted by the EU for the purpose of developing the political economy of the Black Sea, Caucasus and Central Asia. There are 12 countries participating in the project - Armenia, Azerbaijan, Bulgaria, Georgia, Kazakhstan, Kyrgyzstan, Moldova, Romania, Tajikistan, Turkey, Uzbekistan, and Ukraine. The project promotes four areas: (i) the development of traditional forms of transport infrastructure - i.e. road, rail and sea; (ii) the development of pipeline distribution networks (particularly for natural gas and crude oil); (iii) the laying of a fiber optic network across the Eurasian continent; (iv) the development of a space satellite system (Yalcin, 2007, p.28). TRACECA aims to promote trade and economic exchange by using these various developments in infrastructure to build a perfectly integrated distribution network.

Russia and China are not involved in this project, even though their involvement in economic development projects in the Eurasian continent seems important considering that Russia occupies a vast area of the region and China's economy is flourishing. Russia refuses to join the project because the planned pipeline that links Central Asia to Europe would bypass the country. Perhaps the Russians feel that they are being snubbed (Blank, 2004, p.239).

2. TTF: Soft Factors

Next, we will look at the "soft" factors connected with TTF. Typical problems are: (i) "unofficial payments;" (ii) lack of coordination among border agencies; (iii) complicated and unclear customs clearance procedures; (iv) low levels of IT use in customs administration; (v) inefficiencies in carriers and transport services; and (vi) political tensions (Broadman, 2005, p.17).

Bribery is rampant. Figure 6-1 shows the percentage of companies that say they have no choice but to pay bribes. The situation has been rapidly improved in Russia and Kazakhstan since the late 2000s. However, between 30% and 50% of the companies in Tajikistan, the Kyrgyz Republic, and Uzbekistan say they must pay bribes to stay in business.

Figure 6-1 Firms Expected to give Gifts in Meetings with Tax Officials (% of firms)

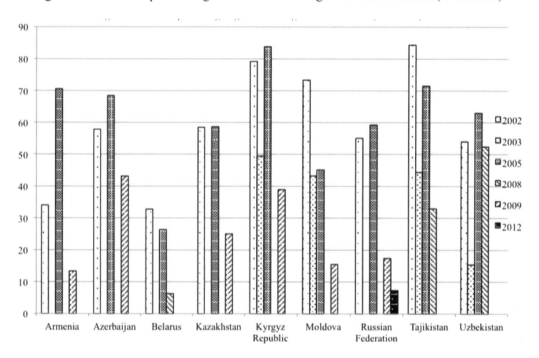

(Source) World Bank Database

Bribes are often paid at customs checkpoints. Figure 6-2 shows where unofficial payments occur in the sequence of transport procedures. It reveals that costs jump during overland transportation, border crossings, and customs inspections. The example in Figure 6-2 shows transport between the Caucasus and Northern Europe. However, the costs are estimated to be higher in Central Asia compared with the South Caucasus (Molnar, 2003, p.14).

Second, there are problems with customs clearance procedure. Despite the fact that new standards have been developed for customs clearance among the nations, it still takes a long time to go through customs inspections (See Figure 6-3). There are five main reasons for the operational delays in customs clearance: (i) uncertainty surrounding the implementation of the

Figure 6-2 Costs Estimated between the Caucasus and North Europe

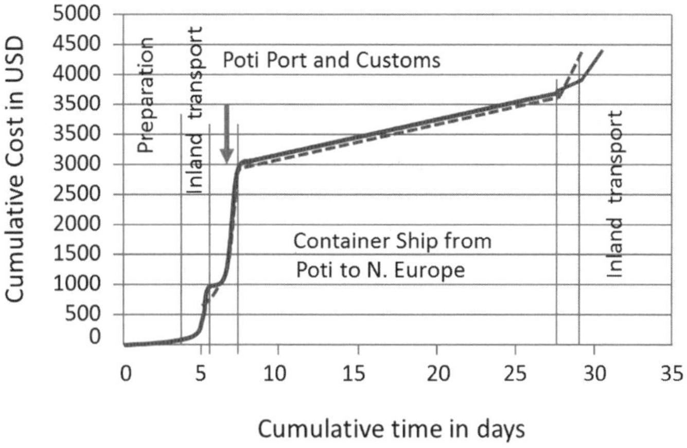

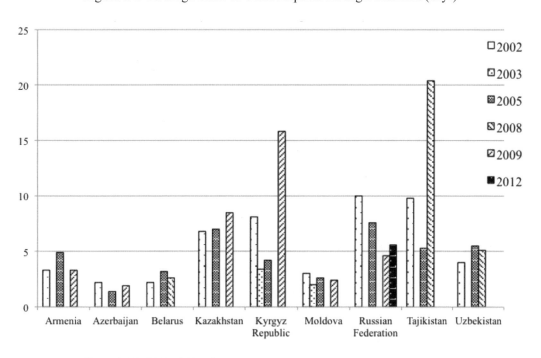

(Source) Molnar, 2003, pp.15-16.

Figure 6-3 Average Time to Clear Exports through Customs (days)

(Source) World Bank Databas

new customs code; (ii) excessive paperwork required in the completion of customs procedures (e.g. Tajikistan requires 18 kinds of documents, certificates, and application forms issued by different agencies); (iii) the inconvenience caused by the fact that border checkpoints are too far away for business operators; (iv) a lack of cooperation between border agencies; (v) a lack of IT utilization skills (Broadman, 2005, p.231). Accordingly, despite its formation, the customs union cannot necessarily be said to have shortened the number of days required to clear customs.

Third, although it is generally accepted that IT can overcome geographic limitations and facilitate the construction of a base infrastructure, this is not necessarily the case in the Central Asian states. Turkmenistan has a poor cell phone network and only one cell phone company. In Uzbekistan, Internet providers are strictly monitored by the government (Broadman, 2005, p.234). The electronic customs clearance system ASYCUDA (Automated System for Customs Data) that computerizes customs clearance operation has not been introduced at this time.

Fourth, carriers and transport services are inefficient. As Figures 6-4 to 6-7 show, there has been some improvement in Kazakhstan and Russia. However, logistics remain highly unsatisfactory, and we can see the need for increasing developments in the soft elements of base infrastructure. Moreover, a characteristic of the transport sector in Central Asian countries is that it is run by a group of small enterprises, meaning that local transport companies are only able to provide services fit for the pre-modern era. For example, multimodal transport is yet to be developed. This generates inefficiencies as separate contracts are needed for each mode of transport (Molnar, 2003, p.30).

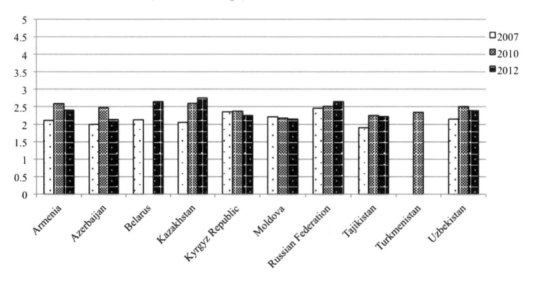

Figure 6-4 Logistics Performance Index: Competence and Quality of Logistics Services (1=low to 5=high)

(Source) World Bank Database

Economic Development in Central Asia and Infrastructure

Figure 6-5 Logistics Performance Index: Efficiency of Customs Clearance Process (1=low to 5=high)

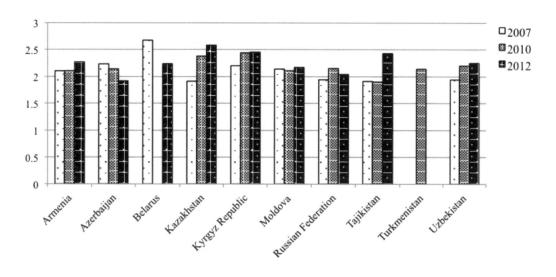

(Source) World Bank Database

Figure 6-6 Logistics Performance Index: Frequency with which Shipments Reach Consignee within Scheduled or Expected Time (1=low to 5=high)

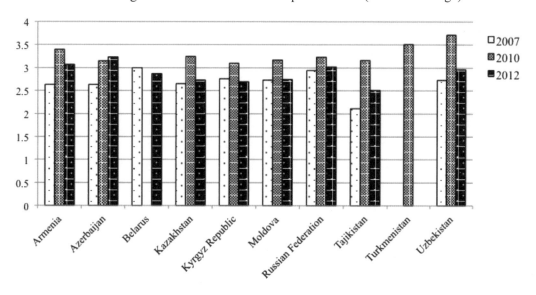

(Source) World Bank Database

Figure 6-7 Logistics Performance Index: Quality of Trade and Transport-related Infrastructure (1=low to 5=high)

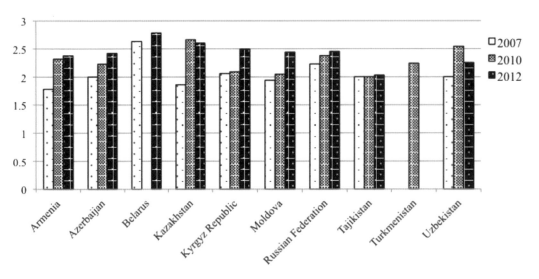

(Source) World Bank Database

3. TTF: Regional Economic Cooperation Factors

The third set of factors affecting TTF is related to regional economic cooperation. The first of these is the construction of a free trade framework. As already mentioned, Central Asian countries have been proactively creating free trade zones by means of cooperative economic frameworks such as the CIS Free Trade Agreement and EurAsEc, as well as bilateral free-trade agreements. However, the outcomes of these initiatives did not become apparent until the start of the Common Economic Space in 2012.

Prior to that, there had been doubts as to the effectiveness of Customs Unions because (i) efforts to list items exempt from tariff eliminations failed, (ii) some exemptions were forced upon unilaterally, (iii) tariffs were never imposed on some items even after exemptions were lifted, and (iv) there were no penalties even when delays occurred (Broadman, 2005, p.168).

The second factor in terms of economic cooperation is the handling of transit goods in the Central Asia region. Central Asian countries are landlocked and therefore any international trade with outside countries must always be carried out through a third country. This means that provisions concerning transit goods are an important element of trade agreements.

Based on the Agreement on Procedures of Transit Through the Territories of CIS States concluded in June 1999, transit between CIS member states should be conducted on the principle of "Free Transit," and must always be handled in an indiscriminate manner, without delay or limitation unless justified (WTO, 2006, p.67). In addition, a transport union was formed between EurAsEc member states to ensure free movement of freight and passengers under the terms of the Agreement on Unified Terms of Transit Through the Territories of the Custom Union concluded in 1998 (WTO, 2006, p.112.)

In reality, however, free transit has not been observed, despite the principles stated above. Let us look at the example of the Kyrgyz Republic (WTO, 2006, p.67). The Kyrgyz Republic has experienced problems in its dealings with Kazakhstan, which ignored the terms of the Agreement on Procedures of Transit through the Territories of CIS States and created barriers to transit with the Kyrgyz Republic. The problems include (i) the introduction of an entry/transit fee of $300 per vehicle for Kyrgyz trucks from 2000 and (ii) the introduction of obligatory attendance at customs for Kyrgyz trucks (with fees of 50-200 Euros imposed) as of July 2004. In addition, (iii) whereas passing through customs on the Kazakh side at border checkpoints took somewhere between two hours and 13 hours for Kazakh drivers, it took between two and a half days and seven days for Krygyz drivers, survey shows. However, a new International Transport Agreement that took effect January 2005 eliminated these discriminatory practices.[3]

The ADB estimates that the proper operation of regional economic cooperation in transit in 2006 should put the real GDP of the Krygyz republic at $2.1 billion (based on 2002 prices), or increase it by 112% in the 15 years from 2006 (WTO, 2006, p.113). But in reality, despite the conclusion of free trade agreements, the rules of the agreements are not being observed due to weak discipline and inadequate systems of execution.

Comprehensive factors need to be addressed to construct basic infrastructure, including not only hard elements but also soft elements and aspects of regional economic cooperation. While hard elements are being steadily developed by the ADB and EBRD, and with assistance from industrialized nations, improvements in soft elements and regional economic cooperation are not so easy. It could be said that one of the major challenges facing Central Asian nations is the development of its infrastructure.

V. Conclusion

In this chapter, we have emphasized the importance of the development of a base infrastructure in order to achieve the formation of a Beads-type industrial city, which requires economic development within a geographic expansion.

Then, we examined the basic infrastructure from three perspectives: hard factors, soft factors, and factors related to regional economic cooperation. We found that steady developments are being made in the hard elements as a result of ADB and EBRD initiatives and

---

[3] However, obstructive behavior is still continuing in the field. For example, (i) Kazakhstan's local authorities charge various road taxes and fees; (ii) in addition to bureaucratically created delays that are deliberate, there is police harassment with requests for bribes; and (iii) sometimes Kyrgyz trucks are forced to reduce the amount of cargo they carry (WTO, 2006, p.67).

bilateral economic cooperation. However, looking at soft factors and factors related to regional economic cooperation, it became obvious that developments in these hard factors alone would not be sufficient to achieve economic development over a widespread geographic area.

It is not easy to build strong ties among countries based on soft elements and regional economic cooperation. Indeed, it can be said that the key to economic development in the Central Asian countries is the development of infrastructure based on these three factors.

References

Asian Development Bank (2006), *Connecting Central Asia: A Road Map for Regional Cooperation*, Asian Development Bank.

Blank, Stephen (2004), "Infrastructural Policy and National Strategies in Central Asia: The Russian Example," *Central Asian Survey*, 23 (3-4), 225-248.

Broadman, Harry G. (ed.) (2005), *From Disintegration to Reintegration: Eastern Europe and the Former Soviet Union in International Trade*, World Bank.

Libman, Alexander (2011), *Commonwealth of Independent State and Eurasian Economic Community*, Centre for Studies on Federalism.

Molnar, Eva, WB Lauri Ojala (2003), Transport and Trade Facilitation Issues in the CIS 7, Kazakhstan and Turkmenistan, a paper prepared for the Lucerne Conference of the CIS-7 Initiative, 20th-22nd January 2003.

RBTH Network (2010), Economic Union, 20 Dec.

RIA Novosti (2010), 2010 a milestone for CIS, 29 Dec.

RIA Novosti (2012a), Russia, Belarus, Kazakhstan are launching common economic space, 1 Jan.

RIA Novosti (2012b), Fraudster Mint Common Currency for Customs Union, 27 July.

World Trade Organization (2006), *Trade Policy Review: Kyrgyz Republic*, WT/TPR/S/170, 4 September 2006.

Yalcin, Serkan (2007), "Revitalizing the Eurasian Trade: Prospects from the TRACECA Project," *Akademik Arastirmalar*, 9 (33), 26-38.

Chapter 7

CHINESE REGIONAL DEVELOPMENT AND THE NEW SILK ROAD:
AN EXAMINATION OF EXISTING MAJOR CITIES AND EMERGING SMALL-TO-MEDIUM SIZED CITIES IN THE CENTRAL REGION OF CHINA

I. Introduction

Research concerning the New Silk Road and regional development began to flourish around the mid-1990s within China. Most of this research dealt with the economic development of Chinese cities and regions along the New Silk Road, focusing on the Jiangsu, Shandong, and Zhejiang provinces, including their eastern sea ports of Lianyungang, Rizhao, and Shanghai, as well as the Xinjiang Uyghur Autonomous Region and Shanxi and Gansu provinces, most notably the Western Chinese cities of Urumqi, Xi'an, and Yinchuan. These cities and regions were mainly characterized as "frontier regions" because of their locations being at the eastern and western extremities of Chinese territory. In an important earlier study by our group, Wu (2000, 2007) presented a study result on these frontier regions from a spatial economic perspective. Expanding on the core-periphery model of Krugman (1991a), this study analyzed a two-country, four-region model, and concluded that industrial agglomeration has a tendency to "international dispersion and national concentration" and that national concentration tends to intensively occur in regions where international transportation is relatively advantageous (i.e., so-called frontier regions). On the basis of these conclusions, further studies (see Wu, 2009; Tsuji, 2009; Riku, 2009) expressed the following views with regard to the economic development of the New Silk Road. As the transportation competitiveness of the New Silk Road improves, further industrial agglomeration is likely to occur in existing major cities, but at the same time also in frontier regions, resulting in the successive appearance of new cities. Accordingly, we can expect to see a Beads-type formation of industrial zones along the New Silk Road, which will serve as a major impetus for the economic development of whole regions.

In this chapter, we want to shift the focus of our research away from the frontier regions to central region of China. More specifically, we turn our attention to some existing major cities of the central region (provincial capitals and seats of government) -Zhengzhou, Hefei, and Taiyuan- as well as some small-to-medium sized cities - Luoyang, Anqing, and Jincheng (see Figure 7-1).

The locations of these cities relative to the New Silk Road are shown in Table 7-1. Zhengzhou and Luoyang both lie along the New Silk Road, but they differ in size. Hefei and Taiyuan are both major urban cities, but they are located distant from the New Silk Road. Jincheng and

Figure 7-1

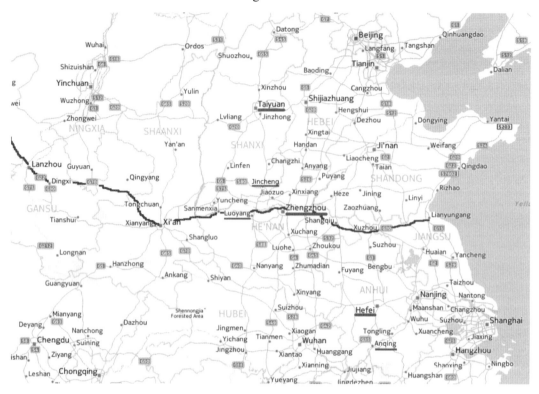

Table 7-1 Distance of Each City from the New Silk Road

	Distance from the New Silk Road (NSR)		
	Along NSR	Close	Far
Major Urban Cities	Zhengzhou		Taiyuan, Hefei
Small-to-medium Sized Cities	Luoyang	Jincheng	Anqing

Anqing are both small-to-medium sized cities, but they are located different distances from the New Silk Road. If we look at the provinces from southeast to northwest, we find that Hefei and Anqing are both in Anhui province, Zhengzhou and Luoyang are in Henan province, and Taiyuan and Jincheng are in Shanxi province.

We believe that looking at the change in economic conditions of these cities can yield some interesting insights. How have these cities, despite not being located in the frontier regions, been influenced by the gradual improvement in the transportation competitiveness of the New Silk Road? In this chapter, we analyze the change in economic performance of these cities over recent years, examining a wide variety of data on industrial structure, foreign trade, foreign direct investment (FDI), transportation costs, postal services, and the tourism industry, and we consider the problem of redressing the economic disparity between the central region of China and coastal regions. In addition, we try to verify that the Beads-type formation of industrial zones on and around the New Silk Road is playing a significant role in the economic development of entire regions. While the level of economic disparity within China remains severe, it is undeniable that substantial change has recently occurred in the underdeveloped central region of China compared to the 1990s. We wish to examine the correlation between this economic change and the New Silk Road.

II. Economic Growth in Existing Major Urban Cities of the Central Region of China

From east to west, China can be roughly divided into three regions - an eastern coastal region, a central region, and a western region. After the reforms and liberalizations of 1983, the disparity in economic development between the regions widened. The eastern coastal region, the first to be liberalized, utilized its great advantage in international transportation to quickly achieve economic development, gradually leaving behind the central and western regions of China. As an attempt at correcting this disparity, the Chinese government in 2000 formulated its "great western development" strategy. This paved the way for economic development opportunities in the central region. Since then, the major cities of the central region of China have steadily grown bigger and they have also developed a more advanced industrial structure. In the Henan, Anhui, and Shanxi provinces in the central region, this economic development is most clearly evident in the major urban cities of Zhengzhou, Hefei, and Taiyuan, which serve as the respective provincial capitals. These three cities have expanded rapidly by industrial agglomeration, with growing populations, changing household consumption structure, and rising consumer spending power.

Firstly, let us look at the sizes of the populations and economies of these three cities. Zhengzhou (capital of Henan province), known as the heartland of China's railway network, developed chiefly through manufacturing conventionally, but since the 1990s, two national-level development zones and one export processing zone have been established in the city and the province has pursued a policy of prioritizing tourism, resulting in a striking shift in the city's industrial structure. In 2012, Zhengzhou's population was over 9.03 million and its gross national product (GNP) was around RMB554.70 billion, up 12% over the previous fiscal year and almost double the city's 2009 GNP of RMB333.04 billion. To appreciate the city's growth over the past 20 years, we can note that its gross domestic product (GDP) is 22 times higher now than in 1990.

Hefei (capital of Anhui province) has seen a remarkable degree of economic development since 1992. In 2012, its population was over 7.52 million and its GNP was RMB416.43 billion, compared to just RMB10 billion in 1991, a stunning level of growth.

For a long time, the pace of economic growth in Taiyuan (capital of Shanxi province) was relatively slow, even by the standards of Chinese inland cities. However, with a swelling population and a focus on policies to reshape the industrial structure of the region, the city by 2012 had a population of 4.23 million and a GNP of RMB231.14 billion, a vigorous 10.5% jump over the fiscal 2011 amount of RMB208.01 billion.

Secondly, if we look at the foreign trade of these three cities, we find that it has followed a similar trajectory to that of China as a whole. The total value of imports and exports grew only sluggishly in the 1990s, but has steadily increased after a distinct turning point in 2001. Of these three cities, Hefei has experienced the fastest growth in foreign trade. Between 2001 and the global financial crisis of 2008, the value of its trade has grown from approximately 2 to almost $8 billion. Then in 2012, foreign trade doubled in value from the previous year, to reach $17.64 billion. As a result, Hefei was ranked ninth among China's major cities (seats of government) in terms of annual growth rate. The total value of imports and exports in 2001, 2008, and 2012 for Zhengzhou was approximately 0.2, 4.27, and 35.83 billion dollars, respectively; for Taiyuan, it was approximately 1.2, 9.38, and 8.47 billion dollars,[1] respectively. These amounts are low compared to those of eastern coastal cities, but they reflect a vigorous level of growth relative to the past. However, it should be noted too that the disparity between these three cities also depends on their degree of international openness and geospatial factors. For example, the fact that Hefei is located closer to the Yangtze River Delta gives it a bigger advantage over Zhengzhou and Taiyuan in terms of international transportation.

Thirdly, let us look at use of the New Silk Road. Over recent years, inland cities of Western Central China have made use of the New Silk Road to make great strides in economic development. For example, in August 2013, a new railway rapid transportation route began operating from the inland city of Western Central China of Chongqing, extending via Xi'an and Urumqi through Central Asia and on to the major ports of Europe - the so-called Yu'Xin'Ou (meaning "Chongqing, Xinjiang, Europe") Railway. With this, the New Silk Road has enabled other cities deep inland in China that suffered like Chongqing from limited accessibility to international transportation to engage in foreign trade more conveniently.

As inland cities, Zhengzhou and Hefei have long served as national distribution hubs. Also, because Zhengzhou lies along the New Silk Road, it is more favorably placed than Chongqing

---

[1] Hefei Municipal People's Government http://www.hefei.gov.cn/n1070/n304559/n310921/n315572/27940062.html

National Economy and Social Development Statistics of Hefei, 2012.

National Economy and Social Development Statistics of Zhengzhou, 2012. Zhengzhou Daily (http://news.hexun.com/2013-03-26/152474278.html, 2013-03-26).

National Economy and Social Development Statistics of Taiyuan, 2012. (Shanxi Provincial People's Government http://www.shanxigov.cn/n16/n8319541/n8319612/n8327840/n8328005/17227463.html)

for international transportation. The strong rise in the transportation competitiveness of the New Silk Road in recent years has given rise to more opportunities for development. For Zhengzhou, it is now important for it to make best use of the advantage that it has in transportation as a central region city. That is, while maintaining its position as a national distribution hub, it is also vital that it bolsters its advantage in international transportation by enhancing its links to the eastern coastal region via Yuzhou and Lianyungang, as well as upgrading its links to the western region through Xi'an, Lanzhou, Urumqi, and Khorgos. Since 1990, the total passenger and freight transportation through Zhengzhou has steadily grown. In 2008, the total value, including railway, express roadways, and air transportation, amounted to 35.48 billion t·km. This amount almost doubled in just four years, reaching 63.09 billion t·km by 2012. Also, by exploiting the advantage of its proximity to the economically vibrant Shanghai region, Hefei is also boosting its passenger and freight transportation sector over the same period. In 1996,

Table 7-2 Statistical Data on Economic Development for Zhengzhou, Hefei, and Taiyuan (1990-2012)

	Population (10,000s)			GNP (100 million of RMB)			Total foreign trade (100 million of USD)			FDI (100 million of USD)		
	Zhengzhou	Hefei	Taiyuan	Zhengzhou	Hefei	Taiyuan	Zhengzhou	Hefei	Taiyuan	Zhengzhou	Hefei	Taiyuan
1990	557.80	380.90	------	116.40	58.20	93.90	------	------	------	0.08	------	------
1995	600.30	411.10	------	389.90	173.50	233.00	1.60	------	------	1.50	------	------
1997	614.80	------	------	574.40	266.10	327.10	------	17.10	------	------	2.27	------
1998	622.70	------	------	620.30	294.60	350.80	1.80	17.00	------	2.38	1.52	------
1999	631.60	------	------	640.80	327.20	364.60	1.82	15.90	------	2.01	1.12	------
2000	665.90	438.20	------	738.00	369.20	396.30	1.90	19.10	------	0.92	1.27	------
2001	677.00	442.20	336.30	828.20	424.00	451.20	2.44	20.50	13.20	0.71	1.76	0.69
2002	687.70	448.10	338.30	928.30	497.40	503.10	2.67	23.00	16.40	0.91	1.82	0.99
2003	697.70	456.60	339.80	1102.30	590.20	613.70	4.24	30.20	20.00	1.57	2.60	1.19
2004	708.20	444.70	341.30	1377.90	721.90	763.80	7.80	35.10	33.90	2.42	3.16	1.43
2005	716.00	455.70	342.80	1660.60	878.40	893.20	11.00	41.80	33.70	3.35	4.07	1.65
2006	724.30	469.90	344.30	2013.50	1073.80	1013.70	18.60	48.80	41.10	6.13	7.22	1.38
2007	735.60	478.90	345.70	2486.70	1334.20	1254.90	23.80	62.50	81.10	10.00	10.12	2.38
2008	743.60	486.70	347.10	3004.00	1664.80	1468.10	42.70	77.10	93.90	14.00	12.00	3.12
2009	752.10	491.40	350.20	3300.40	2102.10	1545.20	36.00	64.30	59.10	16.20	13.00	2.62
2010	862.60	494.95	420.20	4000.00	2702.50	1778.10	51.60	99.58	79.10	19.00	14.30	2.83
2011	885.70	752.00	423.50	4912.70	3636.60	2080.10	160.00	123.10	85.30	31.00	14.56	6.79
2012	903.00	757.20	425.60	5547.00	4164.30	2311.40	358.30	176.40	84.70	34.30	16.01	7.82

(Source) Created from the statistical yearbooks published annually by the national and regional bureaus of statistics of China for each relevant city, and from the statistical reports on "National Economics and Social Development" issued in March each year by regional bureaus of statistics (for the relevant fiscal years).

(Explanation) The statistical data on the population of Hefei for 1990 to 2010 are based on "total population of family register records"; for 2011-2012 they are based on the "resident population at the end of the year". Amounts include both urban and rural populations, and the range resulting from this kind of statistical path is wide.

the city's total passenger transport volume was 9.99 million people; this had grown by 2006 to 78.13 billion, by 2009 to 173.17 billion, and by 2012 to 344.17 billion. At the same points in time, total volume of freight transportation at Hefei was 5.66 million tons, 67.76 million tons, 159.12 million tons, and 337.20 million tons[2] respectively.

Fourthly, without looking at the performance of postal services and the tourism industry in the cities that serve as seats of government in the central region of China (Zhengzhou, Hefei, Taiyuan), we cannot make a complete assessment of how the service industry and urbanization have developed in that region. All the adjustment of industrial structure that has occurred in the central region has been accompanied by continued urbanization. A striking feature of the adjustment in industrial structure has been the expansion of the service industry. One element of this industry is postal services. The total value of business handled by the postal services in each of the three cities in 2009 was RMB10 billion or more. This represents a large increase over 2008, revealing that the impact of the global financial crisis was small.

III. Growth and Development of Small-to-medium Sized Cities of the Central Region of China

Luoyang in Henan province, Anqing in Anhui province, and Jincheng in Shanxi province are all small-to-medium sized cities of the Chinese inland region. Since the 1990s, these cities have established tighter links with surrounding major urban cities, and with the development of the New Silk Road, they have achieved a remarkable degree of economic success. Here, we wish to consider the case of these three cities to examine the effect of the Beads-type formation of groups of industrial cities in and around the New Silk Road.

Firstly, let us consider the GNP of the three cities Luoyang, Anqing, and Jincheng. The population of Luoyang is over 6.80 million, and whereas its GDP in 1978 at the beginning of the period of reforms and liberalizations was just RMB1.69 billion, by 1990 its GDP had climbed to RMB7.45 billion. Concurrently, the GNP per capita rose from RMB357 to RMB13,160. In 2009, economic growth was stalled by the global financial crisis, with GNP falling more than expected to RMB207.50 billion. After economic recovery, however, GNP climbed back strongly, reaching RMB300.11 billion in 2012. In the period from 2009 to 2012, the GNP per

---

[2] *National Economy and Social Development Statistics of Zhengzhou*, 2012. Zhengzhou Daily (http://news.hexun.com/2013-03-26/152474278.html, 2013-03-26).

Hefei Municipal People's Government Homepage, http://www.hefei.gov.cn/n1070/n304559/n310921/n315572/27940062.html.

The data source of 1995-2006 are from *Statistical Yearbook of Hefei*, 2007.

National Economy and Social Development Statistics of Hefei, 2012.

capita of Luoyang rose from 32,314 to 45,699 million RMB.

In Zhengzhou, GNP rose from RMB11.64 billion in 1990 to RMB554.70 billion in 2012, corresponding to a rise in per capita GNP from 44,000 to 63,328 RMB. In effect, although GNP statistics show that a clear disparity remains between the major urban cities and small-to-medium sized cities of the central region, per capita GNP unmistakably demonstrate that the disparity is shrinking.

The city of Anqing with a port on the Yangtze River in Anhui province has a population of over 6.30 million. A look at statistical data for the city since the 1990s shows an astounding level of economic growth. GNP exceeded RMB10 billion in 1994, reaching RMB80.27 billion in 2009 and RMB136.60 billion in 2012. However, compared to other small-to-medium sized cities of the central region, the economic development of Anqing is thought to have been slow.

Table 7-3 Statistical Data on Economic Development for Luoyang, Anqing, and Jincheng (1990-2012)

	Population (10,000s)			GNP (100 million of RMB)			Total foreign trade (100 million of USD)			FDI (100 million of USD)		
	Luoyang	Anqing	Jincheng	Luoyang	Anqing	Jincheng	Luoyang	Anqing	Jincheng	Luoyang	Anqing	Jincheng
1990	570.60	567.00	191.90	74.00	52.90	26.90	------	------	------	------	------	------
1995	598.80	588.70	203.90	245.00	165.90	83.10	2.50	------	------	------	------	------
1997	------	594.50	206.90	335.00	210.80	111.10	2.70	------	------	------	------	------
1998	------	596.70	208.40	364.00	224.30	124.60	2.40	------	0.06	0.22	------	------
1999	------	598.00	210.00	377.00	221.10	133.60	1.70	------	0.06	0.03	------	------
2000	624.30	601.30	210.30	422.00	242.90	146.20	2.10	------	0.10	0.12	------	------
2001	628.40	602.90	210.60	465.00	255.00	161.80	2.30	1.10	0.13	0.15	------	0.08
2002	632.10	604.10	211.20	535.00	275.40	180.40	2.50	1.30	0.20	1.05	0.15	0.18
2003	636.20	605.20	211.80	686.00	307.20	212.60	4.50	1.60	0.30	0.97	0.13	0.09
2004	638.40	604.20	212.20	905.00	376.60	268.30	7.50	2.30	0.45	0.89	0.16	0.00
2005	641.70	605.50	211.90	1112.00	429.90	320.20	9.60	2.30	1.03	1.14	0.45	0.20
2006	646.00	607.90	213.50	1333.00	495.70	374.10	13.20	2.80	0.77	2.11	0.58	0.53
2007	650.50	611.00	214.80	1595.00	587.70	439.80	13.70	3.70	1.56	6.43	1.40	3.23
2008	654.40	613.90	215.20	1919.00	704.70	563.20	18.90	5.30	2.07	8.99	1.80	3.05
2009	657.50	615.90	223.90	2075.00	802.70	606.00	11.20	4.90	2.42	9.15	1.70	0.85
2010	654.90	615.60	227.90	2321.00	988.10	730.50	15.40	6.80	5.30	12.00	2.20	1.30
2011	684.70	618.60	228.60	2717.00	1215.70	895.00	20.80	8.60	11.40	17.70	2.60	2.20
2012	688.50	620.40	229.10	3001.00	1359.70	1011.60	15.80	12.40	12.35	20.00	3.30	2.60

(Source) Created from the statistical yearbooks published annually by the national and regional bureaus of statistics of China for each relevant city, and from the statistical reports on "National Economics and Social Development" issued in March each year by regional bureaus of statistics (for the relevant fiscal years).

(Explanation) 2010 Population Statistics According to Luoyang City, Communiqué of the National Bureau of Statistics of China on Main Data from the 2010 Population Census (No. 1) from Luoyang Bureau of Statistics (May 17, 2011): "Luoyang Daily" May 18, 2011 electronic edition: http://lyrb.lyd.com.cn/html/2011-05/18/content_742422.htm

The population of Jincheng was 2.29 million in 2012 and its GNP was 101.16 billion RMB, almost triple the 2006 GNP level of RMB37.41 billion.

Secondly, let us look at the state of foreign trade and FDI for the three cities Luoyang, Anqing, and Jincheng. In the 1990s, foreign trade was sluggish in each of the three cities, but since 2004, imports and exports have slowly expanded. FDI in the cities has followed a similar pattern. The global financial crisis of 2008 also had an effect, with economic recovery coming slowly for these small-to-medium sized cities.

The total value of international imports and exports for Luoyang was $253.54 million in 1996, and continued growth saw the level rise to $1.37 billion in 2007, to $1.12 billion in 2009, and to $2.08 billion in 2011. However, total imports and exports fell to $1.58 billion in 2012, which is a drop of 34.7% from the previous fiscal year. On the other hand, the growth in FDI remained unchanged over the several years under consideration.

Anqing is located close to the Yangtze River Delta, providing the city with the substantial advantage of ready access to a distribution network for products. The total value of international imports and exports in 2007 was $370.56 million, rising to $498.40 million in 2009, $858.24 million in 2011, and $1.24 billion in 2012. In terms of FDI, we see growth over this same period. After China joined the World Trade Organization (WTO) in 2002, the value of FDI in Anqing was just $14.58 million, reaching $27.20 million in 2011 and then $326.67 million in 2012, an increase of 19.7% over the previous fiscal year[3].

The value of international imports and exports in Jincheng was $156.22 million in 2007, rising to $239.62 million in 2009, an increase of 15.5% over the previous fiscal year. In 2012 the value was $1.23 billion, up 8.9% over the previous fiscal year. Although growth in foreign trade was slightly down, FDI continued growing favorably, reaching $85.39 million (actually used) in 2009 and climbing further to $257.75 million in 2012[4].

The above data on state of foreign trade and FDI for the three cities clearly indicate regional disparities. Leveraging its advantageous access to distribution networks, such as railway and express roadway links to Zhengzhou, and benefiting from improvements in conventional infrastructure, Luoyang has been able to steadily expand its level of trade. Anqing has also been able to utilize the advanced industrial facilities of the economically advanced area of the Yangtze River Delta to serve as an inland port of the Yangtze River and a distribution center, thereby achieving striking levels of industrial agglomeration. At the same time, the city of Jincheng in Shanxi province has also shown a vigorous revitalization in its foreign trade.

Thirdly, we can take a look at the state of the transportation sector and postal services in Luoyang, Anqing, and Jincheng. If we adopt the theoretical premise that clusters of urban centers have developed in a self-organized way along the New Silk Road, in a Beads-type

---

[3] From *National Economy and Social Development Statistics of Anqing*, 2012.

[4] From *Statistical Yearbook of Jincheng (various)* and *National Economy and Social Development Statistics of Jincheng*, 2012.

form, the major cities along the route, which serve like nuclei to absorb people and businesses from their surroundings by means of their latent power of attraction, trace out a process of growth. The city of Luoyang, a small-to-medium sized city along the New Silk Road, has used its resources, markets, and favorable labor costs to become a potential investment destination, and its competitiveness can be expected to grow further. This kind of ripple effect of the New Silk Road on economic development is already apparent in the small-to-medium sized inland cities of China. It is particularly evident in the activity of the transportation sector and postal services.

The total volume of freight transportation at Luoyang in 1992 was 34.38 million tons. By 2002, the volume had grown to 50 million tons, and by 2008, it was 83.03 million tons. Then, by 2012, the volume had expanded to a massive 188 million tons. In the same period, passenger transport volume was also growing. From a total of 77.87 persons in 1992, volume expanded to 89 million in 2002 and 120.49 million in 2008, and eventually reached 1.74 billion in 2012. The postal services agency in China, which handles both postal and telecommunications services, is commonly referred to as the "post and telecom services[5]". The value of these services in Luoyang amounted to RMB81.12 million in 1992, RMB1.61 billion in 2002, RMB8.85 billion in 2008, and RMB5.08 billion in 2012[6].

In the city of Anqing, the volume of freight transportation in 1992 was 16.86 million tons, increasing to 40.18 million tonnes in 2002 and to 58.02 million tons in 2008.[7] Passenger transport volume increased over the same period at a similar pace. In addition, the performance value of post and telecom services in 2002 was RMB1.07 billion, rising to RMB3.84 billion in 2009.

In Jincheng, the volume of freight transportation in 2002 was 77.44 million tons, rising to 86.07 million tons by 2008, but then falling to 39.10 million tons in 2012.[8] Passenger transport volume amounted to 58.00 million persons in 2002, growing to reach 63.07 million persons in 2008. According to Jincheng's national economy and social development statistics report for 2012, the "absolute value" of passenger transportation for the year was only 27.30 million persons. Meanwhile, for postal services, the total performance value of post and telecom services in 2010 was RMB3.94 billion, up 10.7% over the previous fiscal year.

---

[5] In China, part statistical data of the postal service is counted with the communication service.

[6] The reduction in the post and telecom services were resulted from the changes in statistical survey methods by regional statistical offices and calculation methods on 2012. The reduction in 2012 is largely due to the change of investigation method and computing method of local Bureau of Statistics. So it's not suitable to make a simple comparison between the data of 2012 and the data prior to 2012.

[7] Because the data of 2012 is not issued, it is absence.

[8] Data before 2009 are from *Statistical Yearbook of Jincheng*. The data of 2012 are from *National Economy and Social Development Statistics of Jincheng*. Therefore, the changes in statistical methods probably results in the variation of data.

Finally, let us turn to the state of the tourism industry in the three cities of Luoyang, Anqing, and Jincheng. Located in the heartland of the Yellow River (Huang He) Civilization -the cradle of Han Chinese culture- Luoyang boasts many historical sites and a wealth of tourism resources. By 2002, the annual number of tourist visitors to Luoyang was already a substantial 13.84 million, growing further to 53.05 million in 2009 and then further to 77.65 million in 2012, an increase of 13.0% over the previous year. Concurrently, tourism revenue rose from RMB6.83 billion (2002) to RMB26 billion (2009), and on to RMB40.27 billion (2012).

The number of tourist visitors to Anqing was 6.72 million in 2002, rising to 14.95 million in 2009 and 31 million in 2012. Tourism revenue was 2.71, 9.81, and 24.80 billion RMB, respectively. Although these are substantial sums, they reveal a distinct disparity when compared to the tourist economy of Luoyang.

The number of tourist visitors to Jincheng in 2009 was 8.80 million and approximately doubled to 16.97 million in 2012. Tourism revenue for these two years was 6.37 and 15.28 billion RMB, respectively.

If we compare the statistics for these three cities cross-sectionally, we can observe disparities due to spatial and regional factors, but observing the data as a time-series reveals that economic development in these small-to-medium sized cities correlates with the pace of economic growth in China as a whole. In summary, while the tourism industry in the major cities of the central region of China has been developing, as described previously, rapid development is also occurring in the leisure and tourism industries of the small-to-medium sized cities. This demonstrates a shift away from manufacturing industries to service industries as the predominant driver of economic growth. That is, we have evidence that this kind of evolution in industrial structure is also occurring in the inland regions of China.

The most salient feature here is that compared to the major urban cities of the region, the manufacturing industry in the small-to-medium sized cities has developed quickly relative to the service industry. This is because of a relocation of industrial enterprises from coastal regions to these cities, and also a gradual rise in FDI (whereas previously there was hardly any FDI to speak of). The growth of these small-to-medium sized cities due to these factors has been particularly striking since 2004. The examples of these three cities reflect a real transformation in the inland regions of China along the New Silk Road. However, because of such factors as transportation costs and their impact in a market economy, there is thought to still be a disparity in development between China's inland cities, particularly small-to-medium sized cities, compared to the cities of the frontier region. Although the development of manufacturing industries has been especially rapid, tertiary industries remain sluggish, with no substantial growth in evidence. This point seems to reflect a significant difference between these smaller cities and coastal regions or major urban cities in connection with change in industrial structure.

IV. Conclusion

Although economic development in the Henan, Anhui, and Shanxi provinces in China's inland regions still lags behind that of the country's eastern coastal regions, we can expect to see the formation of groups of promising industrial cities, driven by the waves of regional development in western China and along the New Silk Road. The above survey of the state of economic development in the provincial capital cities and small-to-medium sized cities of Henan, Anhui, and Shanxi provinces sheds light on the characteristics of this development. The scatter diagram of Figure 7-2 illustrates the transition toward the upper right corner of the graph, which indicates an upward trend in population and GNP over the past decade or so for all the cities surveyed. Furthermore, a comparison of these indicators reveals the following interesting features.

Firstly, if we look at each of the provinces, we note that not only are each of the capital cities larger than the other (small-to-medium sized) city of the same province,[9] but also their populations and GNPs have grown faster. Next, if we compare the provinces, we see that the cities of Zhengzhou and Luoyang in Henan province, which both lie along the New Silk Road, are larger than the other cities and are also faster growing. Comparing Anhui and Shanxi provinces, which are both distant from the New Silk Road, we find that Hefei and Anqing in Anhui province are larger and faster growing than Taiyuan and Jincheng in Shanxi province

Figure 7-2 Trends of Population and GNP of Each City

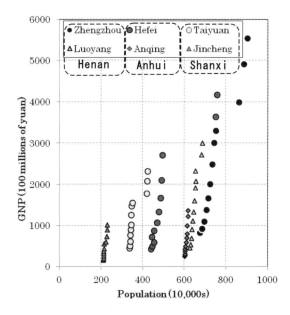

(Source) Same as Table 7-2, Table 7-3

---

[9] The population of Hefei here is resident population.

because they are close to the economically advanced area of the Yangtze River Delta. In addition, a comparison of the small-to-medium sized cities of Luoyang and Anqing shows that, although their populations were almost the same in 2001, Luoyang, located on the New Silk Road, has since grown and developed considerably more. These observations are clear evidence of the impact that the New Silk Road is having on economic development of the cities that lie along it.

Naturally, the economic development of these cities is affected not just by the New Silk Road but also by other significant factors such as the flexibility of government policy and the effects of the market economy system on rural areas. Now, on the basis of our analysis of the cases of the nucleus cities of Zhengzhou, Hefei, and Taiyuan -each a provincial capital and seat of government- and the small-to-medium sized cities of Luoyang, Anqing, and Jincheng as the emerging cities, we can try to identify some characteristics and draw conclusions about the potential for further development.

Firstly, as we can understand from long-term statistical data and a wealth of research findings, economic growth in China's inland regions has been occurring at much the same rate as the overall growth of China. However, there is an underlying and long-standing disparity between the economic development of the China's inland regions and that of the coastal regions. In other words, it is a general feature that economic development of China's inland regions lags behind that of eastern coastal regions. Nevertheless, broadly speaking, economic growth in these regions is keeping pace with that of China's economy as a whole. Since the reforms and liberalizations of 1978, the country as a whole has undergone three main waves of economic growth. Or to put it differently, there have been three turning points. The first was in 1992 ("South Tour Speeches" of Deng Xiaoping), the second was in 2001 (China's admission to the WTO), and the third was in 2008 (global financial crisis).

Secondly, the movement of people, goods, and money into the Chinese inland regions is accelerating. Although there is economic disparity between the different regions of the country, the relatively underdeveloped regions have seen a remarkable degree of growth in recent years because of the expansion of markets and the development strategies and policy support of governments. The movement of people, goods, and money to inland regions from the eastern coastal regions of China and from overseas is happening at an unprecedented pace. Mainly because of the decreasing number of migrant workers in the coastal regions in recent years, more and more small-to-medium sized companies have been closing down in Guangdong province. Two main reasons for this trend are the shrinking disparity between wages paid by companies in coastal regions and those in inland regions, and the decreasing difficulty for people of inland regions to find work closer to their hometowns and villages. Accordingly, we can conclude that in the future there are likely to be large areas of sustainable development within these inland regions.

Thirdly, development in China's inland regions has already entered a favorable cycle.

Recently, the Chinese government has bolstered policy efforts designed to make good use of the overland rail route from inland regions to the western frontier. The national government's "12th Five-year Plan" calls for the enhancement of railway facilities in the frontier regions to connect Xinjiang Uyghur with Yunnan province. This rail route would connect with existing inland rail routes to expand available transportation routes, and this new infrastructure would in turn drive regional development in areas surrounding the railway line. Furthermore, an increase in investment from governments, private enterprise, and foreign companies to promote regional development can lead to a correction in regional economic disparities. This kind of relationship can be thought of as a virtuous cycle of mutual enhancement.

References

Krugman, P. (1991a), "Increasing Returns and Economic Geography," *Journal of Political Economy*, 99 (3), 483-499.

Riku, Yugun (2009), "Regional Economic Development in the New Silk Road and the 'Beads-Type' Development Strategy (in Japanese)," *Kiyo*, 39, 165-180.

Tsuji, Tadahiro (2009), "The Potential for Economic Development in the New Silk Road Regional through a 'Bead-Type' Development Strategy (in Japanese)," *Kiyo*, 39, 181-193.

Wu, Yiliang (2000), "Limited Labor Mobility and Industry Accumulation: Relevancy of Industry Location Facing Borderline (in Japanese)," *Keizaishushi*, 70 (1), 55-69.

Wu, Yiliang (2007), "International Dispersion and Domestic Concentration: An Analysis on a Two-Country Four-Region Model of Industrial Agglomeration," in Mitsuo Honda *et al.*, *Industrial Agglomeration and a New International Division of Labor: a New Analytical Viewpoint of the Globalizing Chinese Economy* (in Japanese), Bunshindo, 1-37.

Wu, Yiliang (2009), "'Beads-Type' Cities Formation and its Process along the New Silk Road (in Japanese)," *Kiyo*, 39, 149-164.

Chapter 8

PATTERN OF THE NEWLY-INTERNATIONALLY TRADED PRODUCTS IN CENTRAL ASIAN COUNTRIES

I. Introduction

Central Asian countries are located at the middle of Eurasian continent and between East Asia and Europe. East Asia has expanded international trade rapidly due to establishing international production networks across borders. International trade of intermediate products has widely drawn the attention from researchers (Amiti, 2005; Amiti and Javorcik, 2008; Athukorala and Yamashita, 2006; Fukasaku, Bo and Yamano, 2011; Feenstra, 1998; Kimura and Ando, 2005; Redding and Venables, 2003; Wakasugi, 2007). EU is the largest integrated economy in the world. Both East Asian and EU countries have achieved the expansion of international trade through inducing the new international divisions of labour such as international production sharing or international outsourcing (Amiti and Freund, 2010; Baldwin and Taglioni, 2011; Feenstra and Taylor, 2008; Olsen, 2006; Yi, 2003).

Multinational firms that take part in international production sharing attempt to find new potential markets and more efficient suppliers in foreign countries in order to make their own global economic activities more productive. The firms develop international business network so as to facilitate international trade between production facilities located across border. With such considerable efforts, international trade expands. In addition, lowering trade costs on a global basis is also an important factor for worldwide trade expansion, since trade costs generally disturb international trade. There are many kinds of trade costs we can consider as barriers of trade between countries such as transport costs, tariff, distance, remoteness, difference in language, culture, religion and institution, infrastructure, and so on.

We can point out that there are two ways to increase the volume of international trade flows between countries. One is the increase in the number of traded products to a partner country. The other is the increase in the volume of the existing traded products to a partner. For these two different ways of trade expansion, we could argue that there would be an individual determinant to the increase of either the number of traded products or the volume of the existing traded products. Similar to this argument, Chaney (2008) discussed that two different trade costs, fixed and variable transport costs by his definition, affect a size of extensive margin and intensive margin of international trade, respectively.

In this chapter, we analyse the changes in international trade structure in 5 selected Central

Asian countries, namely Kazakhstan, Kyrgyzstan, Tajikistan, Turkmenistan, and Uzbekistan, by using disaggregated international trade data in the light of the effects of their independence from the former Soviet Union. According to Pomfret (2003), the 5 selected Central Asian countries (hereafter, CA5) have been gradually integrated to world economy since their independence of 1991. Such economic integration may have been brought by the increase of international trade of CA5 with other countries in the world. Especially, we focus on the pattern of international trade in newly traded products for central Asian landlocked countries that face relatively higher trade costs rather than non-landlocked countries.

The rest of this chapter is organized as follows. In the second section, we explain the importance of newly traded products for the analysis on the structural change of international trade. We also discuss the significant difference between the existing measurement methods and our new measurement method for new trade products or extensive margins in international trade. Then, we examine the trade structure of the 5 Central Asian countries by showing the measurement results of our method in the third section. Finally, concluding remarks will be in the last section.

II. The Trade Growth and Newly International Traded Products

One of the main factors to influence the volume of trade between countries is the change of trade costs. There are many earlier studies which analyse the trade costs matter and actually disturb trade flows between countries. Anderson and van Wincoop (2003) show a comprehensive survey about some relations between trade flow and trade costs. They point out that most traditional trade theories did not include the concept of trade costs which impedes trade liberalization and they also argue some impacts of the trade costs like tariff barriers and non-tariff barriers related to institutional trade costs and of the transport technologies related to transport costs. One of their important arguments, although it is now familiar, is that trade costs are important factors to figure out how trade flow is potentially impacted by and also what sort of trade costs influence trade flow. In our study, we take one of country's geographical characteristics, being landlocked, as one of the trade costs, and CA5 are all landlocked, which potentially face severe trade costs.

Coulibaly and Fontagné (2004) develop one trade model that takes the concept of third country into account and it says that a firm faces not only bilateral trade costs but also the other trade costs due to passing through the third country when landlocked countries trade. Also, they empirically show that the geographical factor, being landlocked, gives the negative effect on trade flow and both hard and soft infrastructures at the border becomes important for trade growth. Besides, the impact of being landlocked on trade flow gives different degree of effect, which is depending on the level of quality of total infrastructure (Behar and Venables,

2010; Limao and Venables, 1999; Shepherd and Wilson, 2006). Limao and Venables (1999) also find that the quality of infrastructure and geographical characteristics can make transport costs higher by using CIF/FOB ratio as a trade costs in their empirical studies. In particular, landlocked countries face much higher trade costs than non-landlocked countries and those landlocked countries have about 50% higher transport costs and about 60% lower trade volume.

In order to achieve trade growth and to lower trade costs such as tariff reductions, common currency like euro, and, economic integration in EU or NAFTA could become driving forces for trade growth (Debaere and Mostashari, 2008; Flam and Nordström, 2008; Hillberry and McDaniel, 2002). In the case of East Asia in comparison with Europe, however, there are not many such strong economic factors to reduce trade costs, although we can observe a rapid economic growth since 1990s due to international trade acceleration. In East Asia, production process sharing in both intra-firms and arm's length trade and decreasing in trade costs are two key factors for wider trade expansion. Many studies discuss these two key words as an important factor to boost international trade, but only some studies focus on trade in newly traded products (Amiti and Freund, 2010; Chaney, 2008; Helpman *et al.*, 2008; Hummels, 2009). In practice, recent trade growth is led by trade in intermediate products. In the recent economic circumstance and under recent international production sharing, firms easily advance overseas to find new market and supplier. It means that firms spread their production place into several places and interconnect them by trading intermediate products. Thus, the volume of trade expands by increasing newly traded products. We analyse how big the volume of newly traded products in CA5 in this chapter.

1. Trade Growth and Extensive Margins

Trade growth due to decreasing in trade costs can explain the gains to consumers and suppliers. One benefit from trade to consumers is the expansion in the variety of products they can consume and to suppliers is the availability of the variety of inputs they can access, and then, it can make consumer's utility and firm's productivity higher. Since trade costs decline, a firm has engaged in global economic activity and such firms' transnational activities that used to be unobservable have dramatically changed the structure of international division of labour and have led to trade growth. It is important to see the trade structure of intermediate products under vertical production linkages to explain recent trade growth, because firms trade many intermediate products across borders to produce a final product (Ando, 2006; Arndt and Kierzkowski, 2001; Athukorala and Yamashita, 2006; Jones and Kierzkowski, 1990, Jones and Kierzkowski, 2001; Kimura and Ando, 2005; Yi, 2003). However, it does not ensure that the worldwide trade growth is accounted for with considerable accuracy from only one perspective that is to look at trade values for some specific products. In fact, it is unclear whether the increase in trade in existing products induces the growth of total trade, or the change of newly traded products influence the growth of total trade. In this study, we investigate how volume of international trade grows in transition era by considering the growth of newly traded products in central Asian countries.

Before analysing the changes in trade structure by the newly traded products in Central Asian countries, we examine the trade components that explain trade growth. Trade growth can be explained simply by two components such as an increase in the intensive margin of trade and the extensive margin of trade. The former is the change in trade values in existing products, and the latter is the change in the number of traded products, the number of partner countries, or its trade values. Following Amiti and Freund (2010), Figure 8-1 shows a structure of trade components that indicate two margins of trade just mentioned above and the other margin of trade which explains change in traded products pulling out of the market (dis-extensive margin of trade).

It simply and clearly expresses the change of trade structure by declining trade costs.[1] (i) in Figure 8-1 shows the trade growth of existing products (the intensive margin of trade), and, it represents that, as trade costs fall in period 1, the volume of trade in existing products in period 1 may increase in period 2. It is relatively easier to observe the recent expansion of trade due to globalization from the aspects of intensive margin, and we generally take an increase in the intensive margin of trade as trade growth. In addition to it, when the value added of a product increases by achieving industrial advances and by rising country's productivity, it is also able to explain the growth of trade volume per product. In contrast, (ii) represents the trade growth of extensive margin of trade. Practically, due to extremely higher trade costs, there are some products that firms cannot trade or some markets that firms cannot enter at all. However, as trade costs fall in period 1, it can enable the firms to start to trade some products

Figure 8-1 Diagram of Trade Components

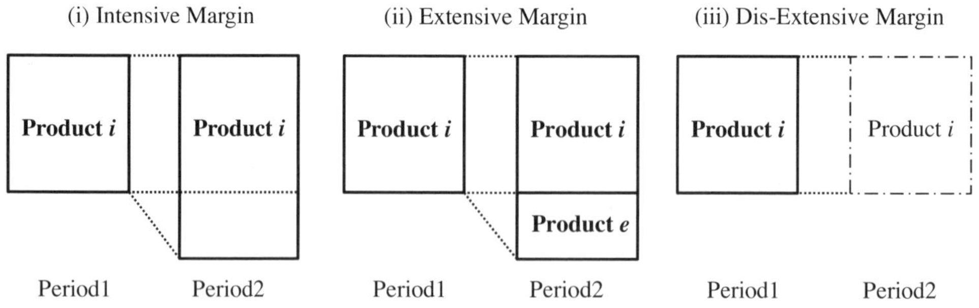

---

[1] Here, trade costs indicate not only the change of tariff or improvement of transportation technology but also any costs to coordinate between production blocks. Jones and Kierzkowski (1990) have called it service link costs.

or gain some new partners in period 2. Thus, we can observe the trade growth in terms of the change of extensive margin of trade from (ii). Lastly, (iii) shows there are some products that disappear from the market due to some impacts (the dis-extensive margin of trade). For example, when trade diversion effect may occur as resulting from concluding FTA between countries, it induces the country to trade with new partners. In this case, the countries that conclude FTA expand to trade in existing products and start to trade in products which they used not to trade each other. In a word, they shift some of traded products from old partner to new FTA partners. Thus, as trade costs decrease by concluding FTA, some products may leave from the market. FTA is only one of trade costs firms face and there are more economic, political, and, social matters that influence the change in trade costs. The similarities among those issues are to make transaction costs change, and it may affect a country's trade structure.

Some studies have theoretically and empirically analysed the relations between changing in trade costs and in trade flows in order to explain the intensive and extensive margin of trade (Amiti and Freund, 2010; Amurgo-Pacheco and Pierola, 2007; Bastos and Silva, 2008; Berthou and Fontagné, 2008; Chaney, 2008; Debaere and Mostashari, 2008; Felbermayr and Kohler, 2006; Flam and Nordström, 2008; Helpman *et al.*, 2008; Hillberry and McDaniel, 2002; Hummels, 2009; Persson, 2008). Traditionally, most trade theories put a strong hypothesis that all firms trade if they exist in the market, but in practical, it is so hard that such hypothesis should be maintained, and, some new stylized facts have proved since a firm heterogeneity is introduced as a factor of trade expansion.

One of the theoretical trade models in terms of the intensive and extensive margins of trade is studied by Chaney (2008). Taking the intensive margin as the exports per existing exporter and the extensive margin as the number of exporters, Chaney (2008) extends the trade model by Melitz (2003) which develops one trade theory with firm heterogeneity and also explains that the sensitivities of the trade components on trade barriers are dependent on the elasticity of substitution. This effect on the intensive and extensive margin of trade is affected in opposite directions. That is, it suggests that, as trade costs fall, its impact on the extensive margin and the intensive margin should not be the same and it depends how much products are differentiated. With decreasing in trade costs, if products are with higher elasticity of substitution, it must be more competitive in the market, so less productive firms capture only small market share. Thus, in this case, the impact of new entrants on aggregated trade is small (less extensive margin). That is, high elasticity of substitution under lowering trade costs means that the volume of the extensive margin of trade is not very sensitive to changes in trade barriers rather than the volume of the intensive margin of trade. The explanation that the change in trade costs has little impact on the intensive margin of trade when the elasticity of substitution is low (higher product differentiation) is one of the main points in the exiting monopolistic competition model in trade theory. However, the relationship between the elasticity of substitution and the extensive margin is more complicated. If products are highly differentiated (lower elasticity of substitution), exporters are sheltered from competition, so the new entrants can capture larger market share when they enter the market. Then, the impact of new entrants on aggregated trade is larger (less intensive margin). That is, low elasticity of substitution means that the intensive margin is not sensitive to changes in trade costs rather than the extensive margin. More specifically, changes in variable and fixed trade costs affect both intensive and extensive margins of trade. To lower variable trade costs can affect both margins in such a way that it makes existing exporters export more and it creates new exporters. Both margins are affected in the same direction. On the other hand, to fall fixed trade costs cannot affect the intensive margin since existing exporters have already paid to enter markets, but can increase the number of new exporters. The new interpretation by Chaney (2008) must require that we need more precise empirical research of trade flow between trade costs and the extensive and intensive margins.

Felbermayr and Kohler (2006) mention that many studies omit two important features when they analyse and estimate the relations between trade costs and trade flows by using the gravity-like model. First one is about an important part of the economic action across time and they call it the time-varying nature of the distance coefficient. Second one is about an interpretation of intensive and extensive margin. They employ panel data for world trade in manufacturing from 1970 to 1990 in order to solve these problems, and, analyse some effects of joining in WTO on intensive and extensive margins. As a result, the importance of distance-related trade costs is falling as time passes, and the effect of WTO membership is statistically significant and economically meaningful on growth of extensive margin.

Flam and Nordström (2008) is one of them which study the impact of economic integration, a common currency like euro, on the intensive and extensive margins. They focus whether some euro effects can be observed between union members and how it affects trade structures. They find that there is a significant euro effect on the extensive margin of trade. More specifically, comparing one period (from 2002 to 2005) to other period (from 1995 to 1998), the extensive margin of trade is increased by 6% between currency member countries, and, also increased by 4% between currency member countries and outside countries. They also attempt to find some different impacts of euro effect on trade on the margins in different industries and conclude that the euro effects can be observed in some semi and final products in pharmaceuticals and machinery industries.

Similarly, Hillberry and McDaniel (2002) consider the effect of conclusion of NAFTA on trade growth between NAFTA countries and between non-NAFTA countries. They focus on three potential sources of changes in trade structures such as the unit of each type of goods (intensive margin in terms of quantity), the unit prices of goods (intensive margin in terms of unit price), and the number of traded varieties (extensive margin). One of their main findings is that there are strong variety effects of NAFTA on trade between U.S. and Mexico which the volume of trade in extensive margin is significantly large. This large change in the extensive margin of trade is observed in import from Mexico, and, this empirical evidence shows that the U.S. domestic producers face higher competition from traded varieties in Mexico, especially in terms of the extensive margin of trade.

Some studies focus on other specific trade costs. Bastos and Silva (2008) take cultural links between countries into consideration. Their analysis investigates whether some cultural links such as conical ties, common language and migrant communities have positive relations for the extensive margin of trade. Also, Persson (2008) takes the number of days needed for trade procedures as trade transaction costs, and analyses the impact of change in trade cost on the extensive margin and the intensive margin. She uses import data of EU 25 countries from developing countries and the extensive margin of differentiated products and the intensive margin of homogeneous products are more negatively affected by trade transaction costs respectively.

2. Difference between Newly International Traded Products and Extensive Margins

As seen in the previous section the preceding papers try to measure extensive and intensive margins of international trade in order to understand how the recent international trade of a country has grown in the era of globalization. However, the measurement method adopted in the preceding papers has the following drawback. It merely measures the difference in the total number of traded products of a country with a partner county between year t and year t-1. It cannot exactly identify the newly traded products with a partner country in a year. In their method, the extensive margin of trade is just a range of the increased total number of traded products compared to specific previous year.

It is important to understand what and how many products each country starts to trade with a partner country, since the emergence of a newly traded product should be brought by specific changes in trade costs, such as transport costs, institutional factors, factor price change, and so on.

Having considered the drawback of the existing measurement method as discussed above, we have developed our own method of measurement for exact identification of newly traded products between countries. This is different from the existing methods of measurement for extensive margins in that our method uses all products in the list of HS 6-digit products for existing and potential trade partners over 4 years to identify a newly traded product, while the existing methods count the total number of traded products in each single year. Our method of measurement is explained as follows.

Our definition of newly traded products is relatively narrow in comparison with that of extensive margin of trade. We exclusively identify a newly traded product (NTP) and partner for each 6-digit product. Specifically, a NTP of country i to a trade partner country j in time t must have no trade value in previous year, t-1, and continue to have more than a certain positive threshold trade value for at least three years in a row. In this study we use US$1,000 as the threshold trade value. For some cases, we observe too small trade values, such as one dollar, in international trade data. Hence, this threshold is intended to exclude such unusual extremely small trade value transaction in the data.

The identification of this NTPs requires setting up a large size bilateral trade panel dataset, which contains all HS 6-digit products and not only existing partners, but also as many potential trade partners as possible. The time range of our dataset is the period between 1996 and 2009. We use HS1996 codes for all years in the dataset. Obviously, the dataset of bilateral trade contains many zero trade values.

III. Evidence of International Trade in CA5

We will examine the trade structure of CA5 in terms of the number of international trade transactions[2] in the period between 1996 and 2009. We use HS1996 trade data at the 6 digits level published in UN Comtrade database. In fact, in order to avoid certain data bias due to the quality of international trade data, we use export data of foreign countries to CA5 as import data for CA5. Similarly, we also use import data of foreign countries from CA5 as export data for CA5.

1. Non-zero Trade Transaction's in CA5

Firstly, we measure the number of non-zero trade transaction and its share among total trade transactions for all potential partner countries. In Table 8-1, the non-zero and share mean the number of positive import or export transaction for CA5 and its share to the total number of trade transactions, respectively. If CA5 could trade all products in HS 6-digit products to all partners in our analysis, the annual total number of international transaction will be 4,057,640 in import and export, respectively. This number can be obtained from the number of products based on HS1996 trade data at the 6-digit level times the number of potential partner countries. According to the Table 8-1, the shares of non-zero trade transaction are only 0.6% in import and 0.06% in export in 1996. However, the number of non-zero transactions increases in both import and export as time passes. The number of non-zero transactions in import is only 24,457 in 1996, but exceed 85,000 in 2009. It has grown more than three-fold in the period. Similarly, the non-zero transaction of export has grown about four-fold in 2009 since 1996, although it remains relatively small to that of import in 2009. Such increases of the non-zero transaction in export and import, which indicates the emergence of newly traded products, could be induced due to CA5's transition to a market economy. As a home market progressively opens, some of

---

[2] The transaction means a trade transaction of each product with a partner country. One transaction indicates that country A exports (or imports) product X to (from) country B in year t.

Table 8-1 Zero-Trade and Non-zero Trade in Total Central Asia: Import and Export

Year	Total Transaction	Import Non-Zero	Share	Export Non-Zero	Share
1996	4,057,640	24,457	0.6%	2,478	0.06%
1997	4,057,640	38,544	0.9%	7,082	0.17%
1998	4,057,640	43,277	1.1%	7,675	0.19%
1999	4,057,640	38,544	0.9%	7,208	0.18%
2000	4,057,640	48,145	1.2%	10,599	0.26%
2001	4,057,640	51,777	1.3%	10,417	0.26%
2002	4,057,640	53,740	1.3%	10,524	0.26%
2003	4,057,640	59,494	1.5%	10,463	0.26%
2004	4,057,640	67,010	1.7%	11,654	0.29%
2005	4,057,640	73,541	1.8%	11,727	0.29%
2006	4,057,640	77,140	1.9%	11,807	0.29%
2007	4,057,640	82,576	2.0%	12,534	0.31%
2008	4,057,640	84,621	2.1%	13,236	0.33%
2009	4,057,640	85,794	2.1%	11,187	0.28%

(Source) Authors' Caliculation using UN Comtrade database.

non-tariff barriers, which are several types of entrance costs, would be expected to become lower. Then, it would attract foreign firms to the market in CA5 as new trade partners.

Figure 8-2 and 8-3 show the number of non-zero trade transaction in import and export, respectively, by each CA 5 country from 1996 to 2009. All of CA5 countries have increased its number of non-zero transactions in import and export in this period. The number of non-zero import transactions of Kazakhstan increased drastically and it has been the largest among CA5 countries through the period. Other 4 Central Asian countries have also increased its non-zero import transactions in the same period. Uzbekistan has the second largest non-zero import transactions, followed by Kyrgyzstan, Turkmenistan, and Tajikistan. On the other hand, as shown in Figure 8-2, the number of non-zero export transactions in each CA5 country remains small and are about one-tenth of import non-zero transactions in the period.

2. Trade Partners of CA5

Secondly, we examine the most frequent trade partner countries of CA5 in terms of the number of non-zero trade transactions. Table 8-2 shows the top 20 exporter countries to CA5 in terms of the aggregate number of non-zero trade transactions in two periods 1996 and 2009. The results indicate that neighboring European and Asian countries, such as Russia, Germany, Turkey, China, Iran, tend to have large shares in CA5 markets. Other European countries, such as Italy, Netherlands, Ukraine, are the common large exporters among CA5 countries in this period. Especially, Russia is the largest exporter to CA5 counties except Turkmenistan. Russia

Figure 8-2 Non-zero Trade, Import

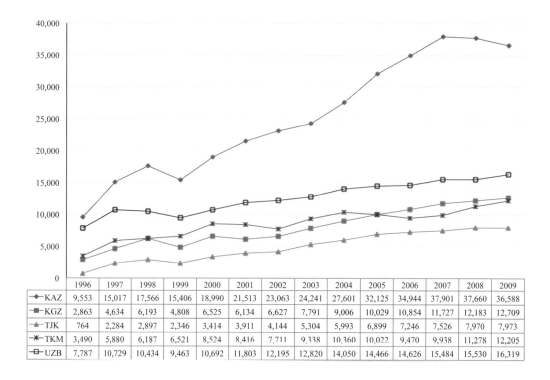

	1996	1997	1998	1999	2000	2001	2002	2003	2004	2005	2006	2007	2008	2009
KAZ	9,553	15,017	17,566	15,406	18,990	21,513	23,063	24,241	27,601	32,125	34,944	37,901	37,660	36,588
KGZ	2,863	4,634	6,193	4,808	6,525	6,134	6,627	7,791	9,006	10,029	10,854	11,727	12,183	12,709
TJK	764	2,284	2,897	2,346	3,414	3,911	4,144	5,304	5,993	6,899	7,246	7,526	7,970	7,973
TKM	3,490	5,880	6,187	6,521	8,524	8,416	7,711	9,338	10,360	10,022	9,470	9,938	11,278	12,205
UZB	7,787	10,729	10,434	9,463	10,692	11,803	12,195	12,820	14,050	14,466	14,626	15,484	15,530	16,319

Figure 8-3 Non-zero Trade, Export

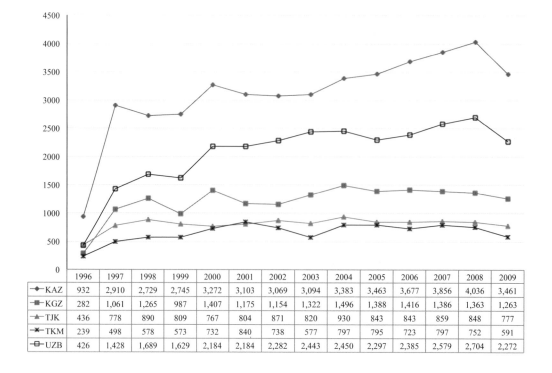

	1996	1997	1998	1999	2000	2001	2002	2003	2004	2005	2006	2007	2008	2009
KAZ	932	2,910	2,729	2,745	3,272	3,103	3,069	3,094	3,383	3,463	3,677	3,856	4,036	3,461
KGZ	282	1,061	1,265	987	1,407	1,175	1,154	1,322	1,496	1,388	1,416	1,386	1,363	1,263
TJK	436	778	890	809	767	804	871	820	930	843	843	859	848	777
TKM	239	498	578	573	732	840	738	577	797	795	723	797	752	591
UZB	426	1,428	1,689	1,629	2,184	2,184	2,282	2,443	2,450	2,297	2,385	2,579	2,704	2,272

Table 8-2 Aggregate Transactions since 1996 to 2009, Import for each C.A. Country

(1) Kazakhstan

	Exporter	Non-Zero	Share
1	Russia	42,977	12.20
2	Germany	29,963	8.51
3	Turkey	27,650	7.85
4	China	19,075	5.41
5	Italy	16,000	4.54
6	Netherlands	14,419	4.09
7	UK	13,055	3.71
8	Austria	10,047	2.85
9	Ukraine	9,976	2.83
10	Poland	9,872	2.80
11	Czech Rep.	9,799	2.78
12	France	9,537	2.71
13	USA	9,051	2.57
14	Lithuania	8,581	2.44
15	S. Korea	7,554	2.14
16	Switzerland	7,399	2.10
17	Belarus	7,352	2.09
18	Finland	7,192	2.04
19	Hungary	6,837	1.94
20	Belgium	6,682	1.90
*29	Japan	3,537	1.00

(2) Uzbekisitan

	Exporter	Non-Zero	Share
1	Russia	25,471	14.43
2	Turkey	24,097	13.65
3	Germany	17,125	9.70
4	China	10,543	5.97
5	S. Korea	7,095	4.02
6	Italy	6,392	3.62
7	Ukraine	5,771	3.27
8	Iran	4,795	2.72
9	Kazakhstan	4,593	2.60
10	UK	4,321	2.45
11	France	4,121	2.33
12	Austria	4,100	2.32
13	Netherlands	3,699	2.10
14	Switzerland	3,692	2.09
15	USA	3,435	1.95
16	Belarus	3,168	1.79
17	Poland	3,055	1.73
18	Belgium	3,017	1.71
19	Czech Rep.	2,860	1.62
20	Japan	2,814	1.59

(3) Turkmenisitan

	Exporter	Non-Zero	Share
1	Turkey	29,025	24.31
2	Russia	15,264	12.79
3	Germany	8,870	7.43
4	Iran	7,994	6.70
5	Ukraine	5,926	4.96
6	France	5,113	4.28
7	China	4,810	4.03
8	Italy	3,249	2.72
9	UK	2,616	2.19
10	Kazakhstan	2,568	2.15
11	Netherlands	2,473	2.07
12	USA	2,205	1.85
13	Austria	2,081	1.74
14	UAE	1,989	1.67
15	Czech Rep.	1,786	1.50
16	Belarus	1,761	1.48
17	India	1,598	1.34
18	Switzerland	1,550	1.30
19	Belgium	1,515	1.27
20	Canada	1,396	1.17
*21	Japan	1,305	1.09

(4) Kyrgyzstan

	Exporter	Non-Zero	Share
1	Russia	20,455	18.24
2	Turkey	14,990	13.37
3	China	11,996	10.70
4	Germany	9,327	8.32
5	Kazakhstan	8,444	7.53
6	Poland	2,914	2.60
7	Ukraine	2,869	2.56
8	India	2,844	2.54
9	Italy	2,838	2.53
10	Iran	2,639	2.35
11	S.Korea	2,532	2.26
12	Canada	2,178	1.94
13	Belarus	1,983	1.77
14	Lithuania	1,921	1.71
15	Netherlands	1,787	1.59
16	USA	1,716	1.53
17	Switzerland	1,713	1.53
18	UK	1,683	1.50
19	Belgium	1,662	1.48
20	Austria	1,526	1.36

(5) Tajikistan

	Exporter	Non-Zero	Share
1	Russia	16,990	24.74
2	Turkey	9,385	13.66
3	China	5,161	7.51
4	Iran	4,325	6.30
5	Germany	3,700	5.39
6	Kazakhstan	3,423	4.98
7	Kyrgyzstan	2,906	4.23
8	Italy	2,126	3.10
9	Ukraine	1,995	2.90
10	Belarus	1,698	2.47
11	Lithuania	1,315	1.91
12	Netherlands	1,227	1.79
13	India	1,110	1.62
14	S.Korea	929	1.35
15	Poland	887	1.29
16	Czech Rep.	815	1.19
17	Austria	758	1.10
18	USA	754	1.10
19	France	737	1.07
20	UK	710	1.03

(Source) Authors' Caliculation using UN Comtrade database.

has its shares from about 12% to 25% in each CA5's import market. Thus, CA5 countries largely rely on Russian products. Especially, its share in Tajikistan is about 25%. So, one-fourth of imported products in Tajikistan comes from Russian. It stands to reason that CA5 and Russia develop close relations politically and economically, because CA5 historically was a part of the former Soviet Union by the time becoming independent from. In practice, Kazakhstan and Russia have concluded the treaty of customs union in 2007, including Belarus.

China and Korea have grown the market share in the Central Asia in terms of the number of non-zero trade transactions. China has the largest market share in CA5 among East Asian countries. China is the 3rd largest exporter to Kyrgyzstan and Tajikistan, and is 4th largest exporter to Kazakhstan and Uzbekistan. South Korea is the 5th largest exporter to Uzbekistan. China has been pulling the global economy along. China's contribution to the global economy is not only achieving the economic growth but also emerging as a major "production plant". Also, because China shares a common border with some regions in central Asia, when China trades products to EU countries or Russia using surface transportation, they must pass through CA5 countries, like New Silk Road. This can be one of the reasons the number of newly international transaction between CA5 and China and its share are relatively higher. Actually, China begins to build up the New Silk Road economic development zone from east coast of China to European regions, and to cooperate with CA5 is necessary for China to make this economic zone be more productive and efficient. In order for the success of the construction of the zone, they need harmonize the institutional constriction in addition to hard infrastructure in order to facilitate international transaction smoothly. For CA5, they are located in the right middle of East Asia and Europe. CA5 is a geographically hub of two regions and potentially they can be incorporated in global production network that has already highly integrated in East Asia and EU in order to maximize their national profit.

Kazakhstan is ranked within top ten exporters to other CA5 countries, namely Uzbekistan, Turkmenistan, Kyrgyzstan, and Tajikistan, while other CA5 countries are not ranked within top 20 exporters to Kazakhstan. In addition, Iran is ranked within top 20 exporters to CA5 countries except Kazakhstan. Turkey is the largest exporter to Turkmenistan. For other CA5 countries, Turkey is either second or third largest exporter in the same period. India is the 8th largest exporter to Kyrgyzstan. Other CA5 countries do not import products from India as much as Kyrgyzstan does. Japan is relatively smaller exporter to its economic and export size in the world economy.

3. Newly Traded Products

Thirdly, Figure 8-4 and 8-5 show the number of NTPs of each CA5 country in the period between 1997 and 2008 for import and export, respectively. These are the results of our measurement method of NTPs explained in the previous section. As shown in Figure 8-2 the import NTPs of all CA5 countries in year 1997 are very high compared to the other years in the analysis period. Kazakhstan has the largest import NTPs through the analysis period. The number of its imports NTPs is more than two-fold of those of other countries. Generally, the import NTPs in all CA5 show increasing trend except the decline of 2008, which are subject to the, so-called, Lehman shock. However, Kazakhstan has increased its NTP at the most rapid rate than other CA5 countries. The NTPs of Uzbekistan has increased at second rapid rate, but it is not significantly different from other countries' growth rate.

Figure 8-5 shows the number of newly traded products in export of each CA5 country. In

Figure 8-4 Number of Newly Traded Products, Import

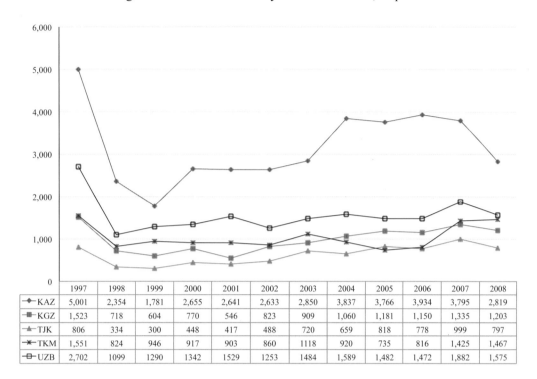

	1997	1998	1999	2000	2001	2002	2003	2004	2005	2006	2007	2008
KAZ	5,001	2,354	1,781	2,655	2,641	2,633	2,850	3,837	3,766	3,934	3,795	2,819
KGZ	1,523	718	604	770	546	823	909	1,060	1,181	1,150	1,335	1,203
TJK	806	334	300	448	417	488	720	659	818	778	999	797
TKM	1,551	824	946	917	903	860	1118	920	735	816	1,425	1,467
UZB	2,702	1099	1290	1342	1529	1253	1484	1,589	1,482	1,472	1,882	1,575

Figure 8-5 Number of Newly Traded Products, Export

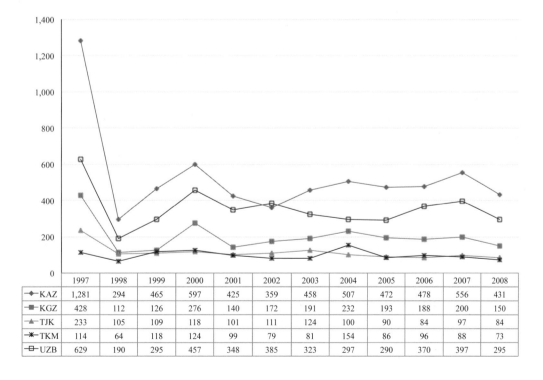

	1997	1998	1999	2000	2001	2002	2003	2004	2005	2006	2007	2008
KAZ	1,281	294	465	597	425	359	458	507	472	478	556	431
KGZ	428	112	126	276	140	172	191	232	193	188	200	150
TJK	233	105	109	118	101	111	124	100	90	84	97	84
TKM	114	64	118	124	99	79	81	154	86	96	88	73
UZB	629	190	295	457	348	385	323	297	290	370	397	295

comparison to the case of import, export NTPs are much smaller in the period. The number of export NTPs in CA5 countries have been fluctuated and not clearly increased in this period. These results indicates that newly exported products to foreign markets of CA5 remains small in comparison to newly imported products to CA5 markets in terms of the number of the transactions. Considering these results, we can summarise that the CA5 countries have been integrated into world economy as rather new markets than new producers.

4. Increases in NTPs by End-use

As stated above, global supply chains or global value chains (GVCs) is an essential point of view to examine the firms' international economic activities. To establish GVCs become a principal driving force behind the recent world-wide trade growth and, thus, economic growth. To examine whether a country makes own industry incorporate into the GVCs or how deep a country gets involved into the GVCs, we should analyse the structure and volume of trade in intermediate product. In East Asia, we can observe and many studies find that most countries have accelerated to trade in intermediate products around early 1990s and so do EU countries (Ando, 2006; Kimura and Ando, 2005). Firms' global activities like FDI strongly influence the rapid growth of intermediate trade and create the stable production network. Firms locate their production blocks through both intra-firm transaction and arm's length transaction for design, production, assembly, distribution, and so on, in the most effective place and connect each production block to produce one final good. To increase in intermediate products trade must affect positively the volume of total trade, because to trade of a final product is one time only but to trade of intermediate products appear several times to manufacture a final product. Under the GVCs that have been complicated to analyse the characteristics and almost impossible to explain by using the traditional trade theories, due to several factors combined when trade takes place, to examine the structure of intermediate products leads us to understand the degree of involvement of the GVCs for related countries.

We use the definition of end-use category of the OECD STAN Bilateral Trade by Industry and End-use (BTDIxE) database. The end-use has the following 9 different categories: Intermediate goods, Household Consumption, Capital goods, Packed medicines, Personal computers, Passenger cars, Personal phones, Precious goods, Miscellaneous, as documented in Zhu *et al.* (2011). It has useful characteristics for analysing the development of structural changes in bilateral international trade. For instance, if Central Asian countries would have been involved in GVCs, they would start to import intermediates goods from other countries -possibly new trade partner- and to export intermediate goods and/or final goods to other countries.

We will analyse the structure of NTPs by considering end-use category shares in CA5. Figure 8-6 shows the total numbers of NTPs in export and import of CA5 countries from 1997 to 2008, respectively. Although the numbers of NTPs differ significantly between export and import, intermediate products (INT) is the largest, consumer goods (CONS) is the second, and capital goods (CAP) is the third in both export and import in the aggregation of NTPs through the period.

Figure 8-7 shows the results of the number of import NTPs by three End-use categories, INT, CONS, and CAP, for each CA5 country. The import NTPs of intermediate products in all CA5 countries is the largest, and that of consumer products is the second. All CA5 countries have a similar import NTPs structure each other. As shown in the Figure, intermediate products' imports play significantly important role in increasing new international trade transactions in these countries. Similarly, Figure 8-8 shows that the results of the number of export NTPs by three End-use categories for the CA5 country. It also indicates that exports of intermediate products are the most important in international new trade transactions. Hence, the growth of NTPs in intermediate products, both import and export, in CA5 countries has led to the increases in the number of their international transactions.

Figure 8-6 Number of Newly Traded Products by End-use in Central Asian Countries, Total Trade

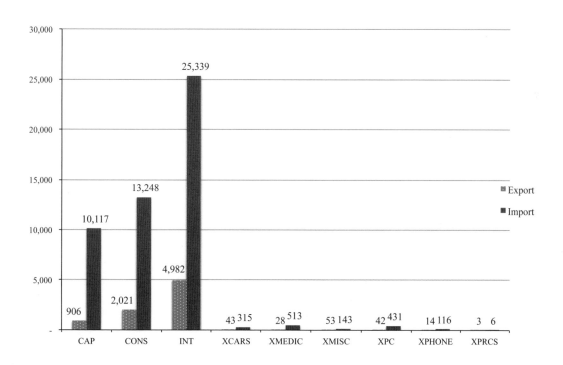

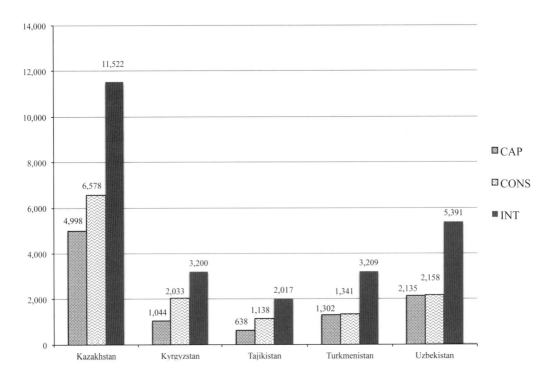

Figure 8-7 Number of Newly Traded Products by End-use and Countries, Import

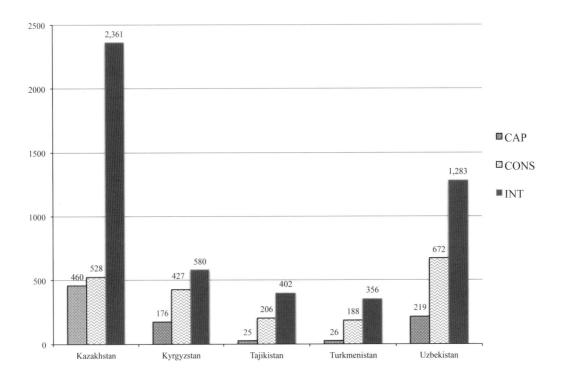

Figure 8-8 Number of Newly Traded Products by End-use and Countries, Export

IV. Conclusion

CA5 have been gradually integrated into world economy after the collapse of the Soviet Union and their independence in 1991. We have empirically investigated their globalization driven by the growth of international trade transactions by using disaggregated international trade data in the period between 1996 and 2009. Unlike the previous researches on the growth of international trade values in these countries, we have analysed their trade growth by counting the number of NTPs in each CA5, based on our measurement method. According to our results of the analysis, the import NTPs in each country have been always larger than the export ones and increasing steadily in the period. Expansions in their import transactions have substantially led the globalization in these countries. Especially, the development of intermediate products' transactions in both import and export has played a significant role in their trade growth. As studied in the previous papers on the analysis of the emergence of GVCs, policy makers have paid their attention to the importance of intermediates inputs trade. Import of intermediate inputs is becoming more important to export its products to foreign markets. Import contents of export (ICE) have been increasing in developed and developing countries in recent decades. As shown in our previous section, our results agree with the empirical results of previous researches in other countries.

References

Amiti, M. (2005), "Location of Vertically Linked Industries: Agglomeration versus Comparative Advantage," *European Economic Review*, 49, 809-832.

Amiti, M. and B. S. Javorcik (2008), "Trade Costs and Location of Foreign Firms in China," *Journal of Development Economics*, 85 (1-2), 129-149.

Amiti, M. and C. Freund (2010), "An Anatomy of China's Export Growth," in Robert C. Feenstra and Shang-Jin Wei (eds), *China's Growing Role in World Trade*, The University of Chicago Press.

Amurgo-Pacheco, A. and M. Pierola (2007), "Patterns of Export Diversification in Developing Countries: Intensive and Extensive Margins," *HEI Working Paper*, No. 20.

Anderson, J. E. and E. van Wincoop (2003), "Gravity with Gravitas: A Solution to the Border Puzzle," *American Economic Review*, 93 (1), 170-192.

Ando, M. (2006), "Fragmentation and Vertical Intra-Industry Trade in East Asia," *North American Journal of Economics and Finance*, 17 (3), 257-81.

Arndt, S. and H. Kierzkowski (eds) (2001), *Fragmentation: New production patterns in the world economy*, OxFord University Press.

Athukorala, P. and N. Yamashita (2006), "Production Fragmentation and Trade Integration: East Asia in a Gobal Context," *North American Journal of Economics and Finance*, 17, 233-256.

Baldwin, R. and D. Taglioni (2011), "Gravity Chains: Estimating Bilateral Trade Flows When Parts and Components Trade Is Important," *NBER Working Paper*, No. 16672.

Bastos, P. and J. Silva (2008), "Cultural Links, Firm Heterogeneity and the Intensive and Extensive Margins of International Trade," *GEP Research Paper*.

Behar, A. and A. Venables (2010), "Transport costs and International Trade", *University of Oxford, Department of Economics Discussion Paper Series*, No.488.

Berthou, A. and L. Fontagné (2008), "The Euro and the Intensive and Extensive Margins of Trade: Evidence from French Firm Level Data," *CEPII Working Paper*, No.2008-06.

Chaney, T. (2008), "Distorted Gravity: The Intensive and Extensive Margins of International Trade," *American Economic Review*, 98 (4), 1707-1721.

Coulibaly, S. and L. Fontagné (2004), "South-South Trade: Geography Matters," *CEPII Working Papers*, No.2004-08.

Debaere, P. and S. Mostashari (2008), "Do Tariffs Matter for the Extensive Margin of International Trade? An Empirical Analysis," *CEPR Discussion Papers*, No.5260.

Feenstra, R. (1998), "Integration of Trade and Disintegration of Production in the Global Economy," *Journal of Economic Literature*, 12 (4), 31-50.

Feenstra, R. (2004), *Advanced International Trade: Theory and Evidence*, Princeton University Press.

Feenstra, R. and A. Taylor (2008), *International Trade*, 2nd edition, Worth Publishers.

Felbermayr, G. and W. Kohler (2006) "Exploring the Intensive and Extensive Margins of World Trade," *Review of World Economics*, 142 (4), 642-674.

Flam, H. and H. Nordström (2008), "Gravity estimation of the Intensive and Extensive Margin: An Alternative Procedure and Alternative Data," mimeo.

Fukasaku, K., M. Bo and N. Yamano (2011), "Recent Developments in Asian Economic Integration: Measuring Indicators of Trade Integration and Fragmentation," OECD Science, *Technology and Industry Working Papers* 2011/3, OECD Publishing.

Helpman, E., M. J. Melitz and Y. Rubinstein (2008), "Estimating Trade Flows: Trading Patterns and Trading Volumes," *Quarterly Journal of Economics*, 123 (2), 441-487.

Hillberry, R. and C. McDaniel (2002), "A Decomposition of North American Trade Growth since NAFTA," *Office of Economics Working Papers* 15866, United States International Trade Commission.

Hummels, D. (2009), "Trends in Asian Trade: Implications for Transport Infrastructure and Trade Costs," in D. H. Brooks and D. Hummels (eds), *Infrastructure's Role in Lowering Asia's Trade Costs*, ADB Institute and Edward Elgar Publishing.

Jones, R. W. and H. Kierzkowski (1990), "The role of Services in Production and International Trade: A theoretical framework," in R. W. Jones and A.O. Krueger (eds), *Political Economy of International Trade*, Oxford: Blackwell Publishing.

Jones, R. W. and H. Kierzkowski (2001), "Horizontal Aspects of Vertical Fragmentation," in L. Cheng and H. Kierzkowski (eds), *Global Production and Trade in East Aisa*, Kluwer Academic Publishers.

Kimura, F. and M. Ando (2005), "Two Dimensional Fragmentation in East Asia: Conceptual Framework and Empirics," *International Review of Economics and Finance*, 14 (3), 317-348.

Limao, N. and A. Venables (1999) "Infrastructure, Geographical Disadvantage, Transport Costs and Trade," *World Bank Policy Working Paper* No.2257.

Melitz, M. J. (2003), "The Impact of Trade on Intra-Industry Reallocations and Aggregate Industry Productivity," *Econometrica*, 71 (6), 1695-1725.

Olsen, K. (2006), "Productivity Impacts of Offshoring and Outsourcing: A Review," *OECD Science Technology and Industry Working Papers* 2006/1, OECD Publishing.

Persson, M. (2008), "Trade Facilitation and the Extensive and Intensive Margins of Trade," *Working Paper* 2008:13, Lund University, Department of Economics.

Pomfret, R. (2003), "Central Asia Since 1991: The Experience of the New Independent States," *OECD Development Centre Working Papers* 212, OECD Publishing.

Pomfret, R. (2009), "Central Asia after Two Decades of Independence," *School of Economics Working Papers* 2009-32, University of Adelaide, School of Economics.

Redding, S. and A. Venables (2003), "South-East Asian Export Performance: External Market Access and International Supply Capacity," *Journal of the Japanese and International Economies*, 17, 404-431.

Shepherd, B. and J. S. Wilson (2006), "Road Infrastructure in Europe and Central Asia: Does Network Quality Affect Trade?", *World Bank Policy Working Paper*, No.4104.

Wakasugi, R. (2007), "Vertical Intra-Industry Trade and Economic Integration in East Asia," *Asian Economic Paper*, 6 (1), 26-39.

Yi, K. M. (2003), "Can Vertical Specialization Explain the Growth of World Trade?," *Journal of Political Economy*, 111 (1), 52-102.

Zhu, S., N. Yamano and A. Cimper (2011), "Compilation of Bilateral Trade Database by Industry and End-Use Category," *OECD Science, Technology and Industry Working Papers* 2011/6, OECD Publishing.

Chapter 9

NEW SILK ROAD AND ECONOMIC DEVELOPMENT IN KAZAKHSTAN

I. Introduction

Kazakhstan as well as all Central Asia has no access to the oceans. Hence from ancient times land routes were very important for this region by which exchange of goods with other countries was taking place. For centuries the Silk Road (also known as the Great Silk Road) originated in the second century BC was joining the Far East, the Middle East and Europe. It was a system of ancient trade caravan routes starting from China to the Middle East and Europe.

Depending on a political and economic balance of powers in Eurasia various routes of the Great Silk Road were becoming more or less popular. Some of them disappeared, leading to the decline of aligning on them cities, while new settlements appeared on the others.

Figure 9-1 Central Asia

The northern part of the ancient Silk Road (Zhibek Zholy - in Kazakh) passed through the territory of modern Kazakhstan. There was a great nomadic empire - Turkic Khanate stretching from Korea to the Black Sea in the 6th century. It was divided into two parts at the end of the 6 century. The center of the Western Turkic part was Semirechye (meaning "Land of Seven Rivers"). During that period trade on the Silk Road had a marked influence on the development of urban culture of Semirechye and South Kazakhstan. Later a part of the Silk Road that lay down through Central Asia, South Kazakhstan and Semirechye came into decay because of the conflicts in Central Asia. The route was running up to the 14th century.

Through the centuries after the Great Silk Road started to disappear there was a hope both for Kazakhstan and other Central Asian countries that the high-speed road will boost economic growth through trade expansion and entrance into the global economy (Figure 9-1). Now its territory is located between China and Europe. The most important component of the New Silk Road is an automobile highway "Western Europe-Western China", an ambitious project costing $7 billion. The transport corridor will pass through three countries: China, Kazakhstan, and Russia. Recreation of the Silk Road should help to accelerate the prosperity of Kazakhstan and Central Asia.[1]

There are also other projects of the New Silk Road. One more attempt to activate the ancient trade route connecting the East and West, is a program of twelve countries of the Caucasus and Central Asia, an international transport corridor Europe-Caucasus-Asia (TRACECA), which will pass through Afghanistan.[2] But according to experts there are serious technical and political hurdles for this project, while the highway "Western Europe-Western China" has no limitations to cross the vast territory of Kazakhstan and Russia united by the Customs Union.

II. Economic Development

Kazakhstan is located in the heart of Eurasia. Most of its territory is in Asia with a small western part in Europe. Yet, in terms of area this portion is greater than the territory of many countries in Europe. Kazakhstan ranks as a ninth largest country in the world by territory (2,725 thousand km^2). Kazakhstan has rich reserves of minerals. Underground resources contain about 100 elements of the Periodic table. Kazakhstan ranks the first in the world in explored reserves of zinc, tungsten, barite, the second of silver, lead and chromate, the third - of copper and fluorite, the fourth - of molybdenum, and the sixth - of gold.

According to economic values the greatest importance are with coal, oil, copper, iron, lead, zinc, chromite, gold and manganese. Ferrous and non-ferrous metals mined in Kazakhstan are exported to Japan, South Korea, USA, Canada, Russia, China and the EU countries.[3]

Kazakhstan has significant oil and gas reserves concentrated in the west of the country. More than 90 % of the oil reserves are concentrated in the 15 largest oil fields. The oil fields are located in six of the fourteen regions of Kazakhstan.[4]

In general according to the Ministry of Oil and Gas of the Republic of Kazakhstan (RK), proven reserves of hydrocarbons, both onshore and offshore, are estimated to be 4.8 billion tons, or more than 35 billion barrels. Moreover according to some experts estimated reserves of oil only in the fields located in Kazakhstan's sector of the Caspian Sea may reach more than 17 billion tons or 124.3 billion barrels. Given oil and gas reserves, as well as the ever-increasing volumes of production in the foreseeable future, Kazakhstan will continue to be at the epicenter

---

[1] United Nations, *Investment Guide to the Silk Road*, New York and Geneva, 2009.

[2] Gorshkov, T. and G. Bagaturia (2001), "TRACECA-Restoration of Silk Route," *Japan Railway & Transport Review* 28, 50-55.

[3] Statistical Yearbook (Kazakhstan in 2011), Agency on Statistics of the Republic of Kazakhstan, 2012.

[4] National Company "KazMunayGaz", http://www.kmg.kz/en.

of world oil production.[5]

Much higher position in proven coal reserves -8th place- Kazakhstan shares with Ukraine. According to BP the coal reserves in Kazakhstan are at the level of 33.6 billion tons (3.9% of world reserves).

The explored reserves of uranium deposits in Kazakhstan make 1.69 million tons, accounting for 21% of world reserves. In 2009 Kazakhstan became the first in the world for the supply of uranium concentrate on the world market, ahead of Canada, which turned out to be on the second place and used to be the first world leader in uranium production for 17 years, having produced 19.5 thousand tons in 2011.[6]

After the collapse of the Soviet Union Kazakhstan, like other countries of the CIS, have experienced a period of deep recession. Compared with 1990 Kazakhstan's GDP fell by 40%. But from the end of the last century the growth rate of GDP has increased substantially and for several years held at a 10% level (Figure 9-2). The main sources of economic growth in Kazakhstan are oil and gas sector, mining and metals industry, transport and communications, and agriculture. The global financial crisis has affected the economy of Kazakhstan. Nevertheless, GDP growth remained positive in 2010-2012 and rose to a level of 5-7%.[7]

Figure 9-2 GDP Growth Rate, 1991-2012

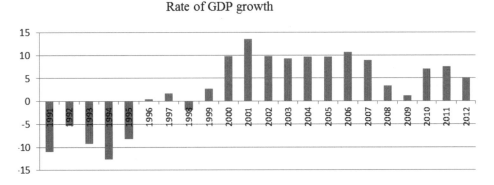

Foreign trade is an important factor of economic development as well. For Kazakhstan, having rich natural resources, trade with other countries, subsequent production of high-tech products and transfer of modern technologies are of particular importance. The dynamics of exports and imports of Kazakhstan are presented in Figure 9-3. Negative rates relate to a period of the world economic crisis.

The export structure is dominated by energy and mineral resources. Figure 9-4 shows the structure of exports in 2002 and 2011 with an exception of oil and gas condensate the shares of

---

[5] The Ministry of Oil and Gas of RK, Министерство нефти и газа РК, http://mgm.gov.kz.

[6] World uranium production in 2011, Мировая добыча урана в 2011 году // AtomInfo.Ru, 22.05.2012, http://www.atominfo.ru/newsa/j0956.htm.

[7] Agency on Statistics of the Republic of Kazakhstan, 2012. http://www.stat.kz/publishing.

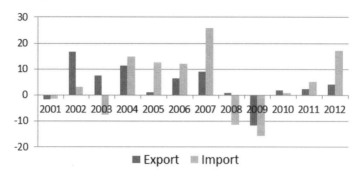

Figure 9-3 Dynamics of Export and Import, 2001-2012

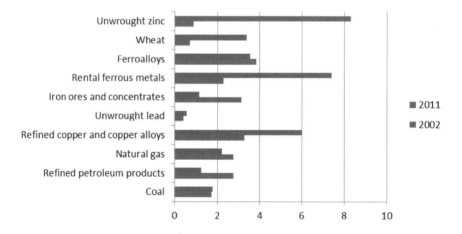

Figure 9-4 Export Structure of Kazakhstan by Main Products

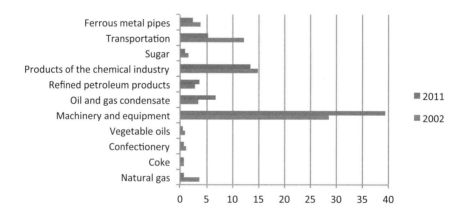

Figure 9-5 The Import Structure of Kazakhstan by Main Products

which reached 52% and 62.7% in the total exports, respectively.

By the year 2011 compared with 2002 proportions of zinc, ferrous metals, and copper and its alloys increased, while shares of iron ores and concentrates, refined petroleum products went down.

Changes in the structure of imports are presented in Figure 9-5. Machinery and equipment, chemical products, and vehicles occupy the largest share in the total imports. In 2011 compared with 2002 a share of machinery and equipment increased in the total imports, while a proportion of vehicles decreased.

The main trading partners of Kazakhstan in 2012 are presented in Table 9-1. It is worth to note that there is no Central Asian country in the top ten of exporting countries, and in the top ten of importing countries only Uzbekistan takes the 10th place. This means that economies of Kazakhstan and other Central Asian countries are not complementary. Moreover, they do not have essential prerequisites for economic integration. A major turnover of Kazakhstan falls on Europe and China, which are at the two ends of the New Silk Road.

Table 9-1 The Shares of the Main Trading Partners in 2012[7) 8)]

Export		Import	
China	17.86	Russia	38.42
Italy	16.76	China	16.83
Netherlands	8.10	Ukraine	6.56
Russia	7.31	Germany	5.10
France	6.10	USA	4.75
Switzerland	5.38	Italy	2.15
Austria	5.37	South Korea	2.15
Romania	3.29	Japan	2.03
Turkey	3.50	Uzbekistan	1.83
Canada	3.34	Turkey	1.77

In 2010 Kazakhstan joined the Customs Union with Belarus and Russia. Customs barriers between these countries were removed and common external tariffs were adopted which on many items were higher for Kazakhstan than they used to be before.

It is interesting to look at the changes in foreign trade in the period from 2009 to 2012. The share of Kazakhstan's exports to the countries of the Customs Union decreased slightly from 8.3% in 2009 to 7.4%t in 2012. The share of exports to Europe has not changed and remained at the level of 55-56%. The share of exports to China rose from 13.6% to 17.9%, and to Japan - from 0.6% to 1.24%.

Increasing rates of import duties at the external borders of the Customs Union should have helped to reduce the share of imports from abroad and increase it instead from Russia and

---

[8)] Agency on Statistics of the Republic of Kazakhstan, 2012, http://www.stat.kz/publishing. Foreign Trade of the Republic of Kazakhstan 2007-2011. - Almaty: Kazakhstan Agency for Statistics, 2012. Внешняя торговля Республики Казахстан 2007-2011. - Алматы: Агентство Республики Казахстан по статистике, 2012.

Belarus. Indeed, the share of imports from the countries of the Customs Union increased from 32.6% in 2009 to 39.9% in 2012, and the share of imports from the European countries fell from 29% to 17.5%, from Japan - from 2.2% to 2.03%. However, the share of imports from China has not diminished but rather increased from 12.6% to 16.8% of total imports.

III. The New Silk Road

A well-developed transportation and logistics infrastructure is of paramount importance for the economy of a country with a large territory. In recent years Kazakhstan has implemented major international projects in all directions of air, sea, road and rail transports. Their implementation will ultimately lead to the same goal - the revival of the Silk Road. Transport routes from Europe reach Kazakhstan from Russia side, whereas on the south and the east they come from China and Central Asia. Roads and railways of the New Silk Road will connect Europe with China, the South East Asia and the Persian Gulf by 2020. The New Silk Road will provide an opportunity to double the volume of transit traffic through Kazakhstan and further bring it up to 50 million tons[9]. The country has almost everything needed for the project: an advantageous geographical location, a constant increase in flows of cargo, a direct access to the markets of countries of the Customs Union and the CIS, a favorable investment climate, political and economic stability.

The New Silk Road involves the creation of a single network of international trade and logistics, financial and business, innovation and technology, as well as tourism hubs. "Over the past 11 years 1,263.1 bln tenge were allocated on the development of the road sector. During these years over 48 thousand km of roads, as well as 1,100 km of railways were built and rehabilitated. Now the New Silk Road is being reborn creating the main transport corridor Western Europe-Western China".[9]

Such projects as a world-class transportation and logistics company based on "Kazakhstan Temir Zholy" (national railways company), the Khorgos International Center of Boundary Cooperation (ICBC "Khorgos") located on the border with China, a free economic zone "Khorgos-Eastern Gates", a seaport "Aktau", a logistics center in the city of Aktobe, a transcontinental corridor Western Europe-Western China, as well as an "A" class multi-functional logistics centers in the cities of Almaty, Aktau and Aktobe are included in the New Silk Road.

New transportation corridors are actively laid to link with markets in Asia and Europe and to minimize transportation costs and time of delivery. The total length of the highway along the route St. Petersburg-Moscow-Nizhnyi Novgorod-Kazan-Orenburg-Aktobe-Kyzylorda-Shymkent -Taraz-Kordai-Almaty-Khorgos-Urumqi-Lanzhou-Zhengzhou-Lianyungang is 8,445 km. The

---

[9] Address by the President of the Republic of Kazakhstan N. Nazarbayev "Strategy Kazakhstan-2050: new political course of the established state," http://www.akorda.kz/en.

largest portion of which (3,425 km) lay through the territory of China, 2,787 km - through the territory of Kazakhstan and 2,233 km - through the territory of the Russian Federation. Currently participants of foreign economic activity freight goods by railway transport via the Trans-Siberian Railway, as well as ship goods through the Suez Canal. If using the marine corridor a travel time equals 45 days, while via the Trans-Siberian Railway it takes 14 days. Via the corridor "Western Europe-Western China" from the port of Lianyungang to the borders of the European states a journey time should be about 10 days. The highway will allow carrying cargos to three main areas: China-Kazakhstan, China-Central Asia, and China-Russia-Western Europe.

Currently large projects are also implemented in construction of railways which occupy a leading position in the country's total cargo traffic. Due to the construction of the railway line Uzen-Turkmenistan's border, an access to the Persian Gulf and the Big East is open. A road Khorgos-Zhetygen opened the eastern gates, paved the route to the markets of China and all Asian subcontinent. The construction of railway Zheskazgan-Beineu has started. The country has a number of large national infrastructure projects. After their launch volume of transit cargo traffic through Kazakhstan will increase by half in 2020, and this figure expected to increase 10 times by 2050.[9]

New Eurasian transcontinental railway line with a length of about 11,000 km begins on the east coast of China and passes through Kazakhstan, Russia, Belarus, Poland, and Germany and ends in Rotterdam, Netherlands. There is a development and expansion of exports of oil and gas resources of Central Asia. A pipeline "China-Kazakhstan" 962 km in length was recently commissioned.

Countries of the Customs Union -Russia, Belarus and Kazakhstan- are already working together to create a single transport corridor. It is expected that by 2020 the volume of trade between the neighboring countries of the Customs Union will reach one trillion dollars. The New Silk Road will substantially remove trade barriers in the central part of the continent, as examination of goods will be made only at the external borders of the Customs Union.

The President of the Republic of Kazakhstan proposed to make the country as a business and transit hub in the whole Central Asia region.[9]

In 2012 implementation of an investment phase of the project New Silk Road to establish the Khorgos International Center of Boundary Cooperation (ICBC "Khorgos") and the free economic zone (FEZ) (Khorgos-Eastern Gate) started.[10]

The ICBC "Khorgos" consists of two parts: Kazakhstani part located in the Panfilov district of Almaty region and Chinese one located in the Ili-Kazakh Autonomous Region of Xinjiang Uyghur Autonomous Region.

The total area of ICBC "Khorgos" is 528 ha, of which 185 ha are on the Kazakhstani side, 343 ha - on the Chinese side. Communication between the parts of the Center is carried out

---

[10] FEZ Khorgos, http://www.mcps-khorgos.kz/en/sez_ptez.

through a special pedestrian-crossing traffic route. Citizens of the Republic of Kazakhstan and China can stay on the territory of ICBC "Khorgos", as on the Kazakhstani and the Chinese part without a visa for up to 30 days.

The railway line Zhetygen-Khorgos with 293 km in length has become a new international transport corridor, which will significantly increase the transit potential of the country, and will also contribute to the expansion of economic ties with China, Kazakhstan and the countries of Southeast Asia. Informal Kazakh name of the "Gateway to the East", while the Chinese consider it as a "Window to Europe".

Figure 9-6

A modern building of the railway station, maintenance depots of wagons, a locomotive depot, and a passenger platform are already built. With the commissioning of them more than 2000 Kazakhstani citizens will have stable employment. Infrastructural objects of the road Zhetygen-Khorgos - it's not just the steel line, but also 14 new stations, 28 bridges and two overpasses. The largest station on the line will be Altynkol.

In 2012 foreign trade turnover through checkpoints "Khorgos" exceeded US$ 11 billion. According to the customs of Xinjiang Uyghur Autonomous Region this is 55% more than in 2011.[11] In the future the FEZ "Khorgos-Eastern Gates" and ICBC "Khorgos" are called to be one of the points of economic growth not only of the Almaty oblast (region), but of the country, which would make a breakthrough step in the establishment of Kazakhstan as a trade, logistics and business hub of the Central Asian region.

---

[11] Investments in "Khorgos" // Business Kazakhstan. No.20 (367), May 31, 2013. Инвестиции в (Хоргос) // Деловой Казахстан. №20(367), 31 мая 2013 г.

IV. The Influence of the New Silk Road on Trade and Economic Development of Kazakhstan

International trade is an exchange of capital, goods and services between countries. It represents a significant share of GDP in many countries. Its importance has increased significantly in recent decades. International trade is vital to economic development of each country. A gravity model to obtain estimates of growth in the volumes of trade and GDP due to the New Silk Road is proposed to use in this article.

The gravity trade model is based on the premise that the volume of bilateral trade is in a direct dependence to a product of gross domestic products of countries and in a negative dependence to trade barriers between trading partners. After the original wording of Jan Tinbergen (1962)[12] of the gravity model significant theoretical and empirical findings in relation to international trade were obtained[13],[14].

A distance D_{ij} in a simple case reflects trade barriers between two countries. In many studies it is a geodesic distance between capitals of these countries or the length of the route, connecting the two cities. In other cases, a distance between the regions with the largest share of production in these countries is taken. Gravity models are widely used in studies of international trade. In addition to GDP and distances between countries other factors that affect the size of bilateral trade: the ratio of prices in countries, cultural and historical factors, existence of a common language, structure of exports, availability of tariff and non-tariff trade barriers, and others are taken into account. In addition, a time factor is taken into account in gravity models, i.e. dynamic models are considered.

In general, the gravity model is represented as following:

$$\ln X_{ijt} = \alpha + \beta \ln Y_{it} + \gamma \ln Y_{jt} + \delta \ln D_{ij} + \mu Q_{ijt} + \varepsilon_{ijt}, \qquad (1)$$

where X_{ijt} - is an export from country i to country j in the year t, Y_{it} is GDP of a country i in the year t, D_{ij} is a variable of distance, trade barriers between two countries i and j, Q_{ijt} is a vector of specific variables, as costs of bilateral trade containing both fixed and time-varying components, ε_{ijt} is a random variable of regression, α, β, γ, δ, μ - parameters.

This study aims to evaluate the impact that the New Silk Road will have on the trade of Kazakhstan with the countries along the Road as well as on the economic development of

---

[12] Anderson, J. A. (1979), "Theoretical Foundation for the Gravity Equation," *American Economic Review*, 69 (1), 106-116.

[13] Tinbergen, Jan (1962), *Shaping the World Economy: Suggestions for an International Economic Policy*, New York: Twentieth Century Fund.

[14] Bergstrand (1985) "The Gravity Equation in International Trade: Some Microeconomic Foundations and Empirical Evidence," *The Review of Economics And Statistics*, 67 (3), 474-481.

Kazakhstan. The main advantage of building a modern highway is to accelerate the freight of goods between the adjacent countries. Based on the goal of research trade barriers are not measured as geographic distances, but as the delivery time of goods between two countries.

Countries adjacent to the New Silk Road include Kazakhstan, Kyrgyzstan, Uzbekistan, Tajikistan, Turkmenistan, Russia, China, Japan, South Korea and the European Union countries. Distances (barriers) are measured as delivery time between capitals of the countries. For the European Union Berlin is selected. In order to compare the effects of the New Silk Road trade estimates are obtained not only for the trade of Kazakhstan, but also for the trade of other countries considered here.

For calculations annual data on exports between the countries of the International Monetary Fund's Direction of Trade Statistics,[15] as well as World Bank data on the GDP of these countries are used.[16]

Table 9-2 Distances between Cities, kilometers[17]

	Almaty	Bishkek	Tashkent	Ashgabat	Dushanbe	Moscow	Beijing	Tokyo	Seoul	Berlin
Almaty		236	837	2114	1202	3861	4355	7831	6573	5661
Bishkek	236		545	1822	910	3569	4592	8068	6810	5369
Tashkent	837	545		1277	365	3300	5192	8668	7410	5100
Ashgabat	2114	1822	1277		1399	3291	6496	9972	8714	5091
Dushanbe	1202	910	365	1399		3665	5777	9253	7995	5465
Moscow	3861	3569	3300	3291	3665		7457	10933	9675	1800
Beijing	4355	4592	5192	6496	5777	7457		3476	2218	9322
Tokyo	7831	8068	8668	9972	9253	10933	3476		1158	12798
Seoul	6573	6810	7410	8714	7995	9675	2218	1158		11540
Berlin	5661	5369	5100	5091	5465	1800	9322	12798	11540	

Distances and delivery times of goods between capitals of the countries were assessed using the so-called calculators of transport companies.[17]

On the basis of panel data the following econometric model (1) for the years 2002-2011 was estimated:

$$\widehat{lnX_{ijt}} = -29.2 + 1.08 lnY_{it} + 0.87 lnY_{jt} - 0.63 lnD_{ij} + 2.71 CIS_i + 1.05 BOR_{ij} - 0.5 TCR_t,$$
$$(0.34) \quad (0.011) \quad (0.007) \quad (0.026) \quad (0.074) \quad (0.098) \quad (0.046)$$

$$R^2 = 0.96,$$

---

[15] Direction of Trade Statistics, IMF, http://elibrary-data.imf.org.

[16] The World Bank, http://data.worldbank.org/country.

[17] Sit-trans, http://www.sit-trans.com.

where $\widehat{lnX_{ijt}}$ is an estimated value of export X_{ijt} from country i to country j in the year t, Y_{it} is a GDP of country i in the year t, D_{ij} is a delivery time of freight between two countries i and j, CIS_i is a dummy variable, which is equal 1, if a country i enters the Commonwealth of Independent States (CIS), and is equal 0 in other cases, a dummy variable BOR_{ij} equals 1, if countries i and j have a common border, and equals 0 in other cases, a variable TCR_t equals 0 for the years 2002-2007 and equals 1 for the years 2008-2011. Standard errors of respective coefficients are presented in brackets.

The coefficient before lnD_{ij} shows an estimate of export elasticity on a duration of delivery of goods from a country i to a country j, i.e. the reduction of a travel time by one percent on average increases exports by 0.63%.

Not all of these cities are located on the New Silk Road. Table 9-3 shows the duration of goods delivery between cities only on the New Silk Road available at this time.

Table 9-3 Delivery Times of Freight between the Cities, days

	Almaty	Bishkek	Tashkent	Ashgabat	Dushanbe	Moscow	Beijing	Tokyo	Seoul	Berlin
Almaty		4	15	34	25	77	65	114	99	107
Bishkek	4		11	30	21	73	67	116	101	104
Tashkent	15	11		20	11	70	74	123	108	101
Ashgabat	34	30	20		26	61	95	144	129	92
Dushanbe	25	21	11	26		80	81	130	115	111
Moscow	77	73	70	61	80		142	191	176	31
Beijing	65	67	74	95	81	142		49	34	175
Tokyo	114	116	123	144	130	191	49		17	221
Seoul	99	101	108	129	115	176	34	17		206
Berlin	107	104	101	92	111	31	172	221	206	

Table 9-4 Delivery Time of Goods between Cities on the New Silk Road "Western Europe-Western China", days[17]

	Almaty	Bishkek	Tashkent	Ashgabat	Dushanbe	Moscow	Beijing	Tokyo	Seoul	Berlin
Almaty		0	11	11	11	77	65	65	65	77
Bishkek	0		3	3	3	69	65	65	65	69
Tashkent	11	3		3	0	70	76	76	76	70
Ashgabat	11	3	3		0	5	76	76	76	5
Dushanbe	11	3	0	0		67	76	76	76	67
Moscow	77	69	70	5	67		142	142	142	0
Beijing	65	65	76	76	76	142		0	0	142
Tokyo	65	65	76	76	76	142	0		0	142
Seoul	65	65	76	76	76	142	0	0		142
Berlin	77	69	70	5	67	0	142	142	142	

Shipping time of goods depends not only on a distance but also on the quality of roads, on the speed with which trucks can move. On existing highways average speed is around 80 km/hour. The New Silk Road is a modern high-speed backbone, and after its completion goods will be delivered faster and at a lower cost. At selected sites, traffic speed can reach 150 km/hour.

Taking into account the acceleration of traffic between the cities on sections on the New Silk Road, it is easy to calculate estimates of exports growth for each country (Table 9-5). Three options for increasing a speed of traffic on the new highway were considered: 1.2 times, 1.4 times and 1.6 times.

Table 9-5 Possible Changes in the Volume of Exports by Increasing the Average Speed on the New Silk Road

Countries	Export to 9 countries in 2011, USD	Increase of average speed by		
		20%	40%	60%
Kazakhstan	4.68E+14	5,6	9,6	13
Kyrgyz Republic	911419317	4,0	6,9	9,0
Uzbekistan	3124409654	6,5	11	15
Turkmenistan	5268784978	1,7	2,9	3,8
Tajikistan	347312065	4,6	8	11
Russian Federation	2,97E+11	1,5	2,5	3,3
China, Mainland	6,44E+11	3,2	5,4	7,1
Japan	3,36E+11	1,3	2,2	2,9
Republic of Korea	2,43E+11	1,2	2,1	2,7
European Union	4,06E+11	3,2	5,4	7,1

According to these estimates, in percentage exports of Uzbekistan, Kazakhstan and Tajikistan can rise faster.

A common feature for all gravitational models is the lack of a direct connection between the dynamics of foreign trade and economic growth. Gravity models are designed to answer the question "what would be if?" But on the basis of such models an answer to the question "what will be?" can not be provided. This is due to the fact that a gravitational equation itself is not embedded in a system of equations that describes an economy. In other words, there is no feedback reflecting the impact of foreign trade on economic growth. Conclusions about the possible development of foreign trade in the past are not sufficient to assess the impact of economic growth in the future. However, assessment of how might a GDP growth change in response to changes in exports can be provided.

Growth of exports helps to increase production in a country; there is an increase in aggregate demand and equilibrium level of gross domestic product. Table 9-6 shows the conditional estimates of GDP growth in the percentage of the level in 2011.

Table 9-6 A Possible Change in GDP due to Increased Average Speed on the New Silk Road "Western Europe-Western China"

Countries	GDP in 2011 (current US$)	Increase of average speed by		
		20%	40%	60%
Kazakhstan	4,68E+14	1,40	2,40	3,15
Kyrgyz Republic	911419317	0,62	1,06	1,39
Uzbekistan	3124409654	0,45	0,77	1,01
Turkmenistan	5268784978	0,36	0,62	0,82
Tajikistan	347312065	0,25	0,42	0,56
Russian Federation	2,97E+11	0,23	0,40	0,52
China, Mainland	6,44E+11	0,28	0,48	0,63
Japan	3,36E+11	0,07	0,13	0,17
Republic of Korea	2,43E+11	0,26	0,45	0,59
European Union	4,06E+11	0,07	0,13	0,16

As can be noticed the highest increase in percentage of GDP to its level in 2011 will be received by Kazakhstan, Kyrgyzstan and Uzbekistan. Different order of countries' ranking on this indicator compared to Table 9-5 is explained by differences of shares of exports in GDP of each of the countries.

The data in Tables 9-5 and 9-6 provide estimates of the benefits for Kazakhstan and other countries that they will receive directly from the acceleration of traffic of goods on the modern highway. But apart from these, there are other favorable conditions for economic development, which occur in countries adjacent to the New Silk Road. And, of course, Kazakhstan will receive a greater benefit from the transit of goods through its territory between Europe and China.

V. Conclusion

Kazakhstan has a favorable geographical position at the crossroads between East and West, North and South. The northern branch of the Silk Road goes through its territory. The revival of ancient ways will increase the flow of goods between the markets of Europe, CIS, China, and South-East Asia. This will give impetus to the accelerated economic development of all adjacent regions.

The New Silk Road route through Kazakhstan and Russia, in particular, the highway "Western Europe-Western China" has undeniable advantages. First, it is shorter than the sea route through the Suez Canal and the Trans-Siberian Railway.

Second, it provides an access to the markets of the Customs Union, within which the smooth movement of goods is ensured, as there is no examination of the goods at internal borders.

Third, Kazakhstan using a favorable investment climate aims to create a major transit hub of the business of the Central Asian region on its territory. Calculations on the gravity model help to assess the positive impact of the New Silk Road on trade and economic growth in the surrounding countries.

Kazakhstan is actively developing its road, rail, sea and air routes. A free economic zone "Khorgos-Eastern Gate" on the border with China is being developed, while an "A" class multi-functional logistics hub is being created. The seaport "Aktau" is being expanded which will serve as "Western Gates" to the Caspian countries and Europe.

Chapter 10

Economic Overview of Uzbekistan:
Cooperation, Free Industrial Zone Establishment, and Financial Stability

I. Introduction

This analytical work encompasses industrial investment opportunities available in Uzbekistan, the main strategic locations of industrial production (for example, the Navoi Free Industrial Economic Zone [Navoi FIEZ]), Uzbekistan's cooperation with other Asian countries, and the status of the national securities market. This research has highlighted several salient observations regarding Uzbekistan's economy: Uzbekistan has been a net energy exporter since 1996, mainly of natural gas, electricity, petroleum products, and uranium; exports of natural gas and electricity can be increased by 15-18% of annual production; and Uzbekistan takes fourth and third places for proven oil and gas reserves, respectively. At the same time, Uzbekistan plans to maximize investment in exploration and production with further economic growth anticipated as drilling activities open exciting opportunities for oilfield service providers and equipment producers.

This paper also includes Uzbekistan's economic cooperation with countries located along the Great Silk Road, such as South Korea, Japan, and China. The People's Republic of China and South Korea both recognized the Republic of Uzbekistan's independence in 1991, with diplomatic relations established in 1992. Currently, 10 joint ventures in the fields of foreign and domestic trade, transportation services, tourism and healthcare, engineering and metalworking, and light industry, including one using 100% Japanese capital, have been established in Uzbekistan. Japanese companies have 12 accredited representatives in Uzbekistan. Since independence, Uzbekistan has offered a favorable investment climate, with a widespread system of legal warranties and privileges for foreign investors backed up by the republic's political and economic stability.

This research provides an analysis of the functioning of the securities market, including examining the methods used in estimating the efficiency of financial tools. This is particularly relevant during financial globalization because financial tools such as shares, bonds, options, and futures play a key role in increasing capitalization levels and the volume of financial operations.

As developing countries have no experience in providing financial operations within a stock exchange, international experience is used as a guide that offers possible ways of implementing the methods used in estimating efficiency levels in terms of financial crises. The paper covers peculiarities in the functioning of the Republican Stock Exchange of Uzbekistan "Tashkent" and analyzes how shares and bond operations have been conducted. A model of the various options for implementing Uzbekistan's options and futures trade in accordance with foreign experience has also been developed.

II. The Republic of Uzbekistan's Cooperation with the Asia-Pacific Region

1. Cooperation between Uzbekistan and Japan

Japan recognized Uzbekistan's independence on December 28, 1991, with diplomatic relations established on January 26, 1992.

Since then, Uzbekistan's President, Islam Karimov, has visited Japan three times (1994, 2002, and 2011), and in August 2006, Japanese Prime Minister Junichiro Koizumi visited Uzbekistan. In May 2010, within the framework of the 43rd Annual Meeting of the Board of Governors of the Asian Development Bank in Tashkent, the Japanese delegation was led by then finance minister and current Prime Minister Naoto Kan.

The Joint Statement of the Republic of Uzbekistan and Japan, dated May 17, 1994, laid the legal foundation for cooperation. In 2002, a Joint Statement on Friendship, Strategic Partnership, and Cooperation between Uzbekistan and Japan was signed. Other agreements followed. During President Islam Karimov's official visit to Japan on February 8-10, 2011, a joint statement was signed, followed by memorandums on economic cooperation; cooperation between Foreign Ministries; and development of foreign trade and investment between Uzbekistan's Ministry of Foreign Economic Relations, Investment and Trade and Japan's Ministry of Economy, Trade and Industry as well as 18 agreements and memorandums between economic units of both countries.

Japan's first ambassador, Ukeru Magosaki (1993-1996), and his successor, Ambassador Kyoko Nakayama (1999-2002), both made significant contributions to strengthening the countries' cooperation. The latter was awarded the order of "Dustlik" ("Friendship"). Inter-parliamentary ties are being actively developed through various forums in association with the parliamentary leagues of friendship, namely the DEMOCRATIC PARTY OF JAPAN-UZBEKISTAN and LIBERAL-DEMOCRATIC PARTY OF JAPAN-UZBEKISTAN. During the Uzbek delegation's visit to Tokyo in December of 2010, led by Senate Chairman Oliy Majlis, the first inter-parliamentary forum Uzbekistan-Japan was held. Since 2002, political consultations between the two Ministries of Foreign Affairs have occurred on a regular basis.

Cooperation within the framework of the Dialogue CENTRAL ASIA PLUS JAPAN initiated by Tokyo in 2004 is an important mechanism to develop bilateral relations. Three Foreign Ministers Meetings (MFF) (2004, 2006, and 2010) and five Senior Official Meetings of participating countries have been held. On August 7, 2010, Tashkent hosted the Dialogue's Third MFF, with the participation of Japan's Minister of Foreign Affairs and the current Secretary General, Katsuya Okada, of Japan's ruling Democratic Party.

To facilitate the implementation of grant and technical aid projects and to establish contacts between business and public groups, regional offices of the Japan International Cooperation Agency (JICA), the Japan External Trade Organization (JETRO), and the Uzbek-Japanese Center were opened in Tashkent between 1999-2001.

Since May 2004, an Honorary Consulate of the Republic of Uzbekistan, led by well-known Japanese businessman, Toshio Toura, has operated in Osaka.

Founded in 1994, the Uzbek-Japanese and Japanese-Uzbek Committees on Economic Cooperation play a significant role in developing trade and economic relations. At these committees' 10th joint meeting held on February 8, 2011, in Tokyo, 18 documents were signed concerning economic activities in oil and gas, chemicals, mining, energy, engineering, and other fields.

An intergovernmental agreement on liberalization, mutual protection, and investment promotion entered into force on September 24, 2009, to facilitate Japanese companies' growing interest in Uzbekistan by helping them establish persistent bonds with Uzbek partners for implementing joint long-term investment projects. In November of the same year, Tashkent hosted business forum UZBEKISTAN-JAPAN: ECONOMIC DIALOGUE AND THE PROSPECTS OF PARTNERSHIP.

In April 2010, a large-scale conference held in Tokyo titled NEW INVESTMENT OPPORTUNITIES FOR JAPANESE PARTNERS IN UZBEKISTAN attracted approximately 400 representatives from official circles and Japanese business groups.

Currently, 10 joint ventures in the fields of foreign and domestic trade, transportation services, tourism and healthcare, engineering and metalworking, and light industry, including one using 100% Japanese capital, have been established in Uzbekistan. Japanese companies have 12 accredited representatives in Uzbekistan. Uzbekistan has been able to execute a number of socially significant and infrastructure projects in healthcare, education, energy, transport, and telecommunications among others owing to Japan's financial and technical assistance.

Most recently, an agreement on modernizing the Talimarjan Thermal Power Plant has been signed, along with a memorandum on economic cooperation between the Ministries of Foreign Affairs of Uzbekistan and Japan (February, 2011.), in which Japan agreed to allocate funds for the electrification of the Karshi-Termez railway.

Cooperation between the two countries is not limited to governmental and business spheres, however. In addition, scientific and academic groups from both countries have also enjoyed long-term successful cooperation. Japanese archeologist Kyuzo Kato made a significant contribution to the discovery in Uzbekistan's southern regions of monuments from the early Buddhist era.

Ties between the two countries also include awarding Dustlik ("Friendship") orders to Toshiharu Kitamura, former first Vice-President of the Banking and Financial Academy and to

Takayasu Okushima, President of the University of Waseda, for their significant contribution to strengthening the two countries' partnership.

In 2002, the Head of the Republic of Uzbekistan was awarded the title Honorary Doctor of Waseda and Soka Universities, and in 2004, the latter erected a monument to Alisher Navoi.

Daisaku Ikeda, President of the Japanese Buddhist Organization Soka Gakkai International was awarded the title Honorary Citizen of Navoi for his significant contribution to popularizing the literary heritage of Alisher Navoi, national poet of the Republic of Uzbekistan.

In 1999, the Uzbekistan-Japan friendship society was established, with the Japan-Uzbekistan Friendship Society and the Fukushima-Uzbekistan Cultural and Economic Exchange Association as its main partners.

In 2001, a Japanese garden was opened in Tashkent on the territory of Uzexpocentre with thousands of young sakura trees planted. The Uzbek-Japanese Scientific and Creative Center Caravansary of Cultures was founded in Tashkent with financial support from well-known Japanese community activist Ikuo Hirayama, who was awarded the title Honorary citizen of Tashkent in 2002. In 2005, the center established a Hiroshima Peace Stone on its grounds. In 2003, the Bell of Peace monument, a gift from the similarly named Japanese social organization, was erected in a cultural and recreational park named after Babur in Tashkent. It symbolizes Uzbekistan's contribution to strengthening peace and stability in Central Asia.

2. Cooperation between Uzbekistan and South Korea

Seoul recognized Uzbekistan's Independence on 30 December, 1991. Since diplomatic relations were established on 29 January, 1992, ten high level meetings have taken place.

Reciprocal state visits in May 2009 in Uzbekistan and February 2010 in Republic of Korea confirmed both parties' commitment to further develop strategic partnerships and implement agreements and arrangements, which were achieved during previous summits.

In 1995, the "Korea-Uzbekistan" Parliamentary Association of Friendship was established at the National Assembly of Republic of Korea (ROK). In 2005, a cooperation group with Korea was established by the Oliy Majlis Legislative Chamber in Uzbekistan. In August, an ROK parliament delegation visited Uzbekistan, while in November 2008, female Parliamentary delegates from Uzbekistan visited Korea. Since 1995, political consultations between the two countries' foreign offices have been held, the 8th round of which took place in November 2010 in Seoul. Close relations at the municipal level have also been established, with cooperation agreements signed between Tashkent and Seoul, Fergana and Yongin, and Namangan and Seongnam.

In accordance with the 1992 Trade Agreement, the status of Most Favored Nation Treatment was achieved. Seoul is currently one of Uzbekistan's lead trade partners in the Asia-Pacific region. According to Uzbekistan's State Statistics Committee, trade turnover increased by 31.5% and accounted for $1.61 billion in 2012: Uzbekistan's exports are $158.2 million and imports are $1.46 billion.

South Korea's total direct investment to Uzbekistan exceeded $5 billion, including more than $2 billion being reclaimed. South Korean businessmen are actively supporting the creation of the Navoi FIEZ.

Since 1992, the Korean Education Center in Tashkent has organized language training, professional development for university lecturers, and courses for students on a contest basis. Korean language, culture, and computer centers are also successfully operating in the Uzbek State University of World Languages and Samarkand State Institute of World Languages. The Embassy of ROK in Tashkent has ensured that these centers are equipped with the latest literature, videos, and audio cassettes. A total of nine departments of Korean studies operate in Uzbekistan's higher educational institutions and 22 schools teach Korean language.

The "Uzbekistan-Republic of Korea" Friendship Society has operated since 1999. From November 2009 to October 2010, an exhibition of Uzbekistan's ancient culture containing unique historical artifacts was for the first time presented in the National Museum of Korea, confirming long-standing cultural and spiritual ties between the countries.

3. Cooperation between Uzbekistan and China

The People's Republic of China recognized Uzbekistan's independence on 27 December, 1991, with diplomatic relations established on January 2, 1992. The two countries enjoy a trusting relationship characterized by friendly and mutually beneficial bilateral cooperation. The leaders of the two countries regularly conduct high level visits and meetings.

President Islam Karimov visited China in 1992, 1994, 1999, 2005, and 2011. In 2001 and 2006, he visited Shanghai to participate in Shanghai Cooperation Organization (SCO) summits, and in August 2008, he traveled to Beijing to participate in the opening ceremony of the 29 Olympic Games.

State visits to Uzbekistan have been conducted by past Presidents of the People's Republic of China: Szyan Szemin (1996) and Hu Jintao (2004, 2010). The state visit of President I. A. Karimov to China raised Uzbek-Chinese relations to a new qualitative level.

Most Favored Nation Treatment was established between two countries by the Economic and Trade Agreement (1994). According to data from Uzbekistan's State Statistics Committee, trade turnover in 2012 accounted for $2,085 million (growth of 1.7%), including exports of $899.9 million and imports of $1185.4 million.

Chinese investors have provided financial backing to 347 companies in Uzbekistan, including 57 companies enjoying 100% Chinese capital. There are 64 Chinese companies accredited by the Ministry of Foreign Economic Relations, Investment, and Trade. These enterprises mainly operate in export-import operations, textile production, agricultural product processing, and IT. Cooperation in the spheres of culture, science, and technology continue to be actively developed. In 2003, a monument of a miniaturist Kamoliddin Behzod, the first monument of a representative of Uzbek culture, was unveiled in the framework of the sixth world sculpture forum in Changchun.

The friendship societies "Uzbekistan-China," established in 1998, and "China-Central Asia," established in 2007, play a significant role. In June, 2010, representatives of the Chan Deguan Friendship Society visited Uzbekistan as part of the international exhibition "Great Silk Road - travel in the name of peace" held within the framework of the SCO summit.

Cooperation exists in education as well, with exchanges of both students and interns occurring within state and inter-agency lines, in particular taking the form of mutual language exchanges and learning. In the sphere of tourism, in June 2009, a memorandum designating Uzbekistan as a tourist destination country for Chinese citizens' travel groups.

III. Free Industrial Zone Establishment

1. "Navoi" Free Industrial Economic Zone (FIEZ)

The Navoi region in Uzbekistan, having well-developed industrial production, skilled manpower, and abundant raw material resources, as well as occupying a strategic location in the central part of the country, has potential to become a sizeable regional manufacturing complex and industrial center.

In an effort to increase the region's production potential, the introduction of innovative technologies and development of new types of essential products demanded on the world market has been accelerated. In addition, the Republic of Uzbekistan's leadership decided to establish the country's first free industrial economic zone (FIEZ) in Navoi city, the region's administrative center.

The Republic of Uzbekistan sits on the crossroads of trade routes between the huge regional markets of South-East Asia, Central and Eastern Europe, the Middle East, and the Commonwealth of Independent States, a fact influencing this decision. Conditions conducive to the establishment of an international transportation and logistics center in Navoi Airport, offering the possibility of immediate transport of finished goods to the ultimate consumers in Europe and Asia, was an important consideration.

The Navoi FIEZ was founded in December 2008 in accordance with the President's decree to create conditions favorable for attracting foreign investment to Uzbekistan, create modern highly technological enterprises, and develop the country's industrial potential as well as its industrial, transport, and social infrastructure.

The FIEZ Concept

The FIEZ in Navoi airport comprises innovation-industrial, transport-logistical, social and recreational complexes in 3 stages covering approximately 500 ha.

The establishment of the FIEZ industrial complex, with a total area of 564 ha, provides a base for organizing the manufacture of products competitive in foreign markets using local raw material resources. The actual production complex is expected to be located on an area of 380 ha near Navoi city. According to the planned layout, the FIEZ will be divided into 21 clusters, each having areas of 6.5 to 25 ha, enabling creation of enterprises having various output and scales during the first stage.

The Terms of Operation

The "Navoi" FIEZ will have a 30 year operational term with the possibility of extension. During this period, special customs, fiscal and tax regimes, simplified entry, stay and departure procedures, and a streamlined application process for foreigners to obtain work permits will apply.

Development of a transport logistic complex is inseparable from the creation of an international logistic center in Navoi International Airport. Navoi International Airport has achieved a certificate of ICAO CAT II Runway, 4,000 m × 45 m with ILS, radar, and lighting. In addition, the airport is equipped with the latest navigation equipment from French producer Thales, and its ground handling equipment can support B747-400F operations. Moreover, the airport has line maintenance capable of handling B747-400s, AN-24s, and TU-154s. Its fuel capacity is 370,000 gal, with 24 tanks.

Currently, construction of a railway connecting the city to the following railway lines is being carried out:
- To the north-west: Uchkuduk-Nukus-Volgograd with access via Russia to Europe;
- To the east: Samarkand-Tashkent-Dustik offering access to China and South-East Asia;
- To the south: Bukhara-Turkmenistan-Bandar-Abbas with the route offering access to the Middle East and Persian Gulf.

Life Environment

To promote effective production processes, comfortable living quarters for recreation and residence are being built on 35 ha of land, along with land set aside for public areas, green areas, and parks. Located 1.2 km from Navoi FIEZ on the picturesque bank of the Zaravshan River, 120 ha has been allotted for construction of world-class residential and hotel complexes, social facilities for cultural centers, recreation and active recreation, and a golf club.

Tax Preferences

The substantial investments behind the development of Navoi FIEZ have been made possible by a wide array of unprecedented preferences and privileges provided by a decree of the President of the Republic of Uzbekistan for FIEZ residents. This system of nearly tax and duty free customs regulations and preferential foreign currency procedures has simplified the region's ability to attract foreign residents and investments.

Business enterprises registered in the Navoi FIEZ are exempt from land, property, profit, social infrastructure development, and unified taxes (for small businesses), as well as compulsory contributions to the Republican Road Fund and Republican School Fund depending on the size of foreign direct investments made:

- 7 years reprieve for investments from 3 to 10 million Euros;
- 10 years reprieve for investments from 10 to 30 million Euros. In addition, firms investing at this rate will enjoy five further years of 50% reductions on profit and unified taxes;
- 15 years reprieve for investments of more than 30 million Euros. Firms investing at this rate will enjoy an additional 10 years of 50% reductions on profit and unified taxes.

Customs Preferences

Business enterprises registered in Navoi FIEZ are exempt from customs duties (excluding customs clearance charges) on equipment, raw materials, and components imported for production of export goods over the entire period of Navoi FIEZ's operation.

In the Navoi FIEZ, all transactions and payments can be made in foreign currency; payment of goods and services rendered by local companies can also be tendered in hard currency.

Free Choice in Payment Forms

Business enterprises registered in Navoi FIEZ are allowed to:

- make calculations and payments in foreign currencies in accordance with mutual agreements and contracts concluded within Navoi FIEZ;
- use hard currency to pay for supply of goods, works, and services performed by business entities belonging to Uzbek residents; and
- choose their preferred terms and forms of payments for exported and imported goods.

2. First Five Enterprises Launched in Navoi Free Industrial Economic Zone

The first five enterprises in Navoi FIEZ were launched on the eve of the country's Independence Day. These enterprises operate in sectors like electronics, car parts production, polymers processing, and the food industry.

The Telecom Innovations joint venture, with a production capacity of 50,000 digital TV receivers per year, was established by Uzbektelecom and Servetechno Pte. Ltd. (Singapore) at a total cost of $1.6 million. The new company provided jobs for more than 30 young specialists.

Two additional new companies will produce polyethylene and polypropylene pipes. One enterprise, Polietilen Quvurlari, will produce 8,600 tons of 75-630 mm polyethylene pipes per year. The project, which employs approximately 70 people, cost $7.2 million. At full capacity, the company is expected to export over $5.9 million worth of products.

The second enterprise, Polipropilen Quvurlari, has capacity to produce 2,300 linear kilometers of 16-63 mm polypropylene pipes per year. The project cost a total of $5.2 million and has employed more than 40 specialists. Up to 50% of the ready products will be exported. The Uz Erae Cable joint venture was established by Uzvtosanoat and Erae cs Ltd. of South Korea to produce 150,000 km of car cables per year, at a total cost of $13 million. The main purchaser of these products is the Uzodji joint venture, which makes car harnesses for GM's Uzbekistan plant. In addition, 20% of the production will be exported to other GM enterprises in the region.

AgroFresh JV, founded by Markazsanoateksport and Kefayat General Trading Co. (UAE), is capable of storing up to 3,000 tons of fruit and vegetable products. The company has modern Italian refrigeration equipment offering a regulated gas environment. The project cost $5.03 million and will employ over 20 people. Up to 50% of its products will be exported.

Currently, 16 more projects are being implemented in Navoi FIEZ, of which five have already started functioning, and seven more will commence operations by the end of this year, as reported by UzA. These new enterprises will produce energy-saving bulbs, LCD monitors, electric gas meters, ready medicines, generators, compressors, and instrument sets for GM's Uzbekistan cars.

IV. Financial Stability

1. Portfolio Investments: Estimating the Efficiency of Financial Tools as Options and Futures in Terms of Financial Crises

Considerable growth in the volume of international investments, stimulated by increasing economic globalization and international financial market liberalization can be recognized as the characteristic feature of the previous decade. Foreign investment has played a central role in the structural transformations of Uzbekistan's economy, because internal financing is insufficient and the republic's productive forces require heavy capital investments for goals such as modernization, reconstruction, and achieving macroeconomic stability, steady and balanced economic growth, continuation of structural transformations, and modernization of leading economic sectors.

Increased economic integration and globalization of the world's financial markets (WFM) are most clearly shown in its dynamic and fundamental structural changes. The emergence of the derivative financial tools is one outcome of these changes. Before such changes, inability to access suitable finance in the market remained a distinct possibility, and the newly-emerging tools provide a mechanism enabling creation of a desirable structure to manage market risks and diversify and insure portfolio risks. This increased value is captured by the financial markets using financial tools most suited for use in developed countries where the financial system is institutionally developed and faces somewhat less risk from financial operations, giving these countries higher opportunity to avoid big losses in any financial crisis. Indeed, the global financial crisis has revealed serious deficiencies that confirm the absence of due control over bank's various speculative operations in the credit and securities markets, activities that basically served corporate interests.

The thesis of this research shows that, first, the current formation process of national and international markets for financial tools is far from finished, as new tools already exist that are ready to be implemented. This process occurs not only in developed but also in developing countries, where it has the specificity.

Second, development of emergent markets directly influences the structure of global financial markets and changes their traditional mechanisms of interaction, a process that helps estimate the development prospects of the world economy as a whole.

Third, derivative financial tools possess unique properties that meet the requirements of a modern global market economy: possess low average cost, enable hedging of various risks, offer huge investment possibilities, and provide high rates of return. These qualities, in turn, provide the possibility of rapid activity replacement at corporate, national, and international levels.

Despite its positive dynamics and existing infrastructure, Uzbekistan's stock market can be characterized as ineffective because it lacks liquidity. Existing problems demand rapid policy responses as lack of governmental leadership on this issue is a certain threat to economic stability. The issue's urgency is obvious: it is caused by the necessity of revealing and establishing an optimum model to estimate the efficiency of financial tools that are able to prevent losses in financial operations at the global level.

Rather than designing an entirely new and untested financial market system, Uzbekistan needs to examine current models that adapt the most suitable financial tools while still taking national features into account.

The growing influence of financial tools, especially derivatives, on the world economic system and their special role in the economy's infrastructure have been the subject of much research by many leading foreign and domestic scientists.

Many researches have examined the financial relations arising from how financial tools function in economy, utilizing theoretical models of the roles of both finance and credit. Specifically, S. Natenberg, U. Sharp, R. T. Deigler. S. Cox, M. Rubenshtein, R. U. Kolb, J. Lederman, and K. F. Luft have all made appreciable contributions to working out the theoretical aspects of problems created by financial tools in the global economy.

Other researchers, such as C. Strickland, L. Galits, T. Lofton, D. Marshall, V. K. Bansal, J. Murphy, M. S. Tomsett, J. K. Hall, and D. R. Siegel, focus on key concepts behind the workings of financial markets, as well as on concrete financial tools including the nonconventional, to formulate a model of pricing. The given tools are also used in formation of trading strategies. Authors focusing on general questions of finance administration and investment management include I. Balabushkin, A. Burenin, A. Feldman, S. Vain, and M. Chekulaeva.

Research intended to determine new models of financial tool efficiency were conducted by J. Berge, I. Brajs, E. Benks, and J. Finerty, whereas O. I. Degtyarev, O. Kandinskiy, T. J. Safonova and B. B. Rubtsov were engaged in studying the functioning of various stock exchanges.

However, the problem of determining the appropriate application of efficiency estimation models for financial tools in a transitive economy demands a model be adapted to incorporate national economic and legal conditions, the history of the national financial market, and global tendencies in working out new financial products. Working out new methods can pose problems of estimating the efficiency of derivative financial tools, as they are not, as a rule, considered independent objects of the analysis; rather, they are described in context of tools already existing in the market.

Uzbek researchers such as S. Shohazamy, K. Tolipov, L. Butikov, D. Ankudinov, I. Ahmedhodzhaev, A. Abdukadyrov, M. Aliev, V. Kotov, S. Muminov, J. Nazarov, M. Hamidullin, and L. Sultanov have conducted studies on problems in the formation and functioning of the national stock market. At the same time, these authors emphasize the difficulties of working out applied aspects of a considered problem due to insufficient theoretical understanding and underdeveloped models accounting for the efficiency of financial tools and their functioning -or lack thereof- in financial markets. The problem of urgency, compounded by insufficient scientific research on the problem's component parts forms the purposes and problems of this dissertation.

2. Methodical Aspects of Stock Markets' use of Financial Tools in Terms of Financial Globalization

The global financial market, which includes the market for loan capital, specializes mainly in securities (the primary market) and their purchase and sale (the secondary market). A normally functioning market economy demands that people in the market have effective and reliable financial tools (bank notes, securities, etc.), allowing physical and legal entities to make sound and productive economic actions. Basic (traditional) financial tools include bank notes, actions, bills and bonds; other financial tools are termed derivatives.

Prior to the beginning of the 1990s, derivatives had been mainly used to insure against market risks (currency, percentage, etc.). However, the scale of the economic crisis phenomena observed over the last few years in the global stock market, generated demand for effective hedging not only of market but also of credit risks.

Analysis of data published by international financial organizations shows that increases in the market for derivative financial tools occurred throughout the past decade. In addition to this rapid increase, the modern world market for derivative financial tools is characterized by its sizeable scope. For example, in 1993, the general nominal volume of both the exchange and off-exchange markets of urgent tools grew 47% and has made more than US$12 billion, an amount that exceeds twice the nominal volume of the US's GNP. By the end of 1996, the total volume of both the exchange and off-exchange markets at conditional face-value had already reached US$34 billion. By the end of 2012, given indicator posit a further three-fold increase.

It is possible to construct a model showing the interrelations between the securities market, financial tools, and investments. Each open economy pursues policy of attracting foreign capital into the country with a view toward improving production and the economy as a whole. However, attracting such investment requires the existence of an international stream of capital. This capital is then used in various transactions and processes. One of the most important and highly remunerative is the stock market. Stock market development, by providing dynamic capital flows, attracts foreign investments into the country. However, bigger than the stock market is the secondary market, or the derivatives market, which owe their popularity to their being short-term, liquid, and high profit. The basic trend of financial globalization at the present stage of the global economy's development are further country specialization, excess rates of gain by international financial operations over international commodities, an information-technological revolution and creation of a universal information field, increased influence for global financial tools, concentration and centralization of capital due to mergers and acquisitions, and reconsideration of the role of the WFM in determining universal norms and standards, integration tendencies, and an increased role for supranational bodies in the world economy.

Activity of the global stock markets shows that the securities markets should be considered in relation to the integrated groups: share markets, bonds markets, and derivative financial tools markets.

For twenty years (1980-2000 years) the global economy saw its capitalization grow by almost 13 times while cumulative gross national product increased approximately 2.5 times. Since 2000, a universal reduction in both absolute and relative capitalization has occurred in connection with the global economic crisis. Nevertheless, in the new decade, the position of the formed markets has considerably improved. By 2010, 67% of global capitalization was provided by only three countries, the U.S., Japan, and Great Britain, while the seven largest provided 75% of the world's capitalization.

As the result, total capital in world economy in 2008 reached US$11.4 billion compared to US$7.5 billion in 2000, having exceeded four times a similar indicator of 1990. For the same time period, capital movements have increased by approximately US$500 billion to reach US$1.2 billion. The processes of financial globalization have been accompanied by increased investor belief in the theory of investment diversification counseling that the international investor can effectively reduce risks by spreading investments across a wider spectrum of activities.

Estimating the efficiency of separate financial investment tools, as well as that of real investments, is conducted on the basis of comparing the volume of investment expenses with the sums of their returnable monetary stream. At the same time, formation of these indicators presents essential distinctive features.

Considering the given efficiency estimate of a specific investment financial tool means reducing it to an estimate of its real cost determined, in turn, by its expected rate of profit. Models of efficiency estimation for bonds are constructed on indicators including the bond's face value, the sum of percent paid by the bond, the expected norm of total investment profit, and the amount of time until the bond's term of repayment. The factor of its current profitableness is used to estimate the bond's current level of total investment profit.

Models for estimating the efficiency of actions are based on the sum of dividends assumed to be received in a given period, the expected share cost at the end of this period, the expected norm of total investment profit under actions, and the number of time periods engaged in the action.

Estimation of efficiency of a financial tool compared with its current market quote price or its calculated expected norm of total investment profit (profitableness) are the basic criteria used to make administrative decisions that ultimately determine global financial conditions - an economic crisis can hinge on the accuracy of these predictions.

Estimates of financial tools' comparative efficiency are based on definitions of profitableness and effect. Defining such criteria as profitableness, risk, and liquidity is central. The estimated profit defines the profitableness level; every possible uncertainty poses risk, and the ability to transform actions in cash concerns liquidity. During the following fundamental and technical analysis, the estimation of efficiency of financial tools is deduced.

The efficiency of any form of investment pays off on the basis of comparing its effect (income) and expenses. For investments in securities as expenses, this refers to the sum of the means invested in securities, and as income, this means the difference between a security's current cost and the sum of the means enclosed in its acquisition. As a security's income can only be received in the future, for comparability, it should be accounted for at this time by discounting.

The basic formula for calculating the efficiency of financial investments is as follows:
$$E_f = (C - I_0)/I_0 \quad \text{or,} \quad E_f = (C - D)/I_0,$$
where E_f = efficiency of investment into a security;

C = present value;

I_0 = the sum of invested means; and

D = the expected income of investment.

A security's current cost is defined by two major factors: the size of the monetary stream gained from investment in said security and the level of the interest rate used for discounting.

Calculation of the resulting net profit as financial investments has certain differences from the definition of the income for real investments.

When estimating the comparative efficiency of financial tools in the stock market, the resulting net profit is estimated as the difference between the resulting cost of separate share tools and the cost of their acquisition. Hence, share tools are characterized by a variety of models providing estimations of their resulted cost in comparison with the efficiency of various financial investments. When estimating the efficiency of an investment, an important role is played by the size of the norm of the discount, used in reducing the sums of the future monetary streams by this time. Inescapable fluctuations in risk level force a choice between corresponding concrete investment and the object of the norm of discount.

Table 10-1 Models of Estimating the Discounted Cost of Financial Tools

Shares		Bonds	
On the basis of stable level of dividends	$C_a = D/r$	Without any percent payments	$C_0 = N_0/(1+r)^n$
On the basis of sustainable rising level of dividends	$C_a = D_0(1+f)/r(r-f)$	With periodical percent payments	$C_a = \sum_{t=1}^{n} P_0/(1+r)t + N_0/(1+r)^t$
On the basis of non-stable level of dividends	$C_a = \sum_{t=1}^{n} D_t/(1+r)t$	With all percent payments at the end	$C_0 = (N_0 + P_t)/(1+r)^n$

Where, C_a = present value of share (stock);
R = norm of income (share of bond);
D_0 = the sum of last paid dividend;
D_t = the sum of paid dividend for the t-period;
F = tendency of dividend increase;
C_0 = present value of bonds;
N_0 = nominal value of bonds;
P_t = the sum of percent paid for the moment of bond discharge; and
N = the quantity of years left until payment discharge.

In foreign practice, the norm of the discount is used when estimating the resulting cost of financial tools and is carried out according to the model of the price of capital actions.

In Uzbekistan's stock market, accounting for its specific functioning using an estimation of comparative efficiency employing financial tools as base of comparison, it is expedient to not apply current profitableness norms on non-risky investments, and average cost of prospective sources of investments. Results of estimations of the comparative efficiency of the financial tools for various investment objects are used at their choice and formation of a bank's investment portfolio.

Analysis of a technique for estimating the efficiency of various financial tools used in the stock market and of global financial conditions leads to the observation that in an economic crisis, modern economic theory recognizes the important role of financial gambles as the motive forcing the market to move continuously in search of equilibrium prices.

3. World Stock Markets: the International Experience of Financial Tools

The modern stock market in modern understanding first emerged during the end of 16th century because of increased state issuing activity formation of the joint-stock companies. These in turn stem from medieval bill fairs and bill markets periodically arising and disappearing throughout the 13th and 14th centuries. Trade bills were predecessors of modern stock markets, marking the first occurrence of professional participants in a securities market, and they evolved into the first stock exchanges on which transactions of both goods and bills were made. The first stock exchanges offering the trade in securities were established in 16th century in Antwerp (1531) and Lyons.

This early securities trade concerned state securities-trade in state promissory notes led to the development of modern stock exchanges and investment institutes.

The current state of the world stock exchanges testifies to the prevailing volume of operations with state bonds (Table 10-2). In the history of stock exchange formation, a special role was played by bonds. Rather low risks provided the opportunity to expand use of the given financial tool in global stock markets. By 2011, Japan took second place in terms of the volume of bonds available a securities market. Orientation on a public debt has helped to avoid losses stemming from financial instability.

Table 10-2 Structure of Bonds Market up to the End of 2012

Country	Market volume (bln. USD)	Share in the world (%)
USA	16.7	46.0
Japan	6.7	18.4
Germany	2.5	6.9
Great Britain	1.4	3.9
France	1.4	3.9
Other countries	7.6	20.9
All	36.3	100.0

The policy of economic liberalization eventually created the preconditions for interaction between and integration of national stock markets, expansion of their scopes of operations, and movement of private capital between countries.

The positive dynamics behind the internationalization of world stock markets can be seen in the data about parity in international operations for bonds (Table 10-3).

Under present conditions, the U.S. capital market appreciably serves as a conjuncture of the world's capital markets because of its level of capitalization, which confidently exceeds that of any other country (Table 10-4).

The high conjuncture of stock markets in developed countries by the end of the year 2000 played an important role in supporting high levels of business activity in Western countries,

Table 10-3 International Operations with Shares and Bonds (in % to GDP)

Country	Year							
	1975-1981	1982-1992	1993-2003	2004	2005	2008	2009	2012
USA	5.9	43.2	108.7	132.6	156.2	207.9	222.8	178.9
Japan	2.8	73.0	84.3	64.8	79.5	95.4	90.6	85.1
Germany	6.9	32.3	102.5	167.3	195.8	256.3	328.9	334.3

Table 10-4 Shares of Security Markets in World Capitalization

Capitalization level	Year			
	1990	2000	2008	2011
All Country (bln. USD; share, %)	9.3	25.0	35.0	20.0
Developed (Excluding the USA)	65.0	42.0	36.0	46.0
USA	30.0	50.0	55.0	50.0
Developing countries	5.0	8.0	9.0	4.0

stimulating scientific and technical progress, modernizing manufacturing, and increasing capital concentrations. Strengthened relations between financial and real economy sectors also developed. The U.S. has now witnessed the emergence of a network of stock exchanges based in cities as far apart and numerous as New York, Chicago, Boston, San Francisco, Kansas City, Los Angeles, Detroit, New Orleans, Dallas, Philadelphia, Cincinnati, and Salt Lake City. The New York stock exchange occupies the lead position as it provides more than 70% of all stock market operations. Out of its 1366 members, 1226 represent the interests of 523 private corporations, and approximately 140 members operate on its own behalf. In December, 2011 alone, the place cost made US$2.6 million. One feature of this network of the American stock exchanges is that they execute operations with back issues of securities, a feature reducing the difference between actions and other types of monetary investments. Stock values have steadily increased.

In 1988, U.S. stock values had increased by 34 times in relation to 1940 values, a figure reaching 251 times by 2003. These figures continue to increase every day.

The London stock exchange, likewise, can be considered the leader in the UK's network of 22 stock exchanges. The London stock exchange conducts more than 60% of all securities operations in the country. The minimum transaction volume in London is one thousand pounds sterling for usual actions and bonds and 100 securities of any kind.

The London stock exchange, unlike New York's, only offers basic attention to derivatives. In spite of the fact that the basic share of operations at the given stock exchange is concentrated in tools such as bonds and actions, the development and wide application of options, futures, and swaps opens the door to involve significant financial assets in the national economy.

Approximately half of the transactions on the London stock exchange involve actions outside national borders. In addition, the number of foreign banks participating in the London stock exchange has overtaken those active in New York. The given postulate has received the truthful proof and in a course of regression analysis.

With the advent of new financial tools in U.S. stock markets, the New York stock exchange began to widely use tools such as options and futures. As the econometrical analysis (correlation, dispersion, regression) shows, gross national product level increasingly depends on financial tools used in the New York stock exchange, including options and traditional stocks.

The New York stock exchange's options trade uses the Black-Scholes model for estimating the efficiency of financial tools. The given model works successfully provided that the secondary market covers a bigger volume of transactions than the stock exchange.

Unlike two previous stock exchanges, results of the analysis determining the definition of effective financial tools in the Tokyo stock exchange have shown that financial tools such as state bonds can serve as a unique factor of influence on stock market development. As the state plays a prevailing role in Japan, this implies that only the state can regulate the profitableness of a country's stock market.

The Tokyo stock exchange is Japan's largest stock exchange. Its greatest volume is occupied by the actions of the private companies, with a rather small share comprised of promissory notes with fixed income. In 1973, with the permission of the Ministry of Finance, the Tokyo stock exchange allowed the first actions by foreign companies: its market began the process of internationalization. The requirements for a foreign company to establish a stock quote were more rigid than for national companies, and this requirement is in keeping with the theory that the state always aspires to support the national economy.

From Table 10-5, it follows that the New York stock exchange is in the lead for all actions. On other parameters, however, the London stock exchange leads; this means that the Tokyo stock exchange generally quotes securities from Great Britain. State bonds, among other indicators, have the lowest value and the tendency of the state to leave the arena of the Tokyo stock exchange is examined.

Table 10-5 Number of Companies, which have Emissions on Tokyo Stock Exchange in 2012

Stock Exchange	Tokyo Stock Exchange	New York Stock Exchange	London Stock Exchange
Shares	1990	2700	2500
Bonds	60	400	500
Foreign emission	500	480	1630
Private emission	480	410	880
State emission	4	7	55

Table 10-5 shows the entities whose securities were quoted at the Tokyo stock exchange in comparison with separate leading stock exchanges in other countries.

In conditions of world crisis, consolidation at the national level is insufficient for active participation in the global competitive struggle. Stock exchanges are compelled to enter markets in other countries to expand and diversify their field of the activity.

As a result, developed countries intend to take long-term measures for preventing the consequences of a world financial and economic crisis by granting state guarantees for those involved with companies' and investors' financial assets, arranging for the sale of banks nationalized by the state, conducting audits of all commercial and investment banks to reveal potential problems, and creating a commission on the management of inefficient financial tools, the structure of which will include qualified stock market participants.

4. Uzbekistan's Stock Market and the Prospect of Applying the International Experience of Effective Implementation of Financial Tools in Conditions of World Financial and Economic Crisis

The dynamics of an exchange over the previous years shows that in 2006-2010, the revival of the market and activation of stock market participants testifies that financial tools function up to the mark. While during 2003-2005, stock exchange annual turnovers fluctuated within 35-42 billion Uzbek soms, in 2006, the given indicator has for the first time exceeded 100 billion Uzbek soms. The share of a turn of the secondary market, which is the important factor behind the development of stock market stability, prevails. As shown in the analysis of the first years of functioning of banks in the Uzbek stock market, ignoring both the general and specific features mentioned above has negatively affected investment rates and dealer activity as well as lowered improvements in quality of service for stock market participants.

Banks occupy the major place in the formation and functioning of Uzbekistan's system securities market, which in comparison with other types of managing subjects, provide optimum conditions for activity in the securities market.

V. Conclusion

According to the stated research aim, the following conclusions have been drawn:
- Currently, securities market development is in many respects defined by the realization of privatization programs.
- Adoption of laws regarding mortgage lending is a precondition to new levels of Central Bank involvement.
- The securities market infrastructure is generated to carry out broker activities including

depositories, consulting, and estimating organizations.
- Currently, an essential reduction in the volume of the corporate bonds exists that is not compensated by new releases; meanwhile in Uzbekistan's debt capital market, corporate bonds are the most profitable tools of investment.

Developing Uzbekistan's market of financial tools requires acceptance of a number of measures that will minimize the risks connected with estimating the efficiency of financial tools. Against rapid rates of development in separate indicators that, in our opinion, characterize successful development of this economic segment, this work has developed a number of options:

1) The current primary goal of applying corporate management principles to joint-stock companies could ensure their adequate participation in stock market.

2) Achieving dynamic development of the stock market requires not only execution of a policy of stimulating the securities market but also other measures that require making policy decisions connected with its further development.

3) A number of reforms and additions to the legal base regulating the securities market, in particular, separate financial tools, are required.

4) As of today, municipal bonds have not received due development. This financial tool can serve as a guarantee for investors and increase their trust in a securities market. On the other hand, municipal loans could solve questions of sufficient financing of various economic spheres and stimulation of economic growth.

5) To create an infrastructure that enables a wide consultation of emitters with a view to activate the securities trade as well as play a part in domestic share holdings of joint-stock companies in international financial markets for attracting foreign investments and use new financial tools.

6) Sufficient development for a securities market has not occurred, according to the consulting organizations. Absence of transparency in a stock market does not offer investors the possibility of adequately estimating the situation and, as a result, to participate. Accordingly, introducing a system of ratings in the financial market could provide a mechanism of market transparency regarding the activity of various types of emitters, and allow uninitiated investors to explore the possibilities of the capital market.

7) Adhering to certain model that offers an optimum strategy of market management, and would provide an effective means of utilizing those or other financial tools.

8) A prominent aspect of the further development of Uzbekistan's stock market is improving the quality of spent privatization and a solution to the problem of fair estimation of enterprises' market cost. This problem can be solved by the stock exchange via analysis of exchange quotations of the securities of joint-stock companies.

9) Currently, institutional investors form one basic component of a market economy, without whom high-grade development of the financial market is impossible. Further development

of institutional investors can promote rapid development of the stock market. In Uzbekistan, various financial institutions, commercial banks, investment funds, and insurance organizations have been created and the principal cause of their insufficient development is lack of investors' financial assets. Therefore, it is necessary to provide auctions of small prizes at the stock exchange to attract investors' participation in the securities market.

10) It is necessary to regulate basic aspects of the infrastructure serving such a specific and rather new sector of economy as the stock market. This economic sector is an integral part of the process of financial globalization. Without a sufficiently developed stock market, foreign investments will not be attracted to the country.

11) Maintenance of strict regulations on stock market activity is necessary for preventing speculative operations that can lead to financial imbalances and, as a result, threaten the country's economic safety.

12) Maintenance of infrastructure for the international exchange trade in the national stock market should be a priority. Integration into the international securities trade could stimulate both domestic and foreign investors as well as offer the use of effective financial tools.

The national securities market processes an insignificant volume compared with other markets; nevertheless, we should ensure that it possesses all necessary attributes of a modern stock market and be adapted to the global system of capital markets. The state should enact a policy to minimize the risks for investors in the securities market, protect investors' and securities owners' property and non-property rights, as well as maintain the economic safety and the law and order in this economic sector. Effective utilization of the potential of a securities market is a fundamental basis for the investment of means in real sectors and building a reliable economic sector in the republic.

VI. Economic Development and Forecast for Uzbekistan:
Economic Development in Uzbekistan up to 2011 and its Forecast for 2012-2013

Uzbekistan's economy has so far shown resistance to the global financial crisis, according to an IMF summary (memorandum of specialists). Its high margin of safety in foreign-economic and fiscal areas, low exposure to risks inherent in global financial markets, rising prices for most commodities exported by Uzbekistan (gold, copper, and gas), renewed economic growth in major trading partner countries, and continuing public investment have all protected the economy from the global crisis.

In the first quarter of 2012, economic growth rates remained high. Following the enactment of policies to stimulate demand, GDP growth, according to reports, amounted to 8.3% in 2011 and reached 7.5% in the first quarter of 2012 (Table 10-6).

The main growth drivers were services, transport, communications, and commerce. Its external position remains strong and is based on high rates of exports and increasing remittances. Imports have shown growth, mainly due to significant imports of investment goods within the framework of Government program to modernize the industry.

A recent decline in world food prices has not impacted Uzbekistan's inflation. Policies to stimulate demand, such as the weakening of the national currency for the purpose of maintaining competitiveness and an increase in administered prices, have led to inflation that has been maintained at an annual rate of around 13% according to an alternative methodology.

The results executing the budget in 2011 and the first quarter of 2012 were higher than allowed for in the approved rates.

The budget surplus in the larger view (including the Fund for Reconstruction and Development) has grown to 9% of GDP, compared to 4.9% in 2010, which is, among other factors, encouraged by favorable commodity prices, while costs were rather lower than envisaged in the budget.

In recent months, monetary policy has significantly toughened. The central bank has stepped up operations to sterilize the excess liquidity formed as a result of the accumulation of foreign assets, while the government continued to accumulate deposits. As a result, in 2011, a significant decline in main monetary and credit aggregates occurred. Broad money supply continues to outpace the official nominal GDP growth rate while the weakening of the official nominal exchange rate was in line with expectations.

The banking sector situation remains stable. The capital injections forming the government's capitalization of the banking sector continue to be adequate.

The recent technical assistance mission has identified the following priority areas:
- strengthening prudential standards;
- on-site and remote testing;
- stress testing; and
- management of foreign exchange funds.

The short-term economic development forecast is favorable. Growth rates in 2012-2013 are expected to remain high, although lower than in 2011 because of increasing uncertainty in the external environment. It is expected that economic activity will continue to rely on investments in industry and infrastructure under the state's leading hand and higher prices for Uzbek export goods.

In recent years, Uzbekistan has intensified efforts to develop the country's economic potential by pursuing a policy aimed at improving the economy's sustainability and competitiveness as well as its investment in human capital. To achieve tangible results, the following measures of economic policy are recommended in the short term:
- Authorities should focus on measures to reduce inflation; and
- A steady decline in inflation to single digits by the end of the level of 2013 remains the main task of a complex macroeconomic policy.

In accordance with the previously proposed recommendations, the authorities should take the following actions:

- Prevent fiscal policy mitigation while continuing to preserve all revenues received in excess of budgeted levels, as well as reduce non-priority spending on goods and services while maintaining expenditure on the social protection system. The budget for 2012 (adjusted for economic cycle phase and commodity prices) involves extending the structural fiscal surplus of 2% of GDP;
- Calibrate monetary policy by reducing reserves accumulation to increase the volume of sterilization and provide positive interest rates in real terms to improve management of demand pressures resulting from government spending. In the event of deterioration in the global economy, the situation will require a reduced degree of monetary tightening; and

Table 10-6 Uzbekistan: Selected Economic Indicators, 2008-2013

	2008	2009	2010	2011	2012	2013
National income	Forecast					
Nominal GDP (in billion Uzbek soms)	37,747	49,043	61,794	77,751	96,893	117,844
Nominal GDP (in million of US dollars)	28,605	33,461	38,963	45,353	51,572	57,886
(In percent)						
GDP at current prices	33.9	29.9	26.0	25.8	24.6	21.6
GDP deflator	22.9	20.2	16.1	16.2	16.4	14.2
GDP at constant prices	9.0	8.1	8.5	8.3	7.0	6.5
Official	8.0	7.4	7.3	7.6		
An alternative (and IMF staff calculations) [a]	14.4	10.6	12.1	13.3	11.0	11.0
Official	7.2	7.8	7.5	7.6		
An alternative (and IMF staff calculations) [a]	12.7	14.1	9.4	12.8	12.7	10.9
Average salary (Uzbek soms a month)	277,589	390,007	506,437	633,660		
(Changes in percent per year)						
Money and credit						
Reserve Money	31.2	30.5	27.1	20.0	20.9	
Broad money	38.7	40.8	52.4	32.3	29.7	
Net foreign assets	39.5	35.1	31.9	35.2	24.9	
Net domestic assets	-40.2	-30.6	-14.2	-38.5	-19.7	
Including. Net claims on general government	-115.2	-22.1	-33.2	-58.7	-25.4	
Credit to economy	33.6	40.4	42.4	32.0	25.5	
The velocity of circulation (in levels)	5.8	5.3	4.4	4.2	4.0	
Exports of goods and services (in million of US dollars)	12,158	11,536	12,453	15,000	16,068	17,074
Imports of goods and services (in million of US dollars)	11,393	11,698	11,215	14,167	15,410	16,395
The real exchange rate eff (avg official course, altern. CPI-reduced)	-1.7	11.4	-4.8	-3.8		

	(In percent of GDP unless otherwise indicated)					
Current account	8.7	2.2	6.2	5.8	4.5	4.5
Outstanding external debt	13.1	15.0	14.8	13.3	12.8	12.3
External debt service ratio [b]	6.2	5.8	4.1	3.9	4.6	5.2
Consolidated revenues and grants	33.7	33.1	32.4	32.0	32.4	32.5
Consolidated expenditure and net lending	32.4	33.5	32.0	31.4	33.6	34.0
Statistical discrepancy	2.6	0.6	1.6	1.5	-	-
Consolidated Balance of balance Budget [c]	39.0	20.0	20.0	21.0	-1.2	-1.5
Revenue of Fund for Reconstruction and Development	7.0	3.6	4.6	8.2	6.2	5.5
Expenses of the Fund for Reconstruction and Development	0.7	1.0	1.6	1.4	1.5	1.4
Balance	6.3	2.6	3.0	6.9	4.8	4.1
Extended Balance of state finances	10.2	2.8	4.9	9.0	3.6	2.6
Public debt (as a percentage of GDP)	12.7	11.0	10.0	9.1	8.8	8.5
Including Foreign national debt	11.5	10.3	9.4	8.5	8.3	8.1
Nominal GDP per capita (in US dollars)	1,039	1,195	1,367	1,559	1,751	1,942
Outstanding external debt (in millions of US dollars)	3,748	5,022	5,753	6,053	6,599	7,097
Exchange rate (sum per US dollar, end of period)	1,393	1.511	1,640	1,795		
Credit to economy (in percent of GDP)	15.2	16.4	18.5	19.4	19.6	19.4
Broad money (percent of GDP)	17.3	18.7	22.6	23.8	24.8	26.3
Population (mln)	27.5	28.0	28.5	29.1	29.4	29.8

(Sources) Authorities of Rep. of Uzbekistan, calculations and forecasts of IMF staff

a) The authorities began to introduce CPI-based formula Rothwell in November 2011. Historical data since 2004 were presented. At the present time data harmonization by the CPI data for past periods is being carried out, which is obtained by the authorities in the framework of IMF staff calculations using internationally accepted methodology.

b) As a percentage of exports of goods and services

c) Based on funding under the line

Statistical Yearbook. Major trends and indicators of economic and social development of Uzbekistan during the years of independence (1990 to 2010) and the forecast for 2011-2015.

○ Step up implementation of an announced comprehensive reform program. In the short term, the priority areas will continue to deepen financial intermediation and trade facilitation.

To this end, the authorities are encouraged to

- Eliminate imbalances in the foreign exchange market. This will help build on the recent advances in the management of cash, foreign exchange market development, and trade liberalization; and

- Continue to strengthen confidence in the banks by further improving banking supervision and cash management, as well as the liberation of the banks of the functions of tax administration.

Consultations in 2012 are tentatively scheduled for October-November. Analytical work will focus on studying the driving forces and barriers to economic growth, as well as methods to improve the efficiency of macroeconomic policy in light of heightened global vulnerability factors, including risks associated with the effects of a sharp fall in world commodity prices.

To regulate outstanding issues related to the CPI methodology, the mission will include an expert from the IMF's Statistical Department.

References

MAIN LITERATURE

Berge, John and E. Beinks (1998), *Advanced Options Trading: The Analysis and Evaluation of Trading Strategies, Hedging Tactics And Pricing Models*, Irwin Professional Publishing.

Cox, John C. (1985), *Option Markets*, Prentice-Hall Inc.

Daigler, Robert T. (1994), *Advanced Options Trading: the Analysis and evaluation of Trading Strategies*, Irwin Professional Publishing.

Finerty, Johnson (2010), *Financial Derivatives*, 2nd ed., Blackwell Publishers Ltd.

Hull, John C. (2000), *Futures, Options and other Derivatives*, 4th ed., Prentice-Hall Inc.

Kolb, Robert W. (1998), *Financial Derivatives*, 2nd edition, Blackwell Publishers Ltd.

Lederman, Jess R. (1998), *Exotic Options: Instruments. Analysis and Applications*, McGraw-Hill.

Luft, Carl F. (2000), *Understanding and Trading Futures: A Hands-On Study Guide For Investors and Traders*, Probus Publishing House.

Natenberg, Sh.(1994), *Option Volatility and Pricing.* 2nd edition, Probus Publishing Company.

Reports from official web sites of Tokyo Stock Exchange, London Stock Exchange, New York Stock Exchange. www.tse.com, www.nyse.com, www.lse.com.

Siegel, Daniel R. (1994), *The Futures Markets: The Professional Traders' Guide to Portfolio Strategies, Risk Management and Arbitrage*, Probus Publishing House.

Strickland, Chris (2000), *Implementing Derivatives Models*, John Wiley & Sons Ltd.

ANALYTICAL PAPERS

DeFusco, Richard A. (2009), *Quantitative Investment Analysis*, Cambridge: Wiley.

Gazieva, S. (2012), Uzbekistan Oil And Gas Industry Seeks Foreign Investment For Ambitious Plans. Asset capital partners, February 2012.

Korjubaev, A. (2007), "Oil and Gas Complex of Uzbekistan in the International System of Energy Provision," *Economy and Management*, 3.

Laura, Wood, Uzbekistan Oil and Gas Report Q4 2010. Eastern Daylight Time. http://www.researchandmarkets.com/research/d4ae61/uzbekistan_oil_and_gas/.

Majitov, Sh. (2012), Investment Potential of Uzbekistan's Oil and Gas Industry. Official Report of "Uzbekneftegas" for 1 April 2012.

Marr, Julian (2004), *Investing in Emerging Markets: The BRIC Economies and Beyond (Securities Institute)*, CA: Wiley & Sons.

Philimonova, I. (2010), "Mineral Resources of Russia and Other CIS Countries," *Economy and Management*, 6.

Salikhov, T. (2012), "Current Status and Prospects for Energy Resources and Infrastructure Development of Uzbekistan, Institute of Power Energy and Automation of Uzbekistan," *Bulletin of the Academy of Science*, 2.

ANNUAL REPORTS AND BULLETINS

Coal Joint-Stock Association, 2001-2012yy.

Energy Efficiency and Energy Supply in CIS, UNECE, 2001.

Initial Communication of Uzbekistan under the United Nations Framework Convention on Climate Change, 1999.

National Statistical Bulletin, 2000-2012yy.

State Committee for Nature Protection, 2010.

Uzbek-Energo Company, 2000-2012yy.

Chapter 11

IMPORTANCE OF INNOVATIVE ENDOGENOUS INDUSTRIAL POLICIES FOR SHRINKING CITIES ALONG THE SILK ROAD

I. Introduction[1]

This chapter discusses about the economic aspect of sustainability and endogenous economic development strategies for shrinking cities in China, focusing on the socio-economic contribution of their small and medium-scale enterprises (SMEs) to their economic resilience. Referring to Walker *et al.* (2010) as the base of theoretical framework, this chapter pursues three purposes. First, this chapter highlights the importance of public policies to improve performance of SMEs in local economies. These policies function as investment for "resilience capital" of the community. Second, this chapter introduces a US-born "Economic Gardening" program as an example of such policies to support local SMEs. Finally, this chapter discusses opportunities and challenges in applying the "Economic Gardening" program to Chinese cities.

Stratfor, a private news and intelligence analysis service in the U.S., reported on March 10, 2014 that Beijing government created centrally coordinated regional economic zones encompassing multiple provinces with similar or potentially complementary industrial structures. Those economic zones were Bohai Economic Rim (Beijing-Tianjin-Dalian-Qingdao), North China Economic Region (Beijing-Tianjin-Hebei), Central Plains Economic Zone (Henan-Shaanxi-Anhui-Shandong), Yangtze River Delta (Shanghai and its vicinities), "Central Soviet" (Jiangxi-Fujian), and Pearl River Delta (Shenzhen-Zhuhai). Stratfor explained that this approach emerged from the central government's struggle to negotiate and maintain relative parity among the often-conflicting interests of China's geographically, culturally and economically diverse regions. This policy will favor the cities and provinces in the above-mentioned

---

[1] Readers will find that the contents of this chapter are different from those of other chapters. This chapter does not have mathematical models, regression equations, or quantitative analysis. Instead, it intends to analyze the social and economic phenomena in shrinking cities, and to prescribe endogenous economic development strategies in those cities. Readers are requested not to confuse "endogenous economic development" in this chapter with "endogenous growth model" developed by Paul Romer and other economists. "Endogenous economic development" refers to the economic development utilizing the resources (i.e. entrepreneurship, talents, small capital, supply network, and market) existing within the locality, rather than recruiting from outside.

economic zones, but will put economic challenges on cities that were not selected.[2]

A city's growth relies on its capacity of value production. When its productivity and production capacity starts to decline and loses its comparative advantage, a city will experience the loss of companies in operation and its population. The topic of "shrinking cities" is a relatively new, especially compared to the topics of economic growth in urban areas and growth management. Considering the coming change in demographic structure in China, however, it is worth learning from various cases in many countries (including Japan, where the society experiences rapid and large scale of aging) and developing strategies and solutions of the issue in China.

Chinese economy has been growing at a very high pace with an average annual growth of over 8% during the past 20 years. For example, economic development in Anhui, Jiangxi, Shaanxi provinces has been promoted through active investment in industries such as natural resource development (coal, oil, and natural gas), steel, non-ferrous metals, plant manufacturing, and electronics. Chang (2010) finds that investment in these industries contributed to higher labor productivity and then higher income of the residents. These industries have been promoted through investment from state enterprises or foreign firms. In spite of the record of the past rapid economic development, some Chinese cities have stagnant or even negative population growth. This may be attributed to external factors such as the loss of competitiveness in the global economy or a natural disaster, or to internal factors like the industrial development cycle, the exhaustion of natural resources, unavailability of quality workers. For sustainable development of Chinese cities, it is important to depart from development strategies relying on low-cost factors of production (such as cheap labor and natural resources in the vicinity), and to seek for industrial policies based on innovation and entrepreneurship by local firms.

II. Shrinking Cities in the World

The Shrinking Cities International Research Network (SCIRN) defines a 'shrinking city' as "a densely populated urban area with a minimum population of 10,000 residents that has faced population losses in large parts for more than two years and is undergoing economic transformations with some symptoms of a structural crisis" (See Hollander *et al.* (2009) for the detail). This paper employs this definition.

UN-HABITAT (2008) provides an overview of shrinking cities in the world. "In 2000, nearly 100 million people were living in cities whose populations were declining, representing 8.3% of the total urban population in developing nations. Half of the population loss in shrinking

---

[2] "China Takes a Regional Approach to Economic Development", Stratfor. Members-only article downloaded from http://www.stratfor.com/analysis/china-takes-regional-approach-economic-development on March 10, 2014.

cities took place in big cities of between 1 and 5 million, and almost one-fourth in intermediate cities of 500,000 to 1 million. These cities are not only experiencing a dramatic decline in their populations, but also in their economic and social bases. Asian cities are the most affected by population decline; they account for 60% of all shrinking cities in the developing world. Most of these cities are in China."[3] The UN-HABITAT analysis of 143 cities with declining populations in the developing world provides a preliminary overview of the causes behind these changes, which can be grouped into four types: suburbanization and the growth of nucleations, economic decline, selective decline (political choices), and administrative reclassification.[4]

Wu *et al.* (2014) provides typology of shrinking cities focusing on the causes of shrinkage, taking into account the national and local contextual conditions. They find three types of shrinkage: (i) shrinkage is imposed either by nature or external forces (including external to the local region); (ii) shrinkage due to comparative disadvantage; and (iii) shrinkage due to societal and global changes. In the first category of "imposed shrinkage", the underlying causes of the shrinkage are such as political and military conflicts, spatial and administrative reforms (initiated by national government) or the depletion of the natural resources. These causes are beyond the control of the local community. The second category of "shrinkage due to comparative disadvantage" reflects many cases where cities become unable to compete with other cities, because of availability and effectiveness of infrastructure, cost and quality of labor force, availability and effectiveness of technology, changes in the performance of their main industries, business environment, and people's lifestyle. The third category of "societal and global changes" refers to the changes such as continuous decline of birthrate and climate changes. Since these are beyond control of any communities, what they can do is to cope with the situation, and to develop strategies that maximize their opportunities.

As mentioned above, there are several types of shrinkage. Solutions to each type are essentially different. It is, therefore, important to identify the cause of shrinkage in a particular city when solutions are formulated and proposed.

III. Shrinking Cities and Depopulation in Japan

Taking Japan as an example, this section highlights the challenges in managing economy in shrinking cities. Residents in Japanese small cities have been expecting that their cities could prosper and avoid circumstances where their communities would become dysfunctional. However, National Land Council (2011) warns that about 80% of the Japanese cities will face depopulation of more than 25% between 2005 and 2050. This publication was prepared before the destruction in eastern Japan caused by the great earthquakes, and the estimate in the report

---

[3] UN-HABITAT (2008), p.43

[4] *Op. cit.*, pp.43-46.

must already be underestimated without the impact of the disaster. Hayashi and Saito (2012) provides more pessimistic forecast, suggesting that some cities will lose the entire population before 2040.

Masuda and Depopulation Research Group (2013) analyzes that municipalities with small population of young women will lose their residents in the future. They use the population of young women in the age group of 20 through 39 as a proxy indicator of "reproduction" capacity of a municipality. They are important in terms of maintaining population because they can centrally engage in bearing and caring children. Municipalities without job opportunities for them and their husband will lose the young women, and the reproduction capacity of the municipalities declines. Using the estimate by the National Institute of Population and Social Security Research, Masuda and Depopulation Research Group conclude that 523 municipalities in Japan (29.1% of all the municipalities) will become unsustainable and will only have population of less than 10 thousand in 2040.

Based on the discussion by Kühn and Fischer (2011), we can see that shrinking cities in Japan and East Germany have similar characteristics in terms of the multi-dimensional interaction of different challenges. First, demographic problems have been caused by a decline in population due to a lack of birth, migration of the youth, and the aging of residents. Second, urban economic problems involve the loss of employment due to de-industrialization, and job losses linked to de-industrialization could not be compensated for by growth within the service sector. Third, urban problems include an overcapacity of public infrastructure, large brownfield areas, and vacant residential and commercial property. Finally, these demographic and socio-economic processes of decline have resulted in weakened financial conditions within the affected municipalities, which have in tern greatly limited local government's scope of action.

Depopulation, comparative disadvantage of local firms, and loss of local amenities are closely related to shrinkage of a city. However, they are not its direct causes. Shrinking cities and low-performance SMEs in those cities are in vicious circles as shown in the Figure 11-1. "Products" here include services.

IV. Model on Economic Resilience in Shrinking Cities

Walker *et al.* (2004) defines "resilience" as "the capacity of a system to absorb disturbance and reorganize while undergoing change so as to still remain essentially the same function, structure, identity, and feedbacks." This definition is comprehensive and fundamental. Building Resilient Regions project at the Institute of Governmental Studies, the University of California at Berkeley, defines "regional resilience" as "the ability of a place to recover from a stress, either an acute blow, as in the case of an earthquake or major plant closing, or a chronic strain,

Figure 11-1 Vicious Circles for SMEs in Shrinking Cities

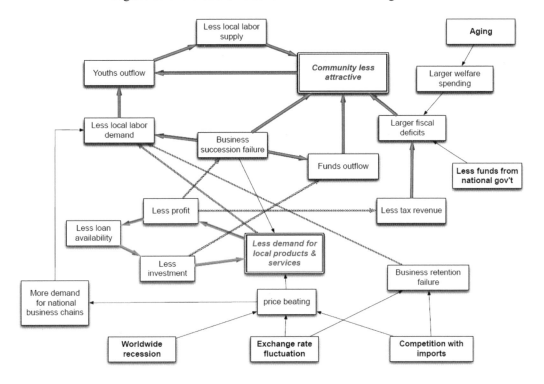

as may occur with longstanding economic decline or unremitting rapid population growth."[5] This chapter employs such definition of the "regional resilience" since it focuses on the resilience of a town or a community.

This chapter introduces a theoretical model based on Walker *et al.* (2010), which incorporates resilience into inclusive wealth model. One of the characteristics of the model is that it does not assume the existence of optimal state or optimizing behavior of actors. This characteristic is attractive because it is unrealistic to pursue dynamic optimal state or optimizing behavior in an attempt to build resilient community. The model pays attention to the relationship between community welfare and sustained business performance of SMEs located in the municipality. This relationship is important because local SMEs are perceived as the sources of income and employment for the residents.

Figure 11-2 shows how we can understand regional resilience in this model. The size of a "stock of resilience", or "resilience capital", is expressed as the distance in the "sustained business performance" from the initial state to the unstable threshold. The closer to the threshold, the lower the resilience capital, and the higher is the probability that the community welfare drops into the alternate regime. Starting from the initial state (point A), the level of the community welfare improves as the sustained business performance becomes better, and the resilience capital becomes higher. This movement is shown on the trajectory from point A

---

[5] The project's webpage (http://brr.berkeley.edu/rci/site/faqs) viewed on March 10, 2013.

Figure 11-2 Resilience Capital

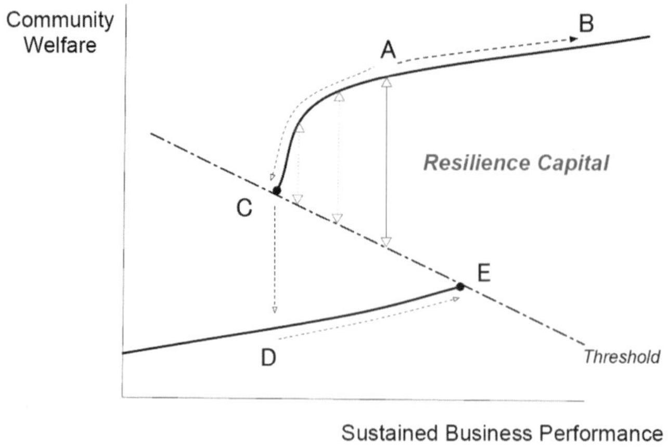

to point B. On the other hand, as the business performance turns worse, the movement toward point C reduces the resilience capital. The business performance exceeds the critical threshold level, the system transforms and the level of community welfare drops to point D. Recovery to the original regime is almost impossible even if the business performance improves, and the community welfare can achieve as low as point E. Investment is necessary to maintain and increase the size of resilience capital and to avoid the negative system change. Such investment would improve the sustained business performance and the community welfare. The next question is: what kind of policies / programs are necessary to enhance economic resilience in shrinking cities?

V. Policies to Enhance Economic Resilience

An OECD report says that sustainable planning models for shrinking communities is one of the seven areas of notable policy and strategic focus for sustainable local economic and job development in view of demographic change scenarios: "addressing the issue of sustainable development models that move away from the growth paradigm requires different instruments and strategies strongly anchored to the local situation and the manifestations of shrinkage."[6]

It is necessary to increase employment of local firms, to raise income of local residents, and to promote fund circulation at local level so that the shrinkage of local economy can be avoided and economic resilience can be enhanced. Young people will have to move out without attractive jobs in local towns. Local economy cannot be sustained if residents' income is kept low or funds continue leak out of the area.

Supporting "basic industries" is usually effective for the growth of local economy. An

---

[6] Martinez-Fernandez and Weyman (2012), p.30.

industry can be recognized as a basic industry when its output is larger than local demand, and the surplus is exported to outside the area, bringing incoming funds in return. Basic industries are the keys in sustaining and developing local economy. Income brought by basic industries can be used to finance imports and taxation. Basic industries can be manufacturing, agriculture, or even tourism depending on the geographical and historical background of the area. Promotion of the basic industries in a city may not directly lead to local economic development, especially when their products are not competitive. Competition of low price will fail to increase income of the residents, and therefore, will not contribute to economic development.

Jacobs (1985) says that ability of import replacement in a city is the key to understand the rise and decline of the city's wealth and its sustained growth. She also explains that successful cities have good pro-business "eco-system": "economies producing diversely and amply for their own people and producers, as well as for others, are better off than specialized economics like those of supply, clearance, and transplant regions. In a natural ecology, the more diversity there is, the more flexibility, too, because of what ecologists call its greater numbers of 'homeostatic feedback loops,' meaning that it includes greater numbers of feedback controls for automatic self-correction. It is the same with our economies."[7]

As Martinez-Fernandez *et al.* (2012) proposes, it is important that unique strategies should be designed and introduced for economic development in shrinking cities. "Designing skills and employment strategies for these cities requires different approaches from cities that are growing and where skills shortages relate to strong industrial demand. Declining cities need to work much harder at offering lifestyle choices together with a dynamic business environment that can attract and keep knowledge workers and their families."[8]

The next section of this chapter introduces a set of programs that are expected to perform well in shrinking cities.

VI. Economic Gardening

This chapter claims that "Economic Gardening" can improve the economic resilience for small cities. Economic Gardening is an entrepreneurial alternative to traditional economic development strategies. This new approach, created in the City of Littleton, Colorado by Christian Gibbons and his supporters in response to massive corporate layoffs, uses high end corporate-level tools and cutting edge scientific concepts to help entrepreneurial growth companies identify markets, monitor competitors, track industry trends, locate customer clusters on maps, and use search engine optimization / Google Adwords / social media for marketing and various customized research.

---

[7] Jacobs (1985), p.224.

[8] Martinez-Fernandez *et al.* (2012), p.221.

Economic Gardening was created in 1987 and implemented from 1989, and some best practices were starting to emerge by the late 1990s. Littleton has outperformed in employment growth when Economic Gardening was in operation. The US Small Business Administration (2006) introduces outstanding performance of Littleton in job creation. "Since its introduction of economic gardening principles in 1989, the number of new jobs in Littleton has grown from 14,907 to 35,163, or 136%. This numbers include wage-and-salary jobs plus self-employment. This growth is approximately twice the rate of the Denver region, three times that of Colorado, and six times that of the United States." The performance in job growth continued to be high even during the recession just after the turn of the century in the U.S. "Littleton's 35 % job growth between 2000 and 2005 well exceeds that of comparable inner suburban Denver communities of similar size: Englewood (7.3%), Northglenn (6.2%), and Thornton (21.4 %)."

Economic Gardening has been picked up by a number of communities and states including Wyoming, Oregon, and Florida. There was an urgent need to maintain the authenticity of Economic Gardening because some economic development consultants might have had temptation to imitate Economic Gardening and damage the brand image. Gibbons and his team in Littleton had official duties to serve their clients and could not travel across the country so often in spite of the growing interests for Economic Gardening. The Edward Lowe Foundation established the National Center of Economic Gardening in 2009. The Center now operates training programs for certified Economic Gardening managers, and provides professional services for state centers or regional centers conducting Economic Gardening.

Economic Gardening is not an application of specific economic theories, while its creators had conversation with David Birch (jobs and SMEs), Paul Romer (endogenous growth), and researchers at the Santa Fe Institute (complexity science).

Gibbons (2010, p.6) writes that economic gardening at Littleton has following underlying principles:
- Power laws (80/20 rule) that revealed a few companies made a whole lot of difference and a lot of companies made a little bit of difference;
- Network theory that described a critical factor in business success;
- Commodity traps which explained why standards of living weren't rising in agricultural areas and "business friendly" manufacturing areas;
- Temperament which turned out to be a big factor in company growth; and
- Complexity science and systems thinking which said that economies were not in equilibrium and in fact were far from equilibrium - which in turn nicely explained the turbulent "gales of creative destruction" identified by Schumpeter a half century before.

To clarify the difference from traditional economic development strategies, Gibbons (2010, pp.6-7) explains what is Economic Gardening:
- An idea that economies are driven by entrepreneurial growth;

- The public has three major roles: information, infrastructure, and connections;
- It is focused on growth companies, especially at Stage II (10-99 employees);
- It uses sophisticated corporate tools, such as database searching, geographic information systems (GIS), search engine optimization (SEO), web marketing, social media and research tools, and network mapping;
- It focuses on front-end and strategic issues of business, such as core strategy, market dynamics, marketing, teams, and finance;
- It is driven by innovation rather than the cheapest place to do business;
- It depends on a highly skilled, elite Economic Gardening staff working in an iterative manner with business owners; and
- The EG organization is as entrepreneurial as the companies with which it works.

The primary beneficiary of Economic Gardening is certainly the entrepreneurs and firms in their community that conducts the program. In addition, Economic Gardening has been serving the community itself because it makes the community more economically resilient through diversifying businesses, developing connection among businesses, universities, and other supportive organizations, and making the businesses more informed and intelligent.

The theoretical model of economic resilience introduced in the previous sections indicates that improvement in sustained business performance will raise the community welfare and enhance the resilience capital in the community. Economic development by business recruitment was popular in the U.S. and Japan, but it did not increase resilience capital because recruited firms or production plants tend to move to another place when they have better business chances. Economic Gardening is one of the effective approaches for building regions with economic resilience, and it has provided practical effectiveness in many municipalities in the United States.

VII. Implementing Economic Gardening in Silk Road Cities in China

Economic Gardening can be introduced in Chinese cities, so long as cities can implement SME-friendly policies. Weng and Woo (2013) identified three factors that provide foundation for continuous business relationship among Chinese SMEs. These are technological complementarity among the firms, difficulty in finding alternative firms in markets, and corporate strategies to secure stable relationship with other firms.[9] Ye and Leipnik (2013) find that not only a Chinese city could implement SME-friendly policies but also their pro-business policies contributed to rapid growth of private enterprises, using the case in Wenzhou Municipality in Zhejiang Province.

"Municipal and county governments in Wenzhou are locally embedded and are pro-business.

---

[9] Weng and Woo (2013), pp.171-172.

They promote local business by protecting private enterprises and improving the business environment. The Wenzhou government has been shaped not only by national policies, but more importantly, by local geographies and institutions. The local institutions of business creation and networks have created a strong presence of business owners in government and business people with strong and long-standing connection to a sympathetic locale cadre of apparatchiks and officials. In this region, business men (most business people are men) not only influence public policy but also are often government officials themselves. Local governments have implemented a series of reform policies, typically one or many steps ahead of other places in China."[10]

Cities like Wenzhou Municipality would be suitable for Economic Gardening. Implementing successful SME-friendly policies requires good staff, broad support from leaders, and sufficient time. There is no specified way to start Economic Gardening in a city, but it is recommended to follow the sequence mentioned below so that the program can be successful and sustainable.

1) A leader (usually, the city mayor) declares that the city starts preparing Economic Gardening. At this stage, it is not necessary that all the leaders in the city agree on implementing Economic Gardening.

2) A feasibility study for Economic Gardening. The study will confirm whether the city has personnel and financial capacity to implement Economic Gardening, and identify potential opportunities and challenges for Economic Gardening.

3) Leaders in the city agree that Economic Gardening will be implemented, understanding that it takes time before the program will bring visible results. They also agree that they will cooperate so that Economic Gardening will be conducted in a timely manner.

4) Detailed survey on industrial structure, supply chains, inter-firm relationship, social capital and profiles of major firms in the city. This survey intends to provide necessary information to design specific programs to support local firms.

5) If necessary, administrative staff in charge of local economic development will be trained so that they can implement SME-friendly policies.

6) Formation of specific programs to support local firms.

7) Test-drive the programs for a selected small number of firms. There is a chance to modify, improve, add, or stop specific components of the programs, depending on the results of the test drive.

8) Full implementation of the firm support programs.

It should be emphasized that each city must uniquely design programs to support local firms. Each city has its own background such as history, geography, natural resources, human resources, economic structure, and social capital. Therefore, the programs should be designed so that they are consistent with the background.

---

[10] Ye and Leipnik (2013), pp.308-309.

VIII. Conclusion

This chapter discussed about endogenous economic development strategies for shrinking cities in China, focusing on the socio-economic contribution of their small and medium-scale enterprises (SMEs) to their economic resilience. This chapter pursued three purposes. First, this chapter highlighted the importance of public policies to improve performance of SMEs in local economies. These policies function as investment for "resilience capital" of the community. Second, this chapter introduced a US-born "Economic Gardening" program as an example of such policies to support local SMEs. Finally, this chapter discussed opportunities and challenges in implementing the Economic Gardening programs in Chinese cities. It is possible to introduce the Economic Gardening programs to Chinese cities, but it should be emphasized that each city must uniquely design programs to support local firms. The Economic Gardening programs should be designed so that they are consistent with the social, environmental, and economic background of the city.

References

Chang, Xin (2010), "Chugoku-Nairikugata Keizai Seicho to Shinko Chiiki Keizaiken no Taito (China: Inland-style Economic Growth and the Emergence of New Regional Economic Zones)," in Fukui Prefectural University (ed.), *Higashi Ajia to Chiiki Keizai 2010 (East Asia and Regional Economy 2010)*, Kyoto University Press, 125-145.

Gibbons, Christian (2010), "Economic Gardening - An Entrepreneurial Alternative to Traditional Economic Development Strategies," *The IEDC Economic Development Journal*, 9 (3).

Hayashi, Naoki and Susumu Saito (2012), "Suuchi de miru shorai no noson (Quantitative analysis of Japanese farming villages in the future)," Downloaded at http://tettai.jp/info/info-10.php on March 10, 2013.

Hollander, Justin B., Karina Pallagst, Terry Schwarz, and Frank J. Popper (2009), "Planning Shrinking Cities," Downloaded on April 15, 2014 from http://policy.rutgers.edu/faculty/popper/ShrinkingCities.pdf.

Jacobs, Jane (1985), *Cities and the Wealth of Nations*, Vintage Book Edition, New York: Random House.

Kühn, Manfred and Susen Fischer (2011), "Strategic Planning - Approaches to Coping with the Crisis of Shrinking Cities," in Bernhard Müller (ed.), *German Annual of Spatial Research and Policy 2010*, Springer-Verlag Berlin Heidelberg, 143-146.

Martinez-Fernandez, Cristina and Tamara Weyman (2012), "The Crossroads of Demographic Change and Local Development," in Cristina Martinez-Fernandez *et al.*, *Demographic Change and Local Development: Shrinkage, Regeneration and Social Dynamics*, OECD.

Martinez-Fernandez, Cristina, Ivonne Audirac, Sylvie Fol and Emmanuèle Cunningham-Sabot (2012), "Shrinking Cities: Urban Challenges of Globalization," *International Journal of Urban and Regional*

Research, 36 (2), 213-225.

Masuda, Hiroya and Depopulation Research Group (2013), "2040 nen Chiho Shometsu Kyokuten Shakai ga Torai suru (Local Cities Disappear in 2040 - Coming of Polar Society)," *Chuo Koron*, December 2013, 26-27.

National Land Council (2011), "Kokudo no Choki Tembo - Chukan Torimatome (Interim Report on Long-term View of Japanese Land),"

Downloaded at http://www.mlit.go.jp/common/000135838.pdf on September 5, 2011.

The US Small Business Administration (2006), "Economic Gardening: Next Generation Applications for a Balanced Portfolio Approach to Economic Growth," Chapter 6, *The Small Business Economy for Data Year 2005: A Report to the President*.

UN-HABITAT (2008), *State of the World's Cities 2008/2009*, London: Earthscan.

Walker, Brian, C. S. Holling, Stephen R. Carpenter, and Ann Kinzig (2004), "Resilience, Adaptability and Transformability in Social-ecological Systems," *Ecology and Society*, 9 (2).

Walker, Brian, Leonie Pearson, Michael Harris, Karl-Göran Maler, Chuan-Zhong Li, Reinette Biggs, and Tim Baynes (2010), "Incorporating Resilience in the Assessment of Inclusive Wealth: An Example from South East Australia," *Environment and Resource Economics*, 45, 183-202.

Weng, Zhenqiong and Jongwon Woo (2013), *Chugoku Minkan Kigyo no Koyo Kankei to Kigyokan Kankei (Labor Management and Inter firm Relationship of Chinese Private Firms)*, Tokyo: Akashi Shoten.

Wu, Chung-Tong, Xiao-Ling Zhang, Gong-Hao Cui, and Shu-Ping Cui (2014), "Shrinkage and Expansion of Peri-Urban China," in Karina Pallagst *et al.*, *Shrinking Cities - International Perspectives and Policy Implications*, London: Routledge, 166-167.

Ye, Xinyue, and Mark Leipnik (2013), "Beyond Small Business and Private Enterprises in China: Global and Spatial Perspectives," in Ting Zhang and Roger R. Stough (eds), *Entrepreneurship and Economic Growth in China*, New Jersey: World Scientific, 289-316.

Chapter 12

ECONOMIC DEVELOPMENT OF THE NEW SILK ROAD AREA AND ITS LINKS WITH JAPAN

I. Introduction

The New Silk Road Area is positioned inland in the center of the Eurasian continent and consequently faces considerable transport difficulties in its trade with industrialized and emerging countries at both the eastern and western fringes of the continent. However, transport within the New Silk Road Area is gradually improving with the development and expansion of an international transportation network in Eurasia, providing opportunities for reconstruction and prosperity to the New Silk Road Area's hinterlands. This is a great economic opportunity for Japan. The country should link its economy with the New Silk Road Area's potential economic growth. That, in turn, will further promote economic development within the New Silk Road Area itself.

In this chapter, we will look at Japan in the context of the New Silk Road Area's economic development and discuss Japan's economic and diplomatic relationships with the New Silk Road Area. Then, we will consider Japan's future role in the economic development of the New Silk Road Area.

II. The Economic Importance of the New Silk Road Area for Japan

Japan's main export markets are the newly industrializing economies of Asia (South Korea, Taiwan, Hong Kong, and Singapore), China, North America, and Europe. With its trading partners spread out over a substantially wide area, Japan conducts most of its trade by sea freight. As can be seen from Table 12-1, the U.S. was consistently Japan's largest export market from the 1960s until the beginning of the 21st century, accounting for about 30% of Japan's exports. However, there has been a rapid expansion in the national and regional markets in Asia's newly industrializing economies since the 1970s. That has led to a rise in Japan's exports to South Korea, Taiwan, Hong Kong, and Singapore, which together purchase more than 20% of Japanese exports. Furthermore, China has come to be regarded not only as the world's factory, but also as its market, due to the country's significant economic growth since the reform and liberalization efforts that began in the late 1970s. Consequently, there has been a marked increase in Japan's exports to China. In 2011, China accounted for 19.67% of Japan's

Table 12-1 Destination of Japan's Exports (%)

Year	Asia			North America		Europe		Others
		Korea, Taiwan, HK, Singapore	China (excluding HK and Taiwan)		U.S.		Germany, UK, France, Netherkand	
1965	32.50	9.58	2.90	34.71	29.33	15.35	6.96	17.44
1970	31.23	13.68	2.94	36.73	30.75	17.41	7.43	14.63
1975	36.75	12.50	4.05	26.36	20.00	18.56	8.18	18.33
1980	38.09	14.82	3.88	29.30	24.23	17.27	10.49	15.34
1985	32.55	12.84	7.13	43.27	37.14	14.70	8.97	9.48
1990	34.11	19.75	2.13	36.34	31.49	23.36	14.24	6.19
1995	45.53	25.03	4.96	31.56	27.29	17.37	11.40	5.53
2000	43.21	23.92	6.34	34.48	29.73	17.91	11.45	4.40
2001	42.94	21.70	7.68	34.69	30.04	17.56	11.28	4.81
2002	45.83	22.65	9.56	33.19	28.54	16.33	10.28	4.65
2003	49.20	23.47	12.16	28.82	24.59	17.33	10.27	4.66
2004	34.73	24.69	13.07	26.67	22.45	17.31	9.84	21.29
	(48.44)	(24.69)	(13.06)		(22.45)	(16.72)	(9.85)	
2005	51.25	24.31	13.46	27.12	22.55	16.51	9.18	5.11
2006	50.60	23.22	14.34	27.53	22.50	16.78	8.97	5.10
2007	51.89	22.39	15.30	25.07	20.13	17.45	9.22	5.59
2008	53.75	22.08	15.98	22.38	17.54	17.66	9.02	6.21
2009	57.95	23.48	18.90	21.62	16.12	14.66	8.29	5.77
2010	59.49	23.69	19.42	20.56	15.39	13.92	7.47	6.02
2011	(55.93)	(22.73)	(19.67)	(16.40)	(15.31)	(13.31)	(8.00)	(14.36)

(Note) Figures in parentheses are calculated from database of JETRO.
(Source) Calculated from Japan Statistics Bureau, Japan Statistical Yearbook and Historical Statistics of Japan (http://www.stat.go.jp/data/guide/download/index.htm).

exports, replacing the U.S. as the biggest importer of Japanese products.

Meanwhile, Japan's trade with New Silk Road Area countries as a percentage of its overall exports is extremely small. Kazakhstan and Uzbekistan, major Central Asian nations, account for less than 0.05% of Japan's exports even as the trade volume is on the rise (see Table 12-2). Japan mainly imports iron alloy from Kazakhstan and exports automobiles, pipes, as well as construction and mining machinery to the country. Japan mainly imports gold from Uzbekistan and exports automobiles and rubber products to the nation. Thus, there exists a typical vertical specialization relationship between Japan and Central Asia.

Therefore, the bilateral trade begins and ends with the New Silk Road Area itself. The New Silk Road Area is not an intermediate location through which Japan conducts trade with third countries. For example, Japan does not trade with Europe via the New Silk Road. In fact, Kazakhstan and Uzbekistan trade only with their neighboring countries for the most part. The overland route through the the New Silk Road Area is not a major international trade route

Table 12-2 Japan's Export with Kazakhstan and Uzbekistan

Year	Kazakhstan				Uzbekistan			
	Export		Import		Export		Import	
	Thousand dollars	%	Thousand dollars	%	Thousand dollars	%	Thousand dollars	%
2001	73,266	0.018	105,345	0.030	17,774	0.004	53,207	0.015
2002	90,262	0.022	98,404	0.029	16,969	0.004	73,359	0.022
2003	99,122	0.021	153,131	0.040	43,138	0.009	92,324	0.024
2004	185,532	0.033	245,927	0.054	51,712	0.009	86,208	0.019
2005	178,518	0.030	335,095	0.065	35,413	0.006	125,071	0.024
2006	250,399	0.039	334,176	0.058	16,451	0.003	179,246	0.031
2007	214,953	0.030	400,688	0.065	64,928	0.009	160,803	0.026
2008	210,082	0.027	851,001	0.113	76,212	0.010	312,453	0.041
2009	148,430	0.026	332,112	0.060	84,784	0.015	103,388	0.019
2010	220,878	0.029	604,082	0.087	77,067	0.010	171,551	0.025
2011	340,633	0.042	759,648	0.089	233,144	0.028	48,164	0.006

(Source) Calculated from JETRO database (http://www.jetro.go.jp/world/japan/stats/trade/)

linking the eastern and western fringes of the Eurasian continent mainly because shipping costs through the New Silk Road are higher than sea freight. Thus, it has a relatively low competitive edge in terms of transport.[1]

Japan began to provide development assistance to Central Asian nations immediately after their independence. In particular, Japan attached great importance to its relations with Uzbekistan, which received Japan's official development assistance and grants more than any other Central Asian nation until 1997 (see Table 12-3). Thereafter, aid rapidly increased to Kazakhstan, a country rich in natural resources, and gradually the amount of foreign aid directed at Kazakhstan overtook that given to Uzbekistan. Consequently, ITOCHU Oil Exploration Co., Ltd. and INPEX Corporation both won rights to develop oil around the Caspian Sea in Kazakhstan and Azerbaijan.

The geopolitical importance of the Central Asian region further increased after 2001 with the establishment of the Shanghai Cooperation Organization and significant changes in the international situation caused by the Afghanistan conflict, the Iraq war, and the September 11, 2001 terrorist attack on the U.S. Accordingly, there was a temporary increase in Japanese aid to Central Asia. However, this assistance took the form of loans that had to be repaid. As a matter of fact, the amount of grants provided by Japan actually declined because of the country's deteriorating economic conditions. In 2004, Foreign Minister Yoriko Kawaguchi toured the countries of Central Asia and released a joint statement with the leaders of Uzbekistan, Kazakhstan, the Kyrgyz Republic, and Tajikistan, declaring the launch of the Central Asia plus

---

[1] Detailed analyses of the reasons for the poor competitiveness of the New Silk Road in transport are given by Hisako Tsuji (2007) and a survey by the Japan External Trade Organization (JETRO) entitled "A Survey of Korean Companies' Trends in Central Asia" (9/2010)

Table12-3 Japan's Economic Assistance with Kazakhstan and Uzbekistan
(Net Disbursements in million of US dollars)

Uzbekistan					
Year	Grants Total			Loan Aid	ODA (Total)
		Grant Aid	Technical Cooperation		
1992	1.25		1.25		1.25
1993	0.76		0.76		0.76
1994	2.55		2.55		2.55
1995	16.05	10.45	5.60		16.05
1996	23.86	19.07	4.79	1.44	25.29
1997	19.86	12.16	7.70	63.30	83.16
1998	13.42	7.81	5.61	89.59	103.00
1999	16.66	10.94	5.72	64.97	81.62
2000	12.39	5.13	7.25	69.81	82.20
2001	17.62	10.19	7.43	13.30	30.92
2002	33.48	23.11	10.37	6.68	40.16
2003	22.32	10.28	12.04	40.90	63.22
2004	21.50	7.17	14.33	78.25	99.75
2005	25.24	15.91	9.33	29.20	54.44
2006	17.84	9.49	8.35	0.77	18.61
2007	15.00	6.25	8.75	41.32	56.32
2008	19.08	10.00	9.08	29.55	48.63
2009	15.00	3.34	11.66	5.41	20.41
2010	20.43	7.37	13.05	-13.39	7.04

Kazakhstan					
Year	Grants Total			Loan Aid	ODA Total
		Grant Aid	Technical Cooperation		
1992	1.04	0.02	1.02		1.04
1993	0.85		0.85		0.85
1994	1.62		1.62		1.62
1995	4.40	0.51	3.89		4.40
1996	8.66		8.66	0.30	8.96
1997	17.25	7.03	10.22	25.84	43.08
1998	12.25	0.82	11.43	82.96	95.21
1999	19.82	8.66	11.15	47.64	67.45
2000	19.54	9.00	10.54	63.79	83.33
2001	19.36	5.80	13.55	24.57	43.93
2002	10.02	0.92	9.10	20.11	30.13
2003	15.51	4.89	10.62	120.76	136.27
2004	14.44	5.58	8.86	116.32	130.76
2005	6.19	1.09	5.10	59.97	66.17
2006	5.46	0.94	4.53	19.40	24.87
2007	8.25	0.94	7.31	35.05	43.31
2008	6.63	0.43	6.20	31.28	37.91
2009	5.51	0.57	4.94	31.62	37.13
2010	5.62	0.72	4.90	-7.43	-1.81

(Source) Japan Ministry of Foreign Affairs

(http://www3.mofa.go.jp/mofaj/gaiko/oda/shiryo/jisseki/kuni/index.php)

Table 12-4 FDI Inflow of Kazakhstan and Uzbekistan (in million of US dollars)

		2006	2007	2008	2009	2010	2011
Kazakhstan							
Total	(a)	6,663.0	7,966.0	13,118.0	10,083.0	2,931.0	8,380.0
	(c)	10,624.0	18,453.0	19,760.0	19,017.0	18,144.0	19,850.0
Korea	(b)	249.4	287.3	823.0	155.7	131.6	113.7
Japan	(c)	342.6	405.3	456.6	588.5	614.5	621.9
Uzbekistan							
Total	(d)	173.8	705.2	711.3	842.0	822.2	na
Korea	(b)	22.1	70.8	65.8	32.7	40.1	51.7

(Note) Japan's FDI to Uzbekistan was 1.4 billion yen in 2008 according to Japan Ministry of Foreign Affairs
(Source) (a) Asian Development Bank, http://www.adb.org/countries/main
(b) Export-Import Bank of Korea, http://www.koreaexim.go.kr/
(c) The National Bank of Kazakhstan, http://www.nationalbank.kz/
(d) European Bank for Reconstruction and Development,
http://www.ebrd.com/pages/research/economics/data/macro.shtml#ti

Japan dialogue. However, this effort failed to produce any substantive results. Japan's aid to Central Asia fell significantly because of the country's prolonged economic slump and huge fiscal deficit.

In the same way that ODA was reduced, there has also been a decline in foreign direct investment (FDI) in Central Asia by the private sector. Table 12-4 shows that although Japan's foreign direct investment (FDI) in Kazakhstan is on the rise and has overtaken that from South Korea, it falls short of the cumulative amounts made by South Korea for the period between 1993 and 2009. South Korea accounted for 3.15% of the cumulative total of foreign direct investment (FDI) in Kazakhstan, while Japan's share was just 2.57%. This is in stark contract with the top-ranking Netherlands (19.87%) and second-place U.S. (18.5%) (both statistics provided by Kazakhstan). Japan's foreign direct investment (FDI) in Uzbekistan was just 1.4 billion yen (2008), significantly less than that of South Korea.

III. The Importance of the New Silk Road Area for Japan in Terms of Diplomatic Relations

In terms of diplomatic relations, Japan's approach to Central Asia seems somewhat tepid. After a succession of countries in Central Asia proclaimed independence with the collapse of the Soviet Union in 1991, Japan was swift to recognize the new independent states. Japan established diplomatic relations with each of the Central Asian countries in 1992 and set up embassies in Uzbekistan and Kazakhstan in 1993. Japan developed proactive foreign policies toward Central Asia, trying to build foundations to establish a presence in the region. This was due to the fact that the countries in the region either had large populations or were rich in natural resources. They were also important from a geopolitical perspective, being located between China and Russia. In 1997, Prime Minister Ryutaro Hashimoto addressed the Japan Association of Corporate Executives and laid out his Eurasian Diplomacy (later renamed Silk Road Diplomacy). In 2004, Foreign Minister Yoriko Kawaguchi declared the launch of the Central Asia plus Japan dialogue. And in 2006, Foreign Minister Taro Aso announced a new foreign policy called the Arch of Freedom and Prosperity.[2]

Have the Japanese government's previous foreign policies such as these had any impact on the relationship between Japan and the New Silk Road Area? The Hashimoto administration's Silk Road Diplomacy regarded Central Asia, the Caucasus, China, and Russia as the Silk Road Area that links Japan and South Korea. The basic objective of the Silk Road Diplomacy was to strengthen mutual trust and understanding. It was a very significant policy in the sense that it proactively promoted mutual cooperation and development across the entire region. However, the subsequent Central Asia plus Japan dialogue and the Arc of Freedom and Prosperity foreign policy excluded China and Russia. In other words, Japan's diplomatic strategy ended up dividing the New Silk Road Area. This could not have improved the landlocked conditions for Central Asia. In 2010, when the government was controlled by the Democratic Party of Japan, Foreign Minister Katsuya Okada visited Kazakhstan and Uzbekistan to attend the Central Asia plus Japan dialogue's third conference of foreign ministers. The conference, held for the first time in four years, produced few results. These changes in Japan's foreign policy meant that it was difficult for the country to be actively involved in the construction of a major international transport route in the New Silk Road Area.

IV. Japan's Role in the Economic Development of the New Silk Road Area

We can see from the above that Japan does not take a great interest in the economic development of Central Asian nations or a plan to build a major international logistics route in the New Silk Road Area. However, that does not that mean Japan will have no involvement at all in economic development in the New Silk Road Area. Japan's position is so vitally important that its removal from the economic development of the New Silk Road Area would be unthinkable, although this point is not much recognized within Japan.

As already mentioned in Chapter 2, the Beads-type Development Strategy claims to be able to achieve economic development across a wide area by means of autonomous economic interaction between each base city. That requires that dynamism of the world economy be captured. The sources of this dynamism are industrialized nations and emerging countries with significant economic development. Japan is located on the eastern edge of the Eurasian continent, meaning it can become a source of global economic dynamism. If Japan is not involved in

---

[2] This was intended to promote "diplomacy of value" based on a philosophy of "universal values" (democracy, freedom, human rights, the rule of law, market economy) in the arc-shaped region formed by the outer edge of the Eurasian continent, including Northeast Asia, Central Asia & the Caucasus, Turkey and the 3 Baltic nations.

Figure 12-1　Shipments of Manufactured Goods of Japan's Four Major Industrial

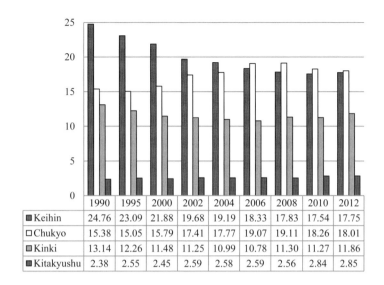

	1990	1995	2000	2002	2004	2006	2008	2010	2012
■Keihin	24.76	23.09	21.88	19.68	19.19	18.33	17.83	17.54	17.75
□Chukyo	15.38	15.05	15.79	17.41	17.77	19.07	19.11	18.26	18.01
■Kinki	13.14	12.26	11.48	11.25	10.99	10.78	11.30	11.27	11.86
■Kitakyushu	2.38	2.55	2.45	2.59	2.58	2.59	2.56	2.84	2.85

(Note) Data of the Keihin zone is derived from Saitama, Chiba, Tokyo and Kanagawa prefectures. Chukyo from Gifu, Aichi and Mie prefectures. Kinki from Osaka, Hyogo and Wakayama prefectures. Kitakyushu from Fukuoka prefecture.
(Source) Japan's Ministry of Economy, Trade and Industry, Census of Manufactures (http://www.meti.go.jp/statistics/tyo/kougyo/result-2.html)

the economic development of the New Silk Road Area, the Area's pace of development will slow.

The economic development of the New Silk Road Area will not only improve its own welfare, but also benefit the Japan, as well. This is because economic exchange with the New Silk Road Area will affect the spatial distribution of economic activity in Japan, leading to increased stimulation of Japan's economy. Such trends are starting to be seen to a slight degree in the Japanese economy as a result of East Asia's remarkable economic development. Namely, there are signs that the core of Japan's manufacturing sector is shifting westwards, due to an expansion of international trade between East Asia and Japan. In particular, there has been a slight increase in manufactured goods produced in the Kitakyushu industrial zone, which is located in relatively close proximity to East Asian countries with strong economic development. This is in contrast to other industrial areas (especially the Keihin zone) (see Figure 12-1.)

Such shifts in Japan's core economic activity associated with the economic development of neighboring Asian countries are also closely related to Japan's strategy on international logistics (particularly the strategy of the country's ports that are responsible for bulk transport). However, Japan has lost the initiative in its strategic responses in this regard. The status of Japan's ports is under threat from the enlargement and upgrading of major ports in neighboring Asian countries.

Logistics is one of the keystones of global economic activity. Consequently, any fall in the status of Japan's ports may lead to its economic activity being excluded from global dynamism. Alternatively, Japanese industry may move to regions that are more competitive in terms of location, leading to a hollowing out of industry.

In view of such necessity and urgency, the Japanese government launched measures to strengthen port functions at the start of the 21st century. The Super Hub Port Project was a proposal set out by the Council for Transport Policy of the Ministry of Land, Infrastructure, Transport and Tourism (MLIT) in a report published in 2002. It sought more efficient management and use of ports leading to increased international competitiveness via the development of large deep-water docks and the large-scale operation of port facilities. The goal was set for 2010, and Keihin Port, Ise Bay, and Hanshin Port were designated as Super Hub Ports in 2004. With the start of 2010, the government began to view the construction of a seamless distribution network to provide links inside and outside of Japan as an essential policy issue (MLIT Port Authority, 2012, p.9). This policy instituted specific measures to develop ports in rural areas of Japan (not the Tokyo metropolitan area or areas around Nagoya, Kyoto, Osaka, or Kobe) for use as international and domestic distribution centers.

Distribution between Japan and the Eurasian continent, where Central Asia is located, crosses the Sea of Japan. While there is the option of air freight, sea freight is the predominant means of transporting cargo. There are regular international shipping routes along the seaboard of the Sea of Japan, many of which are in service between Japan and the South Korean port of Busan. In fact, approximately 80% of the container cargo shipped to Busan is transferred to third countries (MLTI Port Authority, 2012, p.7), and much of the cargo dispatched from Japan uses logistics services provided by South Korea. To overcome this situation and reduce the number of transshipments via Busan, the Japanese government seems to have recognized the need to coordinate the country's multiple ports and implement initiatives to enhance their role as bases for international logistics.

In this regard, it is worth noting the Seamless Asia Plan proposed by the cities of Fukuoka and Kitakyushu. The aims of this plan are (i) to form major distribution routes centered on Asia; and (ii) promote cooperation within Asia using increases in FTA and EPA (Fukuoka-Kitakyushu, 2010, p.1). The idea was to promote cooperation among regional reports by changing their former relationship as competitors (international cooperation was also in view).

The concrete measures thought to enable the realization of the Seamless Asia Plan are (i) to make the ports in northern Kyushu the gateway for Japan's distributions with Asia on the Sea of Japan board, and (ii) to try to achieve seamless distribution between Japan, China and South Korea (Fukuoka-Kitakyushu, 2010, p.6). It is hoped that the plan will be achieved by enabling smooth distribution in the port areas with the development of large deep-water container terminals furnished with coastal distribution centers under point (i), and shortening lead times and ensuring punctuality by increasing the number of international RORO vessels in service, and reviewing customs clearance procedures by means of deregulation (e.g., streamlining customs clearance and bonded management by introducing IC tags) under point (ii).

We can see from the current conditions listed below that the plan is quite feasible. First, there are a variety of sea freight services among Kitakyushu and other Asian countries. Every month, there are 38 routes to Asian destinations for container ships, with 204 vessels in commission. On the Busan route, there are one or two international RORO vessels in service (these are low-vibration shipping) and six international ferry services each week.[3] Second, Kitakyushu has various distribution routes with services connecting it to all of Japan's other regions. There are five domestic ferry services a day to the Kansai and Kanto areas, and one a day to Shikoku. Meanwhile, domestic RORO vessels provide seven services a week to Kanto and Nagoya, respectively.[4] In addition, the rail network stretches from the Kitakyushu cargo terminal to all regions throughout Japan and there is also a high-speed road network providing access to all areas of the country via the Kyushu expressway, East Kyushu Expressway and the Sanyo Expressway. Third, in Kyushu, there is a concentration of industries that are focused on Asia (Fukuoka-Kitakyushu, 2010, p.5) The area accounts for a little over 20% of the total domestic output by the semi-conductor and electronic-component sector (with companies such as Toshiba Semiconductors, Kyocera, Asahi Kasei Electronics operating in the area), 10% of the domestic production volume automotive sector (Bridgestone, Honda Kumamoto factory), and 20% of the domestic production capacity of solar-cell related industries (Fuji Electric Systems, Showa Cell, and Mitsubishi Heavy Industries), respectively.

As such, there is already a substantial industrial base in Kyushu and it seems that the northern Kyushu ports have great potential to become the gateway to Asia on the Japanese seaboard of the Sea of Japan by improving the seamless aspects of domestic and international modes of transport. In light of this situation, the MLIT Port Authority have selected Kitakyushu Port and Shimonoseki Port as an integrated hub to act as the Hub Port on the Sea of Japan Board to strengthen the international competitiveness of ports on that seaboard.

This port strategy was never formulated with a view to the economic development of the New Silk Road Area per se. It was developed in relation to Japan and the coastal areas of the Eurasian continent, and the main export destinations of Europe and the U.S. However, there has been remarkable economic development in China and the country will not necessarily remain a production base forever. Instead, China will be transformed into a leading market. In that sense, we cannot ignore the potential for Russia as a market. Given that the structure of economic power in the Eurasian continent, including the New Silk Road Area, is expected to change considerably in the future, the importance of an international distribution

---

[3] Figures for container routes were as of August 2013; vessel numbers for international ferries are for 2011; and those for RORO routes are for 2010.

[4] Vessel numbers were as of August 2013.

route through the New Silk Road Area may continue to increase from now and is unlikely to decrease. Therefore, Japan should cooperate with the individual countries concerned, in both the public and private sectors, to develop transport infrastructure in the New Silk Road Area and be actively involved in the economic activity.

V. Conclusion

How much importance is Japan likely to attach to economic development in the New Silk Road Area? At the moment, the New Silk Road Area is not as important for Japan as Central Asian countries claim. But Japan is starting to show an interest in Central Asia's abundant natural resources. Improvements in the transport competitiveness of the inland regions will lead to the development of distribution routes to Europe using overland modes of transport. Japan has also begun initiatives to improve the status of its ports. With great future changes expected in the structure of economic power on the Eurasian continent, the importance of an international logistics route across the New Silk Road Area is likely to continue to increase from now on. If this happens, the interests of Central Asian countries will also translate into the interests of Japan. In order for this to occur, Japan should build a relationship of dialogue and cooperation with the individual countries concerned to promote economic development in the New Silk Road Area. Japan should be involved in developing basic infrastructure to allow for more economic exchanges between both sides.

References

Fukuoka-Kitakyushu (2010), *The Plan Directed to the Selection of the International Container Strategic Harbor* (Summary Edition) *(Kokusai Kontena Senryaku Kowan no Sentei ni Muketa Keikakusho)*.

MLIT Port Authority (2012), *About the Change of Present Harbor Policy (Imamadeno Kowan Seisaku no Hensen ni tsuite)*.

Tsuji, Hisako (2007), *Siberian Land bridge: The Main Artery of the Russia and Japanese Business (Siberia Rando Burijji: Nichiro Bijinesu no Daidomyaku)*, Seizando Shoten.

Closing Remarks

The grand and enduring history of the Silk Road has for the most part been a subject of research by historians, archaeologists, and writers. It has also been a source of inspiration for artists. They have captivated us with several breathtaking works of art. Naturally, interest toward the Silk Road varies from person to person. Our interest in the Silk Road was sparked by the following question: Is economic development possible in Central Asia, an inland region handicapped with numerous restrictions? Mineral resources such as crude oil and natural gas will remain indispensable to sustain our high energy consuming life styles. Some Central Asian countries with abundant deposits of fossil fuels have been able to ride the wave of soaring energy prices to achieve favorable economic results. However, this only underlines Central Asia's dependency on high energy prices for its prosperity and is plagued with an inherent economic vulnerability. Can the interior regions promote economic development and if so, how? Is such development sustainable? These are the questions that confront us. In order to resolve these questions, we have given the area a new identity called the New Silk Road to replace the old Silk Road. This allows us to envision the economic development of the Eurasian Continent as a whole, including the New Silk Road regions.

In this book, we have considered the possibilities of economic development of the New Silk Road regions situated in the interior areas of the Eurasian Continent, based on the knowledge we gleaned from our research conducted during the past fiscal year regarding how the underlying geographical and spatial conditions of China's core cities influenced the economic development of these cities. We came to a common awareness that changes in transportation technologies had a large impact on the rise and decline of the interior regions. The Age of Navigation led to great strides in marine transport technologies. Land transportation spanning the east-west trade routes over the Eurasian Continent was replaced by transportation by sea. Consequently, goods and money flowed to the coastal areas and the economic foundation of Eurasia's central regions was gradually lost. The past glory of many cities along the old Silk Road such as Chang'an, Kashgar, Samarkand, and Bukhara became but a site in a historical tale to be passed on to the next generation. Over the centuries the cities never again witnessed an economic revival. Ancient cities such as Loulan, which was an oasis for the caravans that traversed the deserts at the time, were reduced to ruins and disappeared into the sands. In their place new cities emerged along the coastal regions, some of which (such as Singapore, Hong Kong, Guangzhou, and Shanghai) grew to become modern-day metropolises. The impact of transportation technologies on the geographic distribution of economic activity has also been explained by the theory of spatial economics. If we interpret the mechanism of spatial economics correctly, the key to economic development of the landlocked regions of the New Silk Road lies in the improvement in the transportation competitiveness of land transportation.

Progress in present-day land transportation technologies has increased the competitiveness of land transportation in two ways: First is speed. Land transportation is now considerably faster than marine transportation. Second is systems and infrastructure. The technical difficulties involved in building a systems and infrastructure to support land transportation are not as ominous as in the past and can be accomplished more efficiently and quickly. Furthermore, considering the opportunity cost of foregoing the production of other goods, construction costs have declined considerably. Advancements in land transportation technologies have allowed for the possible revival of an east-west trade route over land across Eurasia and provided us with the basic conditions necessary for the regional development of the New Silk Road. However, although development possibilities have emerged, systems and infrastructure supporting land transportation alone by no means lead automatically to economic development.

The present railroad and highway transportation networks crossing the Eurasian Continent have been constructed and are being operated by the Trans-Siberian Railway and the China Land Bridge. Added to the rail transport routes are areas where highway networks alone exist. Transportation infrastructure such as these supports the logistics for east-west trade in the present-day Eurasian Continent. Noteworthy are the railroads and highways connecting China with Kazakhstan, which are proceeding as planned, and have contributed considerably to the economic advancement of the two nations. Signs of a "Beads-type" industrial distribution advocated in this book are already starting to show in the form of economic growth of major cities along the railway and the birth of new cities. Especially noteworthy is the development underway at Khorgos located on the border of China and Kazakhstan. Straddling the border of the two countries, the Khorgos International Center of Boundary Cooperation (ICBC "Khorgos") commenced operations in December 2011 and an international railroad system opened to traffic in December 2012. These events open the doors for Khorgos to demonstrate its potential to become a strategic hub for international distribution. Subsequently, the pace of development at Khorgos has accelerated and the Chinese side of Khorgos, which has a population of 85,000, was recognized by the central government in July 2014 as a city directly under the jurisdiction of the regional prefecture. These events remind us of the development of Shenzhen when the city was still an unnamed location neighboring Hong Kong during the Chinese economic reform era. There are high expectations in the near future for Khorgos to grow into a modern city on the far western end of China.

However, if we examine the record and capacity of land transport across the Eurasian Continent, it is still not on par with marine transportation. The reason for this is mainly the lack of international cooperation. This is manifested in the form of transportation time loss and pileups at the borders with regard to soft aspects and the fact that international railway networks have been limited to only a small number of countries with regard to hard aspects.

Several international railway construction projects have not moved forward as planned given that the concerned parties had to contend with conflicting geopolitical interests. As a result, a bipolarization of the economies of the Central Asian nations occurred depending on whether an international trade transport route ran through the country. Economic disparities that appeared among the countries in the region are widening.

In considering solutions to these problems, it is important to understand the following points: First, the development of a regional New Silk Road must be consistent with the interests of the concerned nations and must be carried out with their cooperation. Interests and mutual cooperation among each nation are inextricably linked, i.e., without the presence of interests, there would be no mutual cooperation. At the same time, without mutual cooperation, a country cannot attain its interests. Therefore, there should be no doubt that this cooperative relationship through the development of the New Silk Road region is for the benefit of all concerned countries and in no way should it be monopolized by a handful of countries or regions to the exclusion of others. Additionally, hopes to fulfill a common interest are consistent with the desire on the part of all concerned countries to advance their economies, which can serve as a strong inducement for cooperation overriding all other contradictions and conflicts.

Second, with the development of a regional New Silk Road, a Beads-type geographic distribution of cities with active economies will emerge and industrial centers are established in each country. If an international trade transportation route crossing the Eurasian Continent is constructed along the New Silk Road regions, the economies among the countries along the route will naturally become increasingly entwined, leading to further globalization. Against this backdrop, manufacturing will relocate from the advanced regions in the eastern and western far ends of Eurasia to the emerging inland regions of the continent, triggering industry agglomeration and urbanization within the region. This is the so-called international decentralization and domestic concentration phenomenon. International decentralization in this case refers to the relocation of manufacturing to the countries of the New Silk road region, especially the emerging countries located inland. Domestic concentration increases the competitiveness of domestic manufacturers. This phenomenon increases productivity and stimulates growth on a global scale.

Third, the New Silk Road regions enjoy an abundance of natural resources, which works as a positive condition for forming industrial sites. However, this is not a necessary condition. New York, Tokyo, Singapore and other major cities developed not because they had natural resources but because of their logistical accessibility. The ease of access is indispensable for international trade. Therefore, the foremost priority should be to revive the international trade transportation routes that will serve as a catalyst for growth in the New Silk Road regions. After accomplishing this, we can turn our attention to utilizing the existing natural resources available in the area. The effective utilization of natural resources means the creation of a strategy that includes the export of natural resources as a means of attracting development funds and the development of the manufacturing sector that uses such resources.

Finally, the formation of an international trade transportation route and regional development of the New Silk Road regions have a circular as well as a cumulative relationship with each other. As both proceed simultaneously, a realistic order of progression is for both to expand gradually. However, in the initial stages, aid from the industrialized nations for the construction of transportation infrastructure in the less advanced regions is indispensable. An ideal relationship is that of mutual cooperation through the use of natural resources on the part of the less advanced regions in return for support in the form of funding and technology from the industrialized countries.

Given the strides accomplished in modern land transport technologies, to ignore the needs for an international trade transport route along the New Silk Road regions runs against the tides of history. This natural progression will not change in the long-term. Our ancestors left behind a rich history on the stages of the Eurasian Continent called the Silk Road when marine transport technologies were still in their infancy. Now that land transport technologies have advanced significantly, the competitiveness of land transport is on par, if not superior, with marine transport. Therefore, like our ancestors, we should be able to create a new rich history on the stages of the Eurasian Continent as we move forward to revive the New Silk Road. This is what we seek to convey the most in this work.

Index

Beads-type Development Strategy 1, 2, 4, 5, 28, 29, 33, 37, 38, 42, 57, 95, 200
Beads-type industrial city 1, 4, 5, 8, 27, 28, 33, 36, 37, 38, 107
Beads-type industrial distribution 206
Break-even distance 79, 81, 82, 85, 86, 87, 88

CAREC 101
China Land Bridge 18, 27, 37, 86, 88, 206
Common Economic Space 99, 106, 108
Council of The European Union 64, 73
Customs Union 97, 98, 99, 106, 108, 133, 144, 147, 148, 149, 155

Dis-extensive margin of trade 126, 127
Domestic concentration 34, 35, 43, 207
Dynamic catch-up 4, 45, 50, 51, 54, 55, 56, 57

Economic corridor 93
Economic disparity 1, 14, 30, 31, 111, 120
Economic Gardening 6, 183, 189, 190, 191, 192, 193, 194
Efficiency of financial investments 169
EU as a normative power 70
EU Central Asia Strategy 61, 64, 73
EurAsEc 97, 98, 99, 106
Eurasian Diplomacy 72, 200
Eurasian Land Bridge 5, 12, 18, 27, 28, 31, 37, 42, 88
Eurasian transcontinental railway line 149

European Commission 59, 60, 62, 63, 64, 69, 73
European External Action Service 64, 73
European Parliament 60
EU Trade Policy 59, 71
Extensive margin of trade 126, 127, 128, 129

Flying geese 4, 31, 32, 33, 45, 47, 49, 50, 55, 57
Fragmentation type division of labor 48, 53, 56

Generalized System of Preferences 61, 70
Geo-Economic 9, 10
Geopolitical importance of Central Asia 12, 25
Global economic dynamism 40, 45, 54, 55, 56, 200
Globalization of corporate economic activities 54, 55, 57
Global value chains (GVCs) 136
Gravity equation 4, 80, 152
Gravity model 5, 151, 154, 156
Great western development 12, 111

ICBC "Khorgos" 148, 149, 150, 206
Industrial agglomeration 1, 2, 4, 7, 29, 33, 34, 37, 38, 39, 40, 42, 43, 52, 53, 54, 55, 56, 57, 94, 95, 109, 111, 116, 121
Industrial distribution 35, 206
Industrial structure 11, 17, 18, 19, 25, 31, 47, 49, 110, 111, 112, 114, 118, 183, 192

Intensive margin of trade 126, 127
Interests of the concerned nations 207
International decentralization 207
International division of labor 7, 37, 38, 42, 45, 46, 47, 49, 51, 53, 54, 55, 56, 57, 58, 94, 121

Khorgos-Eastern Gate 148, 149, 150, 156

Landlocked countries 16, 18, 25, 72, 75, 77, 124, 125
Lisbon Treaty 60, 62, 63, 73

Navoi FIEZ 157, 161, 162, 163, 164, 165
Newly traded products 124, 125, 126, 129, 130, 134
Non-zero trade 130, 131, 132, 133

OECD STAN Bilateral Trade by Industry and End-use (BTDIxE) database 136
Order of "Dustlik" ("Friendship") 158

Resilience 6, 183, 186, 187, 188, 189, 191, 193, 194

Seamless Asia Plan 202
Shanghai Cooperation Organization (SCO) 21, 161, 197
Shrinking cities 6, 183, 184, 185, 186, 187, 188, 189, 193, 194
Siberian Land Bridge 27, 88, 204
Silk Road Diplomacy 200
Silk Road Economic Belt 7, 92
Small and medium-scale enterprises 183, 193
Spatial distribution 36, 38, 42, 52, 53, 55, 201

Super Hub Port 202
Sustainable development 120, 184, 188

TRACECA (Transport Corridor Europe-Caucasus-Asia) 101, 108, 144
Transportation competitiveness 4, 5, 6, 37, 75, 76, 77, 80, 82, 87, 88, 89, 91, 92, 93, 109, 110, 113, 206
Transport corridor 72, 101, 144, 148, 149, 150
Trans-Siberian Railway 18, 72, 76, 77, 88, 149, 155, 206
T-shaped development strategy 30, 31, 37
TTF 99, 100, 102, 106

U.S. Intervention in Central Asia 23

WTO 60, 61, 70, 106, 107, 116, 120, 128

Yangtze River Delta 112, 116, 120, 183

Zhibek Zholy 143

Π-shaped development strategy 31, 37, 39